KAKADU

A GUIDE FOR ALL SEASONS

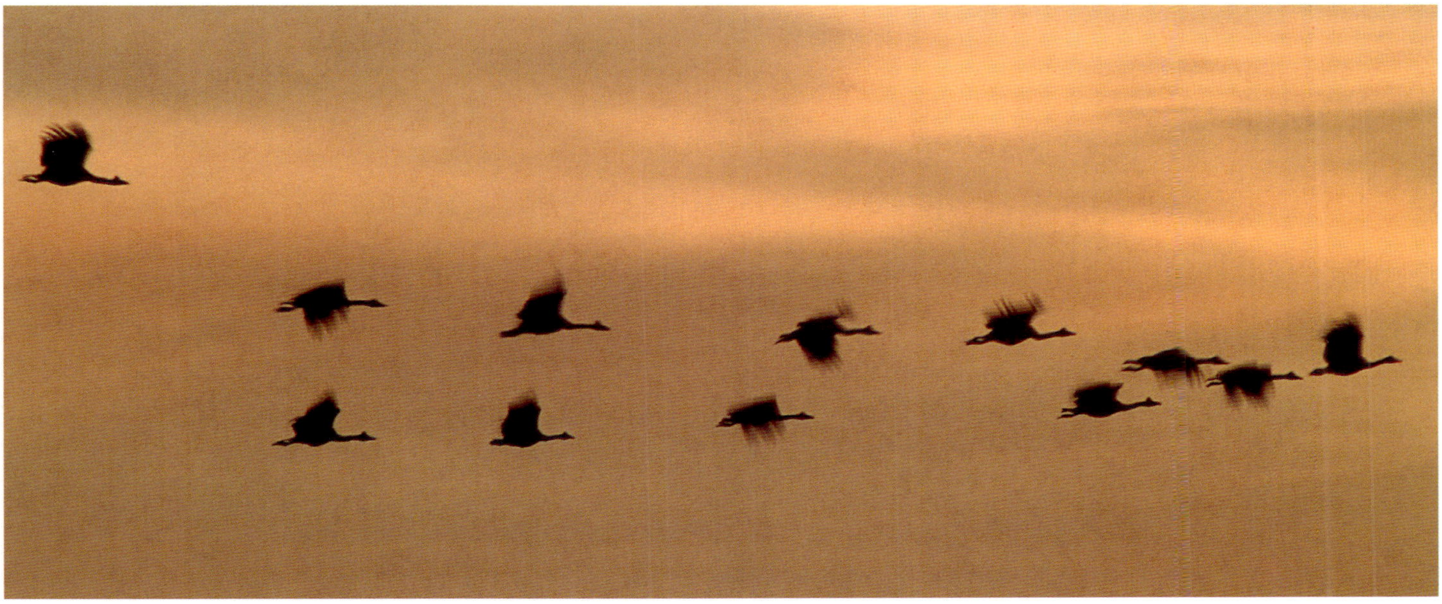

PHOTOGRAPHY BY PETER JARVER

Master of Photography AIPP

TEXT BY QUENTIN CHESTER

BOOKS BY PETER JARVER

The Top End of Down Under

The Heart of Australia

Darwin, Australia's Northern Capital

Cairns, Reef to Rainforest

Daintree to the Coral Sea

Snowgums to Sand

KAKADU NATIONAL PARK

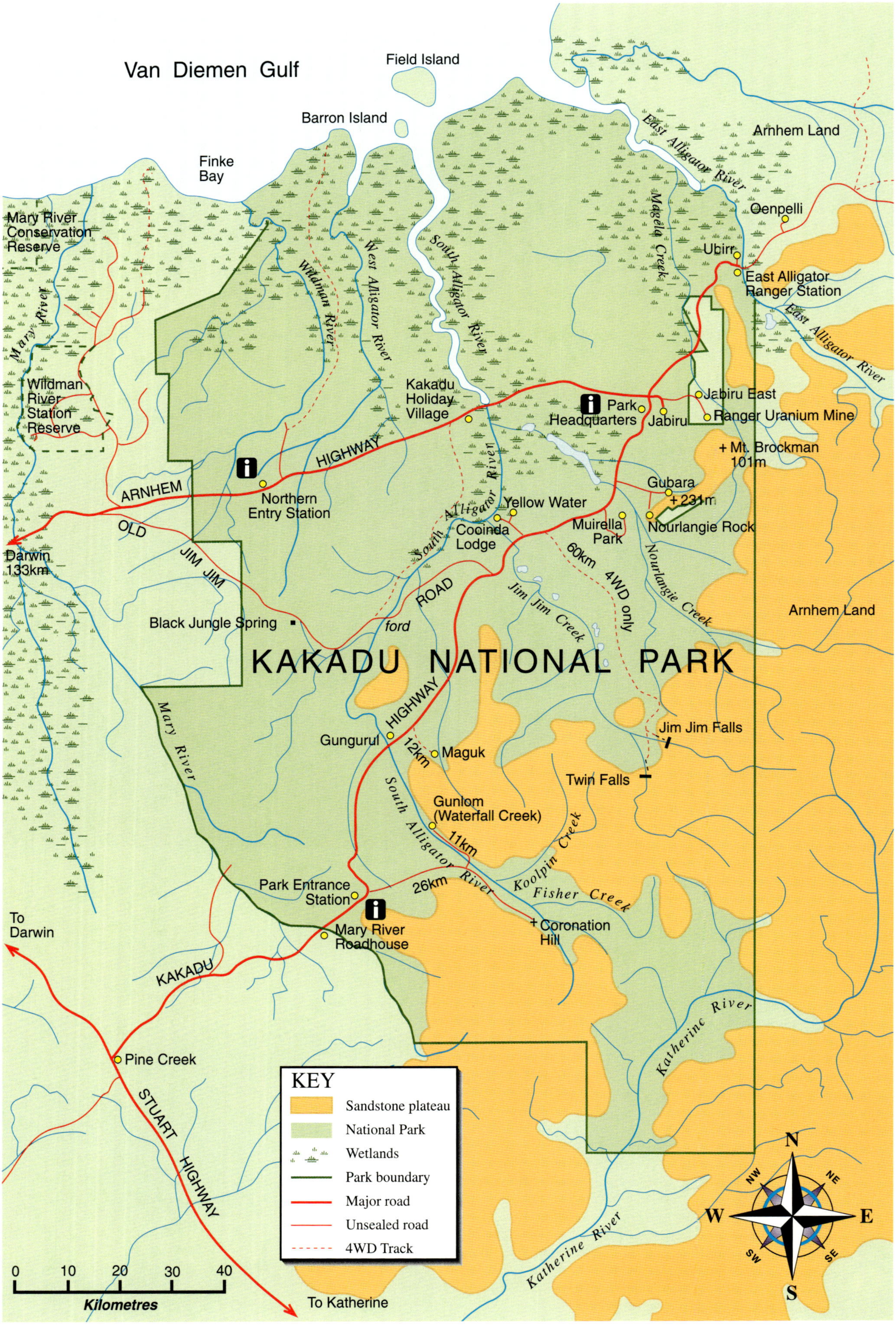

CONTENTS

MAPS

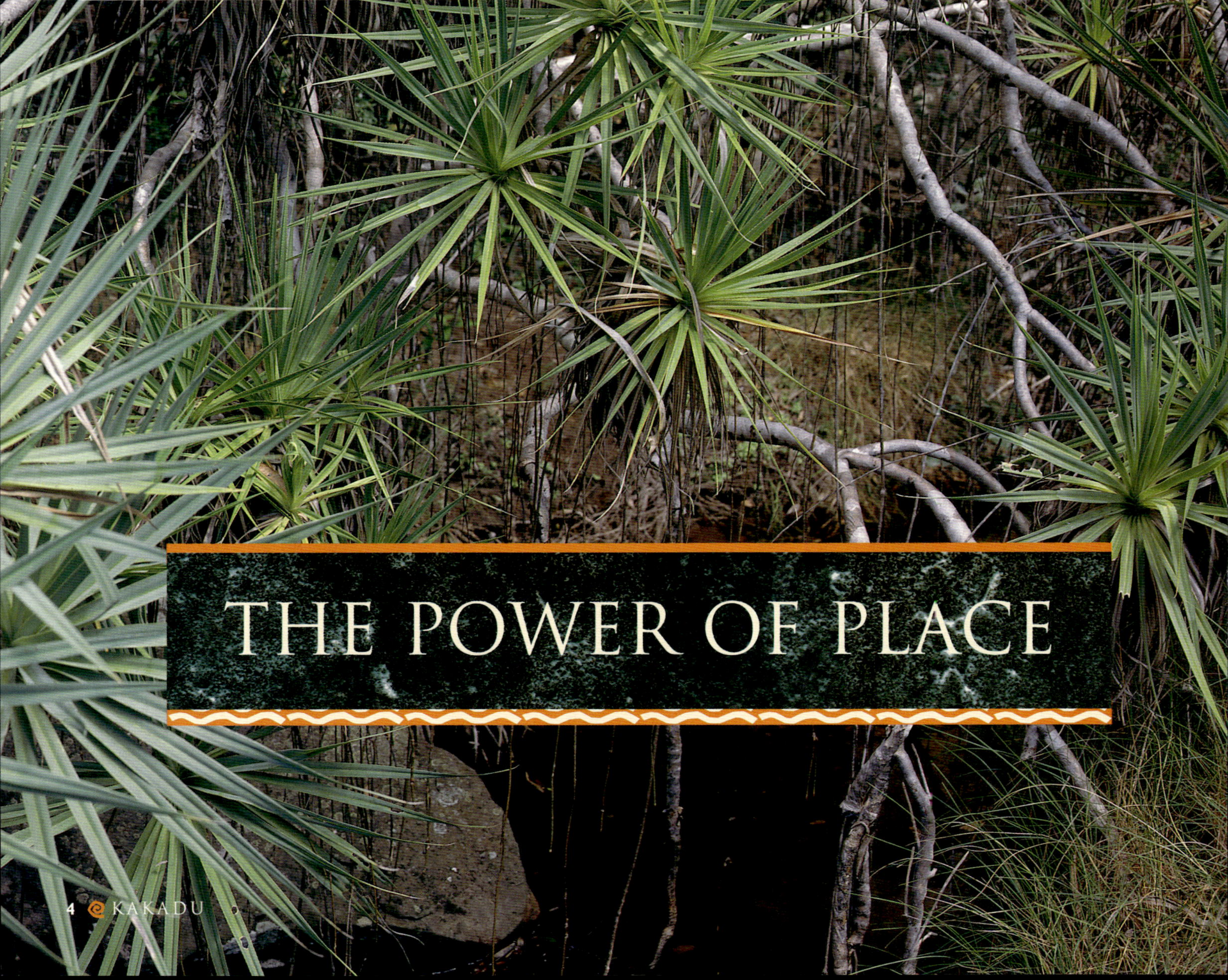

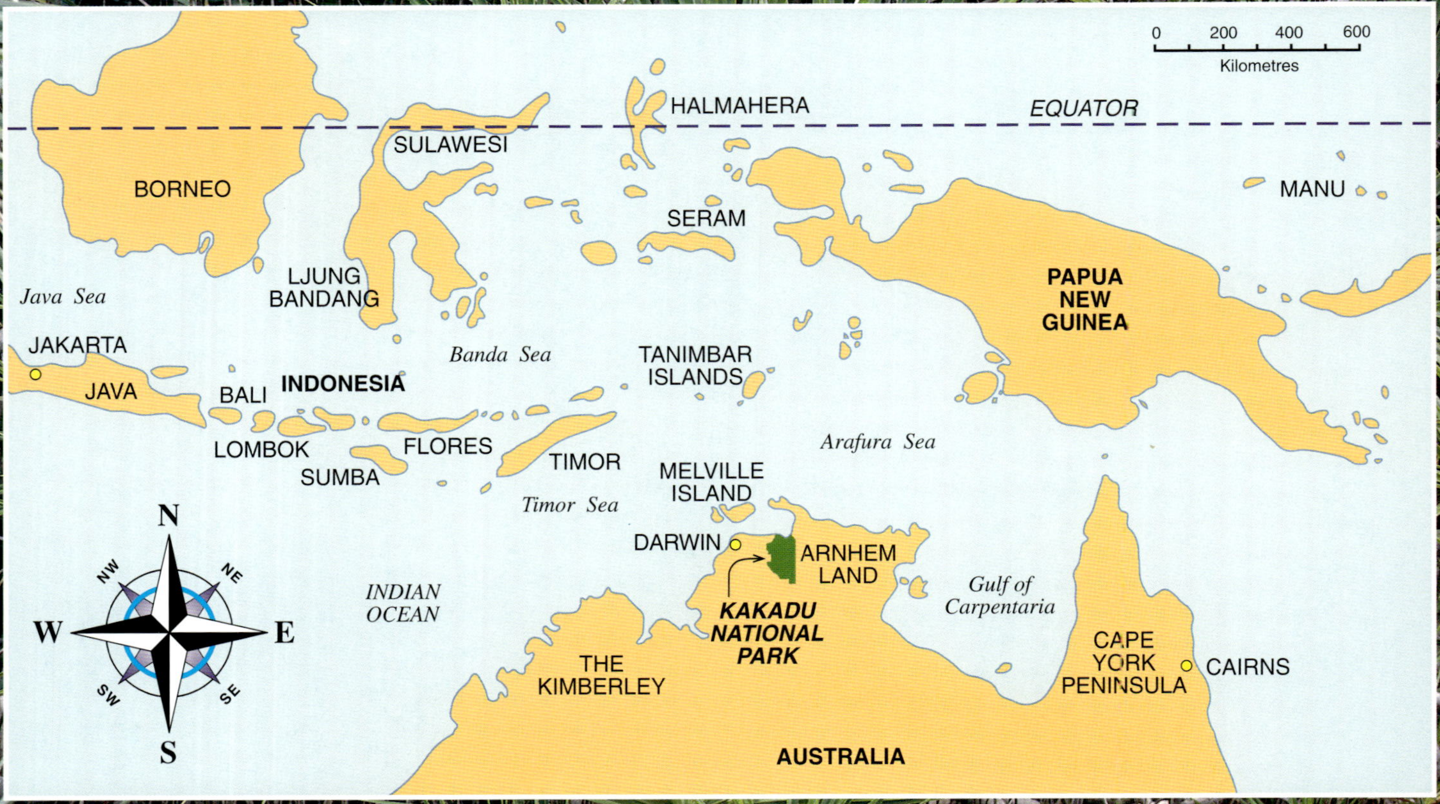

THE POWER OF PLACE

THE POWER OF PLACE

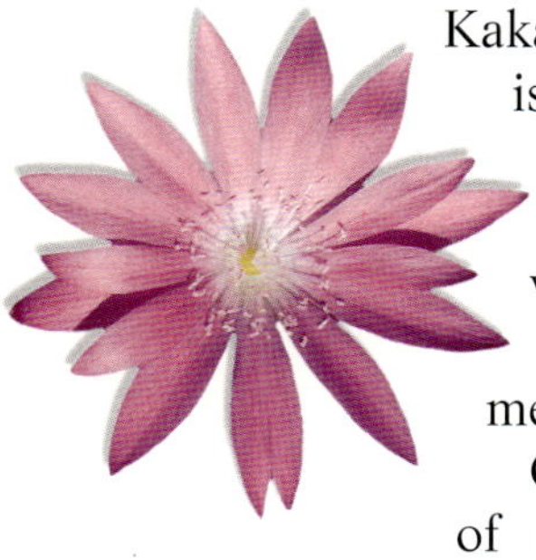

LEFT A small, unprepossessing herb of the woodlands, (Calandrinia uniflora) *does however produce striking flowers through the early months of the year.*

Kakadu is unique. To walk the woodlands and cruise the billabongs is to encounter life in rare abundance. To stand beneath the mighty waterfalls is to be confronted by the antiquity of the land. To enter a rock shelter and stare at a ceiling resplendent with ochre images of animal life and spirit beings is to glimpse a vision of another world. These encounters - and many others - merge to make Kakadu an experience like no other.

One of the first challenges confronting visitors is the sheer scale of the place. Kakadu National Park covers 19,804 square kilometres - nearly half the size of Switzerland. In the east it's bounded by the Arnhem Land Plateau with its lofty sandstone escarpment. To the west sprawls an expanse of open forest and wetlands, while the southern margins are dominated by hills and weathered granite rises. Although both the Arnhem and Kakadu highways give the traveller a cross-section view of these landforms, it takes time to fathom the true character of the park and its remote reaches.

Within its boundaries Kakadu is home to an extraordinary mix of domains, from broad estuaries where silty tides swirl among mangroves, to pockets of luxuriant rainforest perched high among the rocky battlements of the escarpment. More than three-quarters of the park is taken up with a patchwork of eucalypt lowlands. This is breached by three major river systems - the East, South and West Alligator Rivers - and a complex network of billabongs and paperbark swamps.

These habitats provide sanctuary for one of Australia's most profuse concentrations of flora and fauna. Nearly 1700 plant species have been recorded in Kakadu. Here you can find 64 different native mammals, 50 species of fish and around one-third of Australia's bird species. The tallies are remarkable. So too are the rhythms of life and the restless struggles between predators and prey that makes this such a wild, vital place.

The driving force behind this vigour is the Top End's boom and bust climate. From June to September conditions are typically dry, warm and stable. By October much of Kakadu has a dusty, withered look. Gradually, however, thunderheads gather and from November to April the region is rocked by storms and monsoon rains. Large areas are flooded and there is a boisterous surge of plant and animal life.

In its own way Kakadu's recent evolution has been no less turbulent. Anyone who spends enough time here will be aware that taking responsibility for such an enormous estate presents many demands. A bewildering array of issues converge within the national park, from controlling fires and ferals, and the uneasy coexistence of conservation and mining, to balancing the needs of mass tourism and traditional ownership.

Above all else, any visitor to Kakadu has to recognise that this is an Aboriginal place. The local people - or Bininj as they refer to themselves - have made these environs their cherished home for at least 50,000 years. Nowhere else on earth is there such a history of continuous human habitation and few places offer the potential that exists here to share in the knowledge of indigenous people.

Over the past 30 years Kakadu has won international recognition for its cultural and natural riches. More than 200,000 people now visit the park each year. Yet, despite the changes, the power of place endures. For those prepared to respond to Kakadu's extraordinary challenges there are abundant rewards.

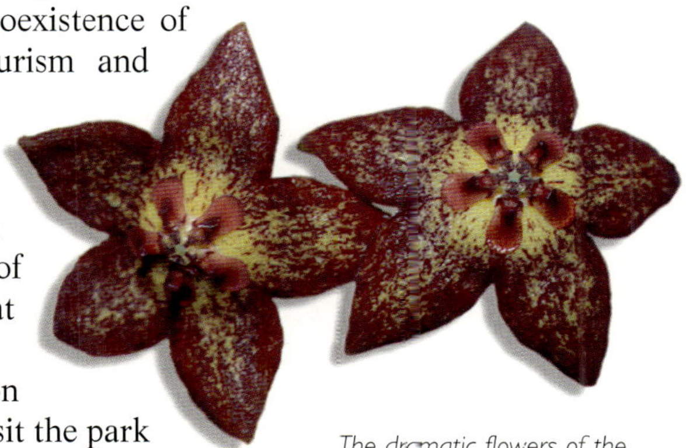

The dramatic flowers of the Heterostemma calcarata, *just one of Kakadu's 1700 plant species.*

LIVING TRADITIONS

Aboriginal customary life is founded on the intimate connections between the land, the seasons and all living things. Over countless generations Bininj have developed a deep understanding of their natural realm and its vivid, telling details. They read the signs all around: bushes in flower, gathering clouds, ripening fruits, creatures on the move. These patterns determine when to harvest, to hunt, to take shelter or to move on.

Inseparable from this practical knowledge are the Bininj spiritual beliefs about the origins of the land and the forces that continue to shape their lives. There are many linked stories and characters which relate to the time of creation. These include the journey of Warramurrungundji (also known as Imberombera), an ancestral mother figure who journeyed from across the sea bringing food plants and a digging stick. She made features in the landscape and bore her spirit children - the Nayuhynuggi or first people - giving each group their language and social structure. Other powerful characters include Ngalyod, the rainbow serpent who travelled the stone country creating waterholes and other resting places, and Namarrgon, the Lightning Man with stone axes on his head, elbows and knees which he strikes against the clouds to make thunder.

According to traditional beliefs many of these creation figures and their descendants are still present in the landscape. The stories - which resist summary and in the telling are complex and vividly detailed - are thus much more than tales from long ago: they embody an active organic philosophy which underpins social interactions, language and the obligations to care for country.

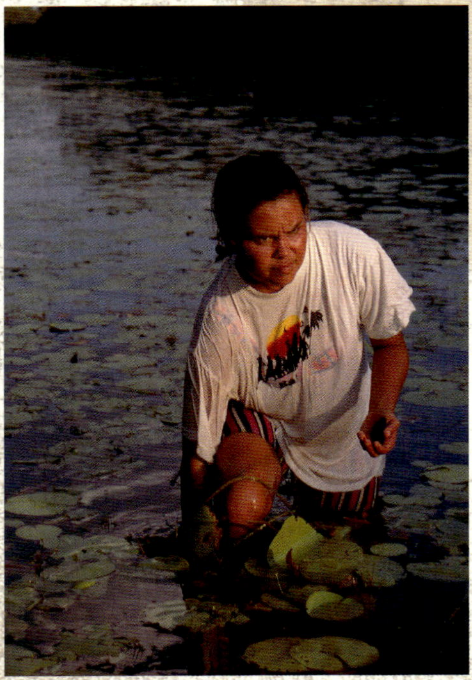

Sandra, of the Murrumbur clan, uses her toes to feel for freshwater mussels in a billabong. She holds one in her hand.

In Kakadu, as elsewhere, contemporary Aboriginal life takes many forms. Traditional owners identify with individual clans which are based on language groups and extended family associations. These clans are in turn tied to estates within the park. Traditional languages include Gagudju, Gun-djeihmi/Mayali, Kunwinjku and Jawoyn. Kakadu's Bininj population numbers some 300, many of whom live on estates, while others make their home in Jabiru. Bininj play an active role in park management, day to day operations and tourism.

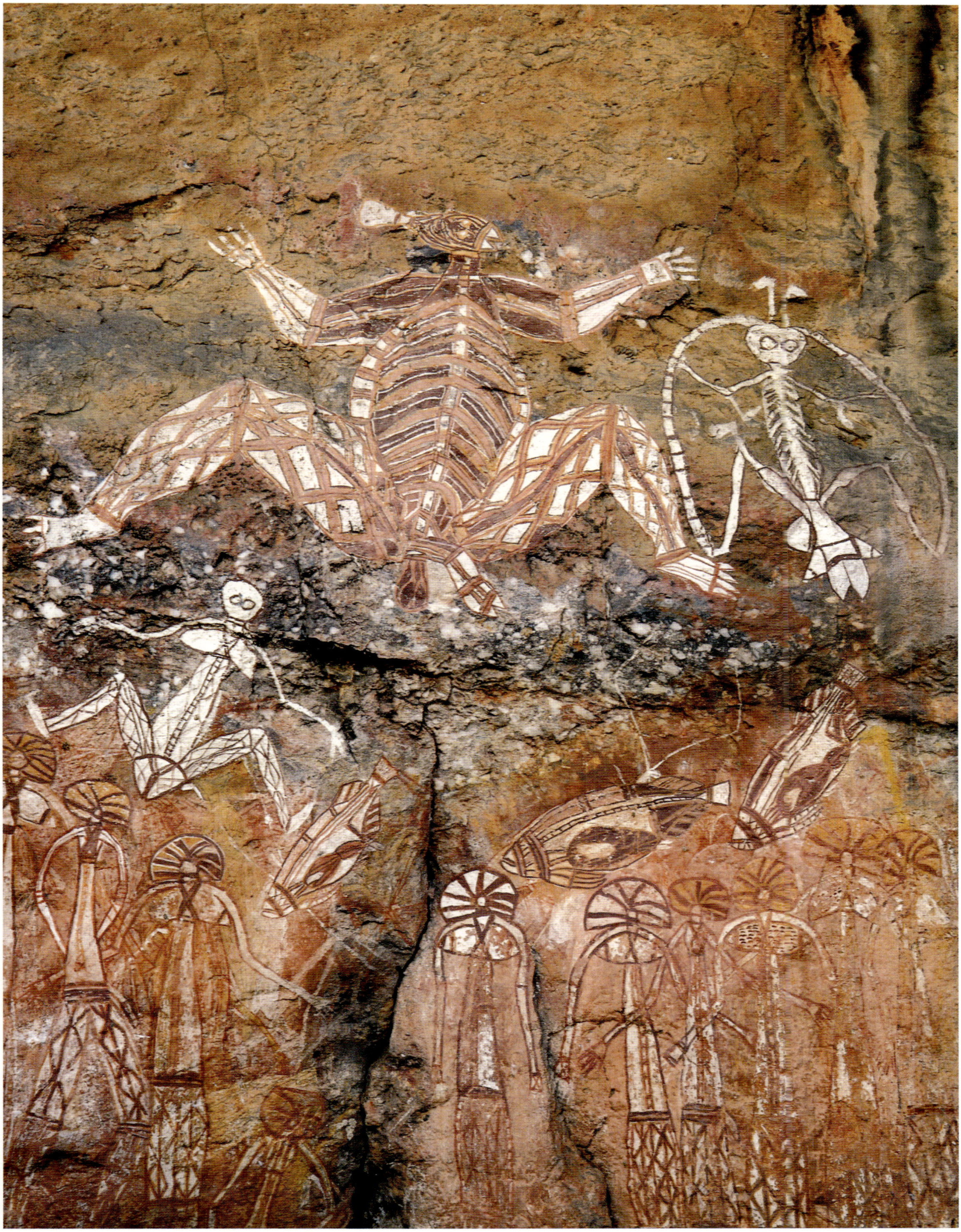

Kakadu's abundant rock art forms a palpable link to the mythology and traditions of Bininj life. These paintings at the Anbangbang Gallery at the foot of Burrunggui (Nourlangie Rock) are a graphic example. Images include a dangerous spirit figure Namondjok (top centre), Namarrgon the Lightning Man to the right and his wife Barrginj below Namondjok.

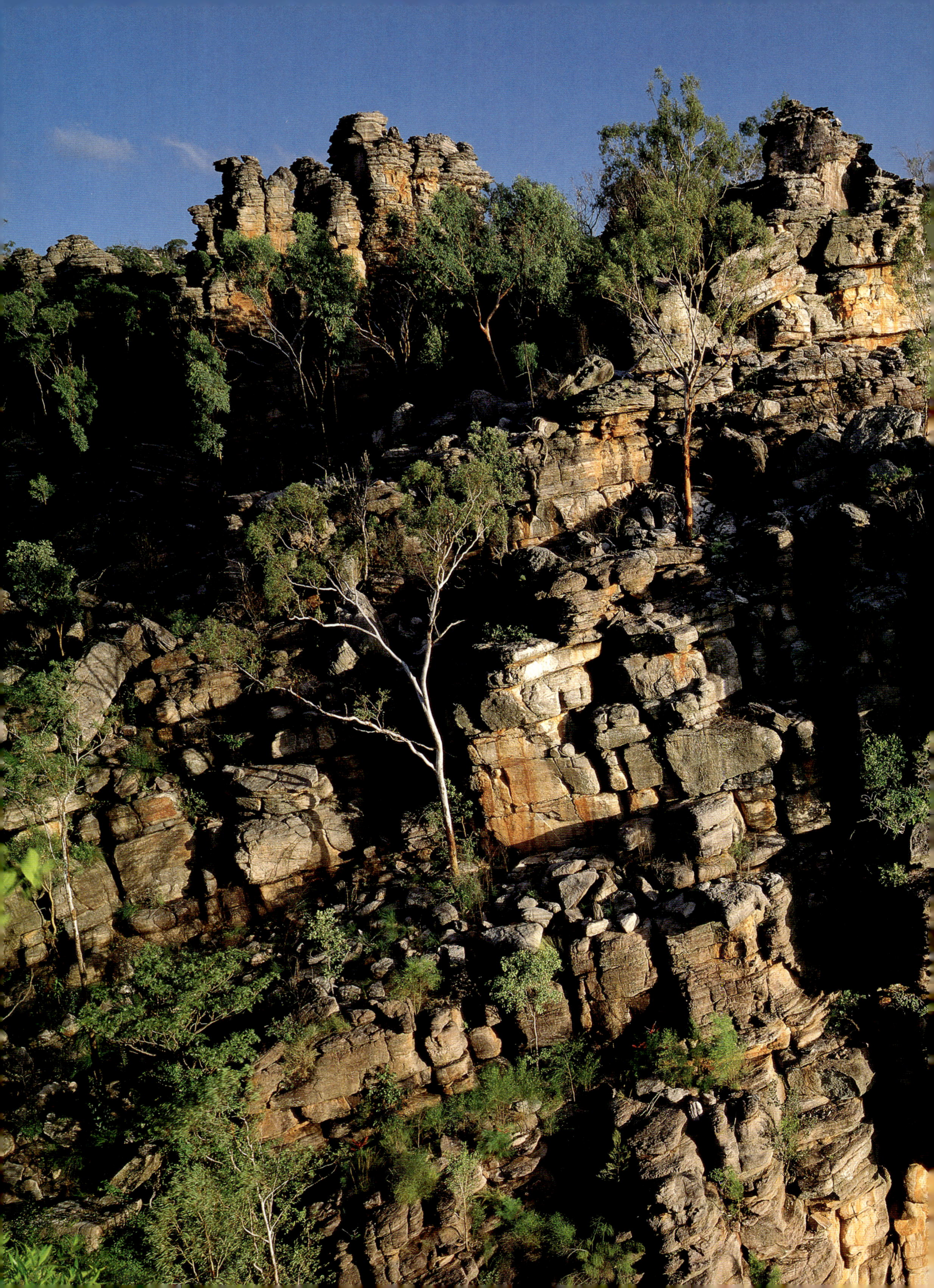

LIE OF THE LAND

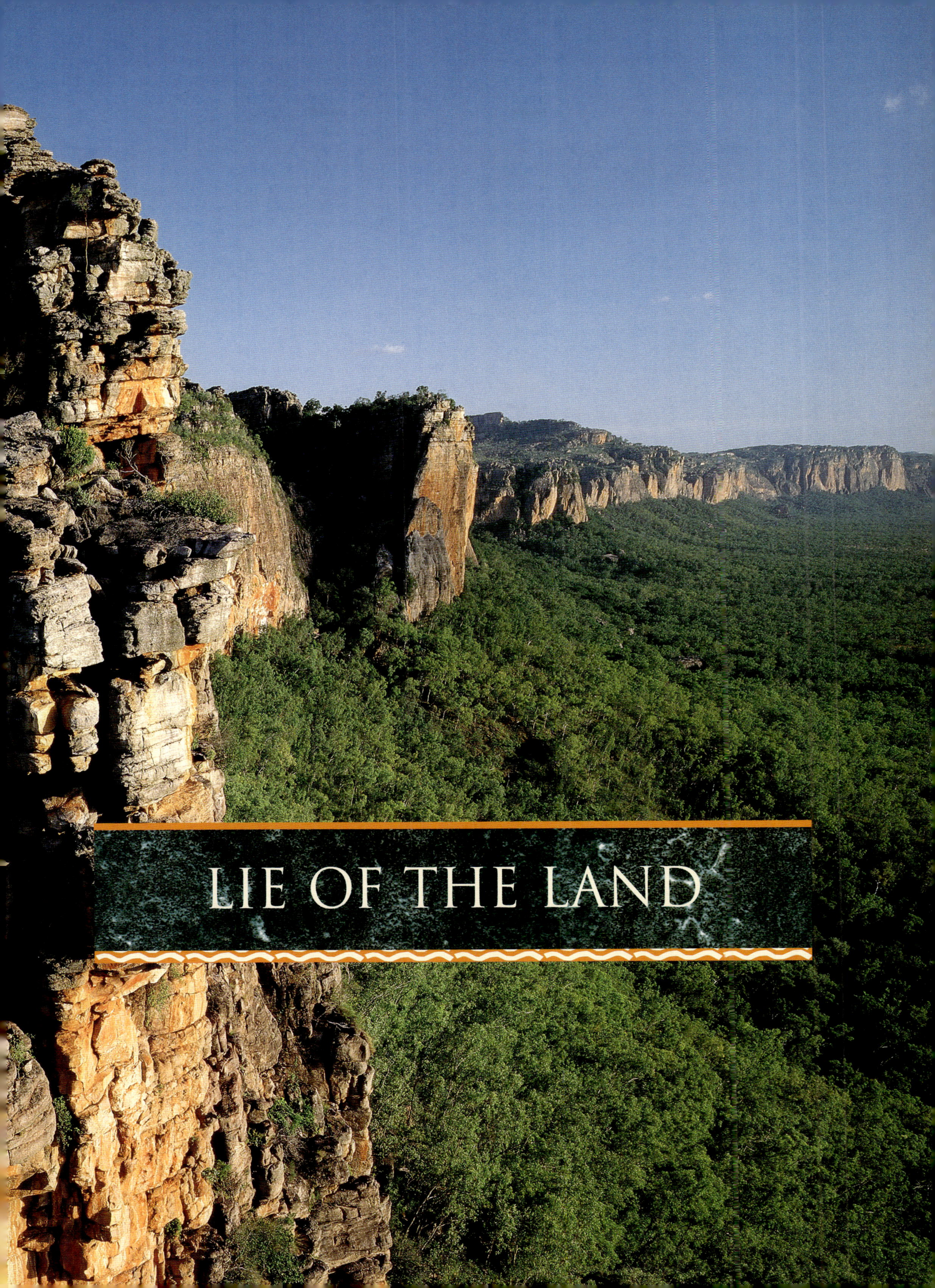

LIE OF THE LAND

PREVIOUS PAGE *Exposed to the western sun, the sheer sandstone face of the Arnhem Land Escarpment forms an imposing natural barrier winding hundreds of kilometres along Kakadu's eastern boundary.*

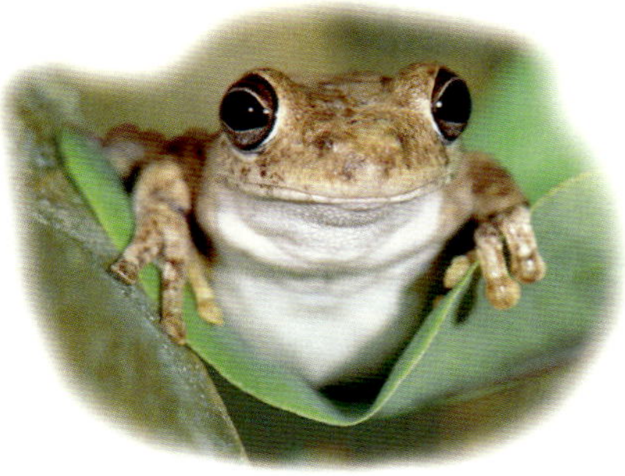

The Brown Tree-frog or Roth's Tree-frog (Litoria rothii) *lives in moist woodland sites, waiting to breed in the deep pools replenished by the monsoon.*

Sandstone formed some 1800 million years ago endures as these massive escarpment walls loom over Jim Jim Gorge.

Standing at the base of Jim Jim Falls you are confronted by a lofty amphitheatre of rust-red cliffs. These 200-metre-high ramparts are quartz sandstone, part of what geologists call the Kombolgie Formation, a massive sedimentary structure that endures as the Arnhem Land Plateau and its outliers. This landform has remained essentially stable since the rocks that make up the formation were laid down in ancient rivers and seas an astonishing 1700 million years ago.

By contrast, if you follow Jim Jim Creek as it winds its way 60 kilometres or so from the escarpment down to the lowlands you arrive at Yellow Water. These freshwater wetlands are among the youngest precincts in the park with the surrounding floodplain coming into existence less than 2000 years ago.

This juxtaposition of features, both ancient and modern, is just one extraordinary aspect of the physical environment that confronts the traveller in Kakadu. While the persistence of the Arnhem Land Plateau is a major theme in the park's geological evolution, it is a story with many many strands.

Over an immense span - more than one and half billion years - the region has been subjected to long bouts of volcanic activity and tectonic stress. Ructions in the earth's climate have caused the oceans to ebb and flow, and countless changes to the emerging river systems. All this combined with long intervals of weathering and deposition have cast and recast Kakadu's topography.

A fascinating history in its own right, the geology of the region has also profoundly shaped the lives of the plants and animals and people that have come to inhabit the region.

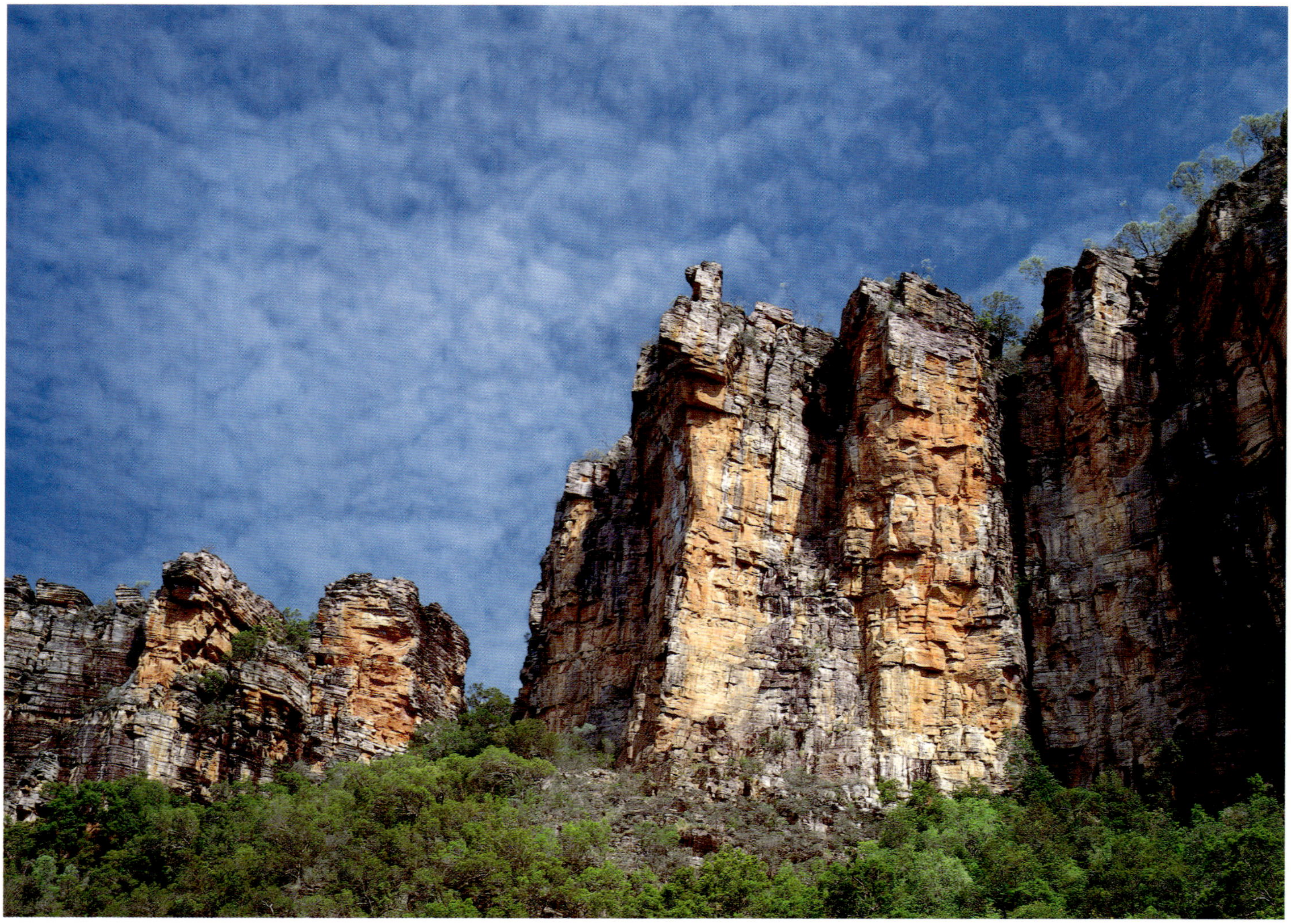

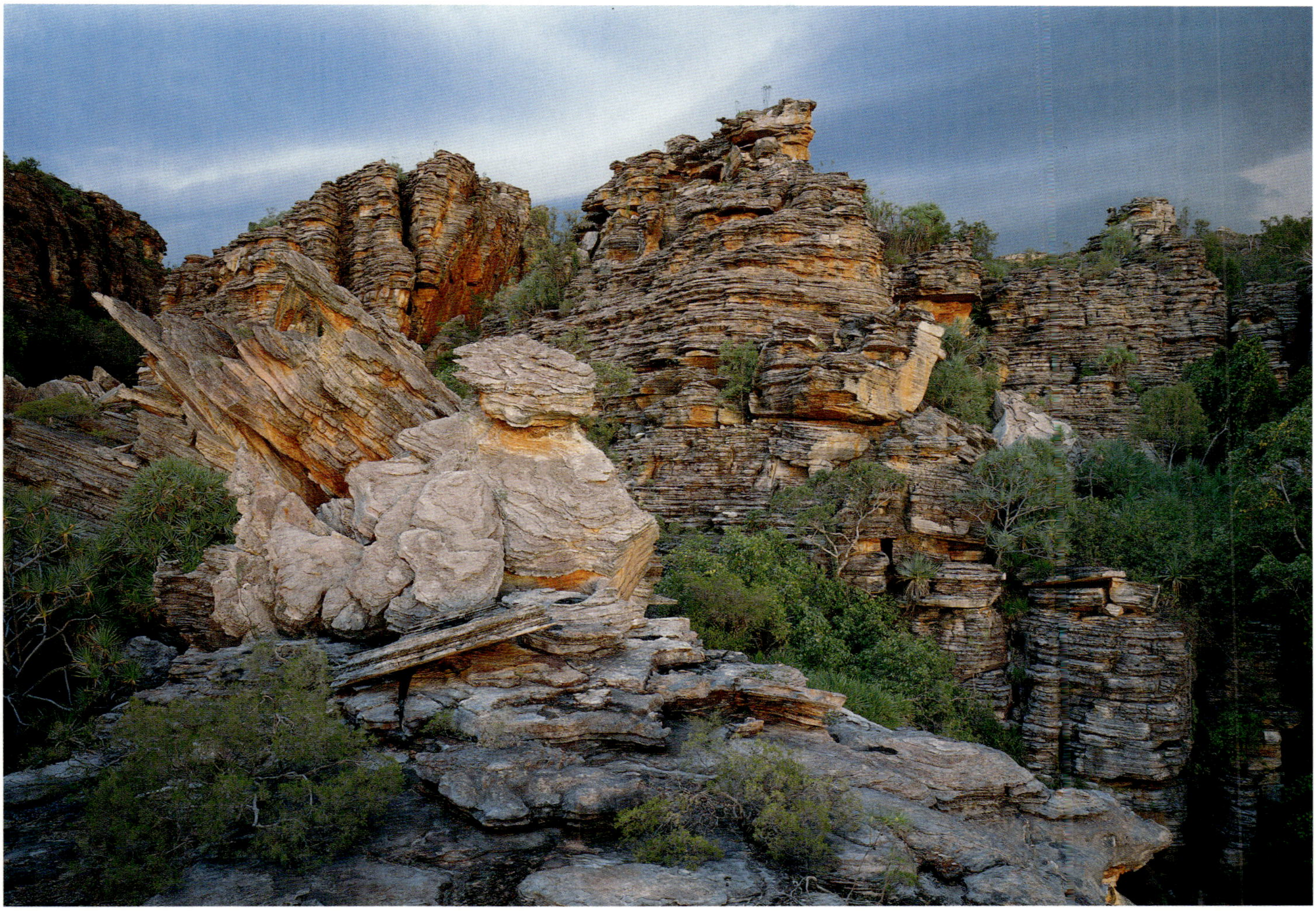

Millions of years of scouring wind and driving rain have hewn the plateau's outcrops into fascinating labyrinths and fanciful forms.

ANCIENT TURMOILS

The Kombolgie Formation may be the outstanding geological feature in the park but its rocks are by no means the oldest. Underlying the plains to west of the escarpment, in the area roughly between the South Alligator River and Magela Creek, is a foundation of granites and gneiss dating back nearly 2500 million years. These rocks belong to the Pine Creek Geosyncline, a major geological depression that extends beneath much of Arnhem Land and reaches as far west as Darwin.

As this structure subsided, vast quantities of sedimentary material were deposited in ancient rivers and shallow seas about 1900 million years ago. A period of intense activity followed, in which these sediments as well as volcanic rocks and ancient granites were subjected to folding, faulting and metamorphosis. Igneous activity around this time saw the intrusion of granites, basalts and other volcanic rocks.

In the wake of these upheavals, widespread erosion gradually levelled the land surface, paving the way for the Kombolgie Formation. Hundreds of metres of sand, gravel and other material accumulated in flat-lying sediments across a broad plain. For 1700 million years these deposits have remained in place.

Over this gulf of time it's likely that the Kombolgie Formation has spent long periods interred beneath a mantle of more recently deposited sediments. There have also been phases of tectonic uplift and a steady undermining of the escarpment, such that some sections of the plateau have retreated by as much as 25 kilometres. Ultimately, however, Arnhem Land was exposed to the sculpting forces of the elements that fashioned the weathered plateau and clifflines that fortify Kakadu's eastern border.

The Northern Brushtail Possum (*Trichosurus arnhemensis*), a nocturnal forager found throughout Kakadu's wooded lowlands.

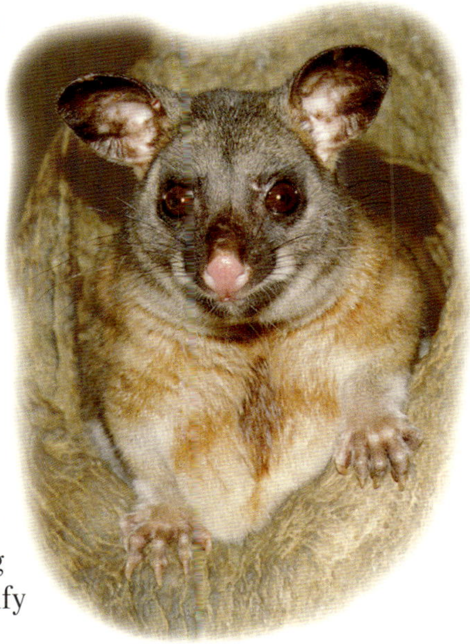

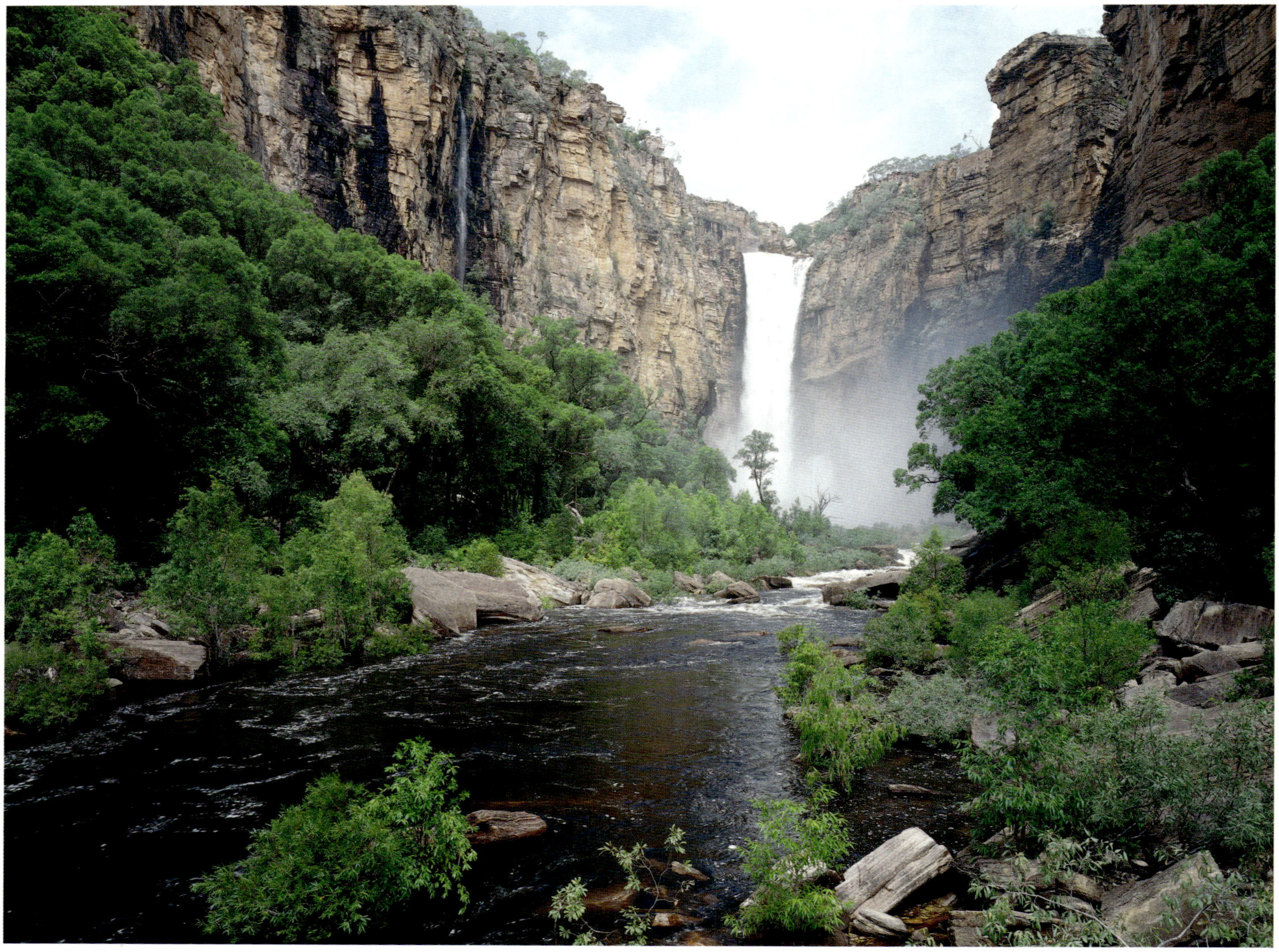

A luxuriant Anbinik forest at the foot of Jim Jim Falls is reinvigorated by run-off from wet season downpours.

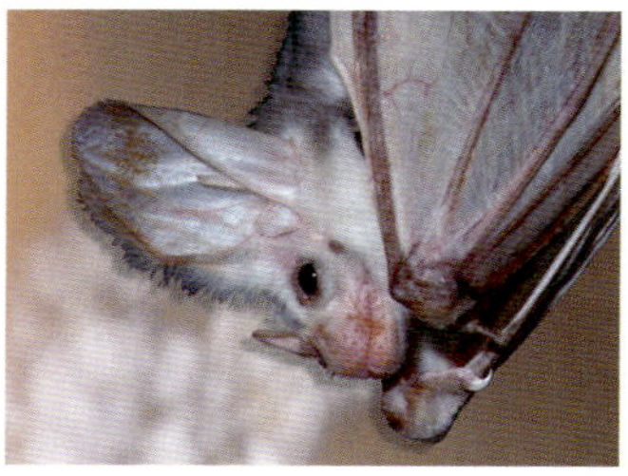

The Ghost Bat (Macroderma gigas), *Australia's only carnivorous bat finds daytime refuge in the escarpment's deep caves and fissures.*

GONDWANAN TIDES

Looking west from the outer rim of the Arnhem Land escarpment, the wooded plains stretch to the horizon like a sea of mottled green. For significant spans of Kakadu's geological past this impression of an ocean below has not just been an illusion but a physical reality.

It is thought likely that saltwater lapped the edge of Arnhem Land as much as 150 million years ago. After the fragmentation of Gondwana, when India parted company with the supercontinent, a huge expanse of northern Australia was washed by seas that invaded when the continental margins slumped and subsided. For millennia the escarpment stood as a line of coastal cliffs before the Late Cretaceous sea.

Shifts in the global climate, including periods of widespread glaciation, produced many more changes in sea levels during the evolution of Kakadu's landforms. At the height of the most recent glacial age some 14,000 years ago the coastline lay more than 300 kilometres to the north of its current position. During this period Australia and New Guinea were yoked together as a single landmass and the sea level had dropped approximately 150 metres. With the subsequent melting of the polar ice sheets the world's oceans rose again, arriving at their present levels around 6800 years ago.

The Millipede inhabits Kakadu's forest environs.

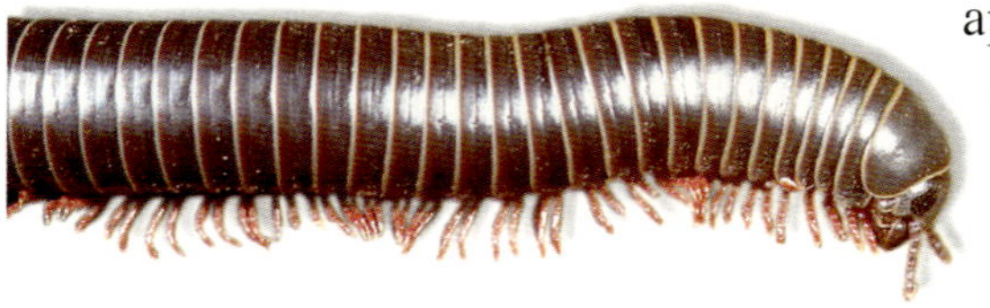

This incursion transformed the rivers and drainage network that had cut deep into Kakadu's undulating surface. Wide river valleys were steadily

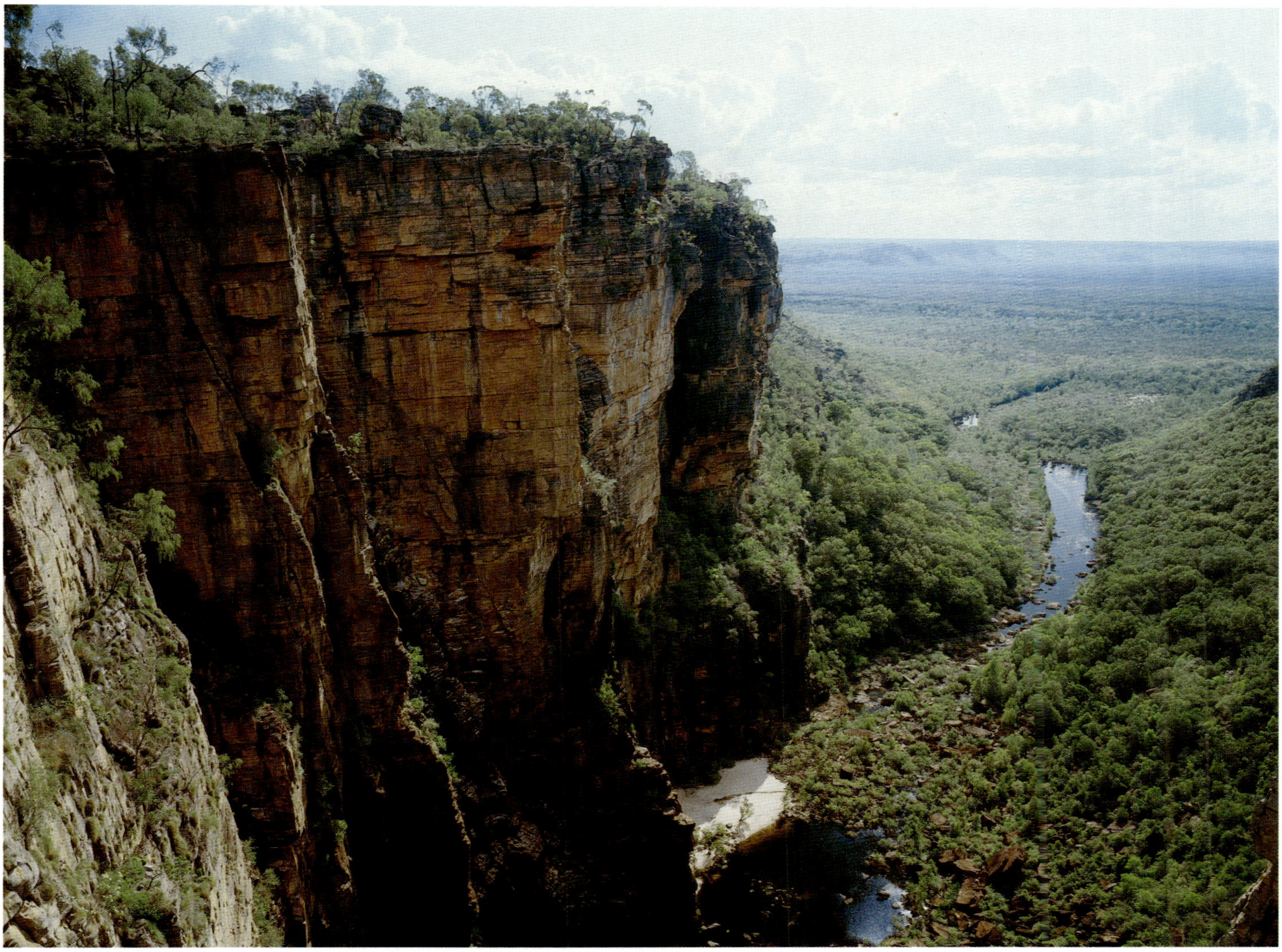

Towering cliffs shadow Jim Jim Creek as it begins its journey across a sea of woodland.

reclaimed by the advancing sea and tides reached far inland. Meanwhile the constant sluicing of silt and coarser sediments from the plateau filled these drowned valleys. This massive build-up of deposits created a broad, flat-lying shoreline with extensive mangrove swamps fed by tidal flows.

However, over a 2000 year period, the continued accumulation of deposits reached a level where they formed natural levee structures. As a result large areas of the lowlands became isolated from tidal influence. Mangrove communities and associated marine life gradually gave way to an array of freshwater flora and fauna adapted to the seasonal inundation in the wake of the monsoon.

These rich floodplains are Kakadu's most dynamic seasonal landforms. Yet they remain acutely vulnerable. The levee banks are a precarious line of defence against a restless sea and encroaching tides. Any breach of this barrier has the capacity to cause widespread disturbance. The impact of such saltwater intrusion is already evident on the Mary River floodplain just beyond the park's north-western boundary.

Similarly, any rise in sea level, such as that predicted from the effects of global warming would be potentially catastrophic for Kakadu's freshwater ecosystem. For example Yellow Water, the park's teeming freshwater heartland, is more than 100 river kilometres inland from the coast, yet lies barely three metres above sea level.

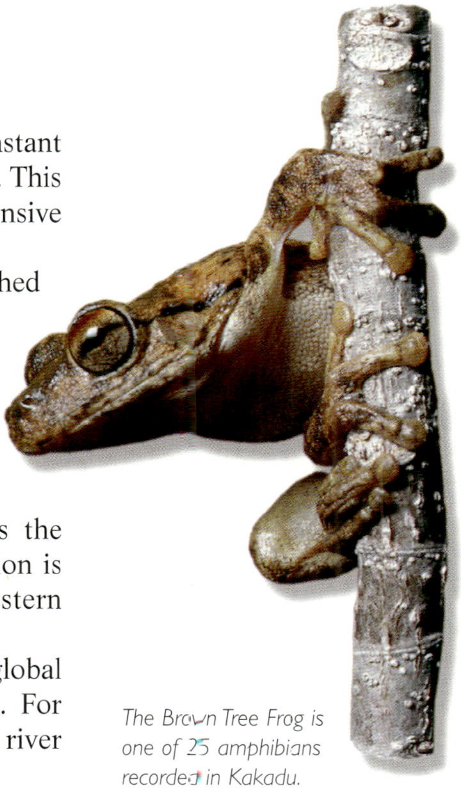

The Brown Tree Frog is one of 25 amphibians recorded in Kakadu.

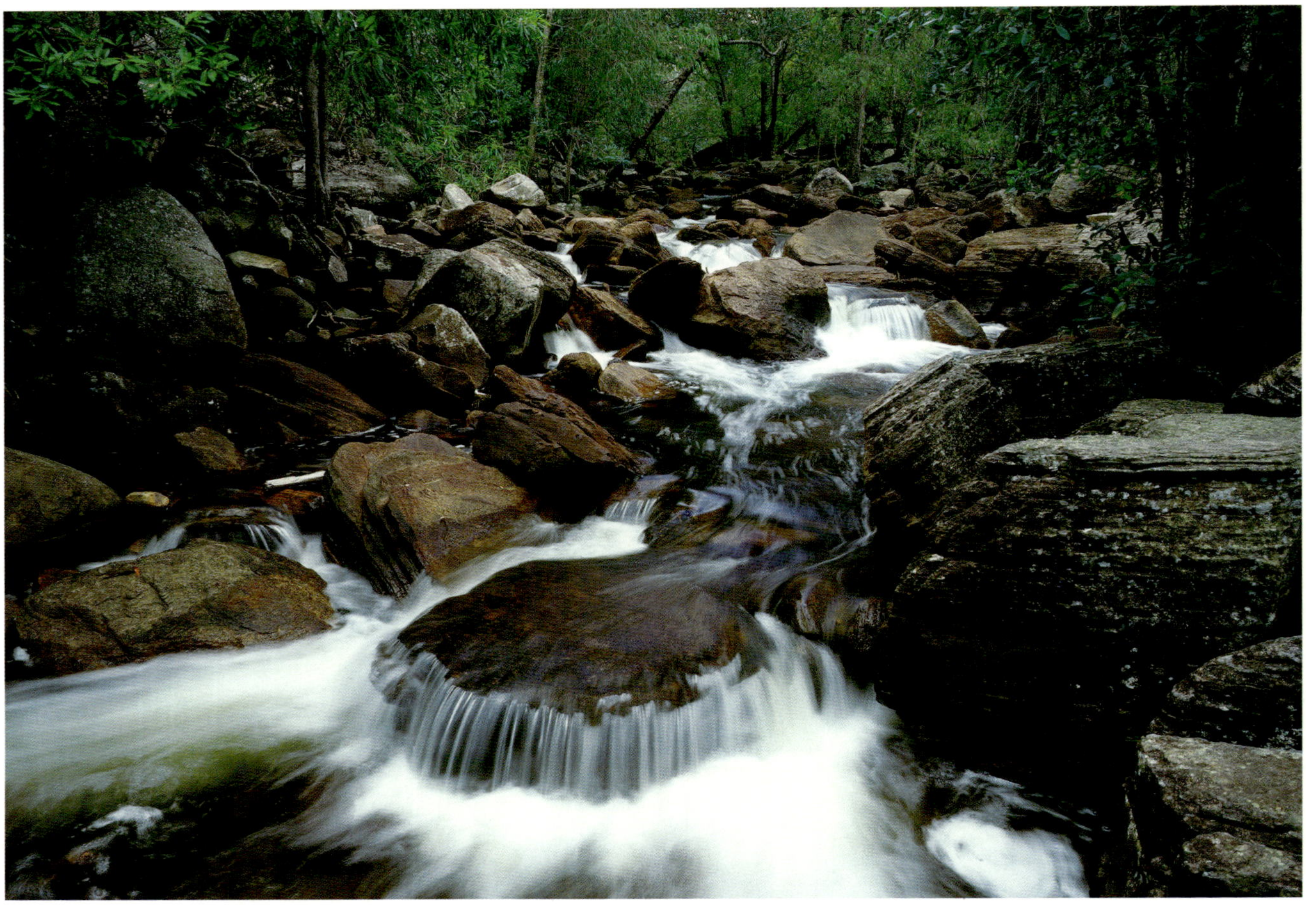

Cool, clear water spills from the Arnhem Land Plateau via a succession of rainforest-lined creeks.

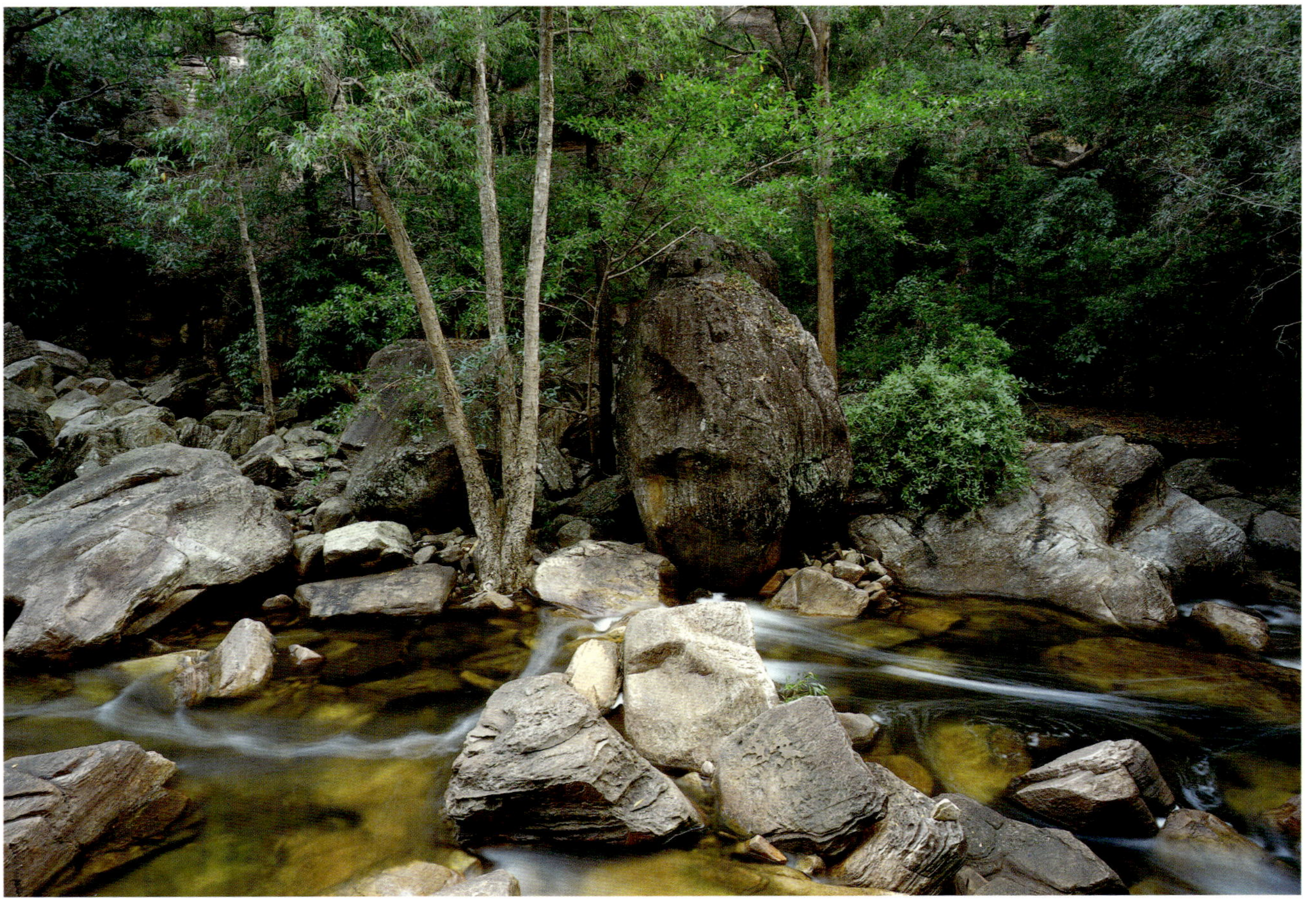

The rocky pools and enclosing vegetation in the upper reaches of Burdulba Creek - one of Kakadu's most enchanting hideaways.

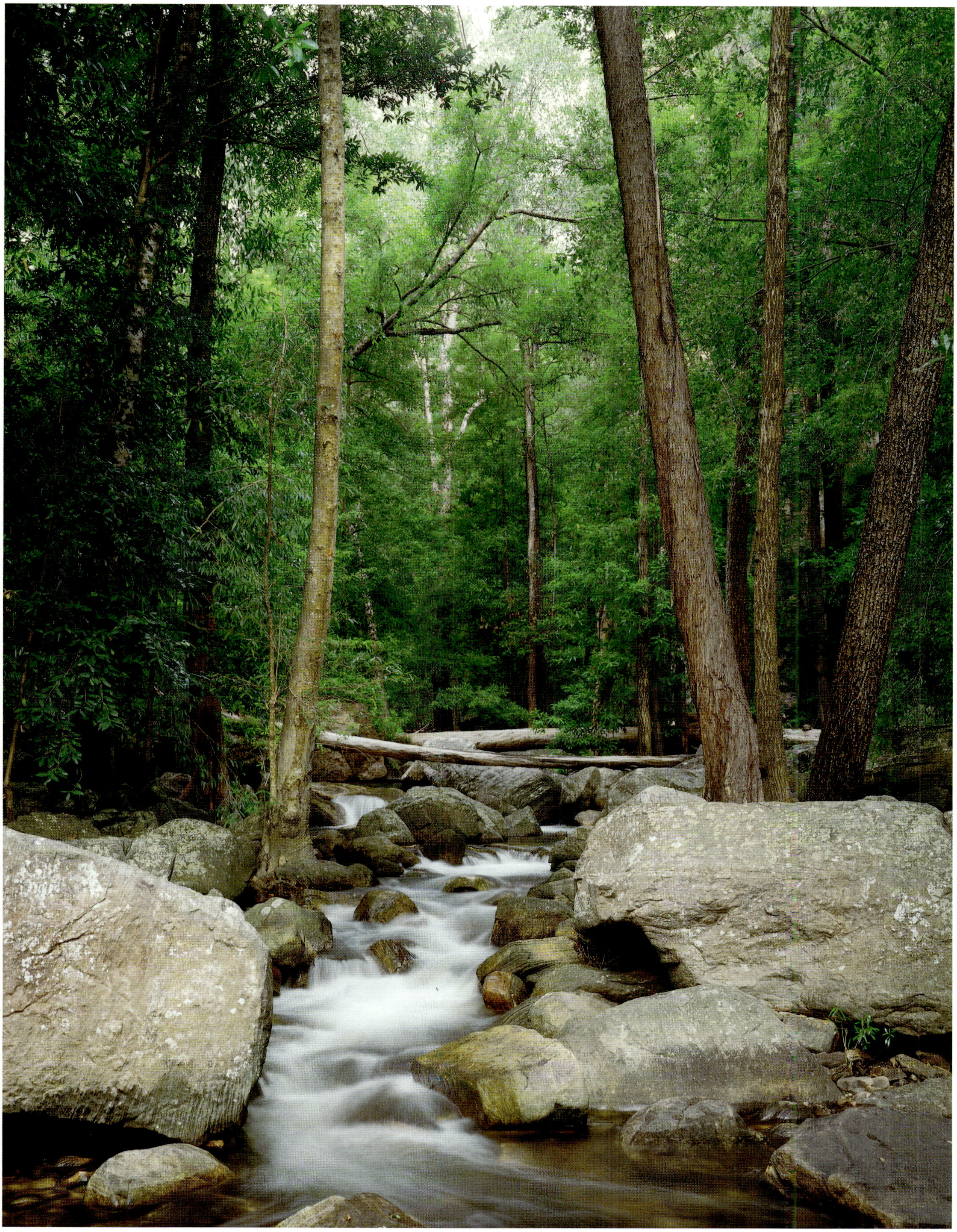

A high canopy of Anbinik trees creates a leafy bower in Burdulba's secluded gorge. Closely related to Gondwanan ancestors these trees are the hallmark of the remaining strongholds of monsoon forest.

BOUNTIFUL HABITATS

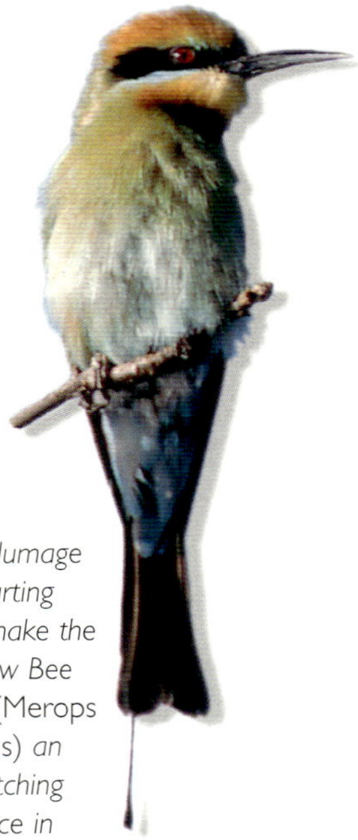

Vivid plumage and darting flight make the Rainbow Bee Eater (*Merops ornatus*) an eye-catching presence in many habitats.

The pattern of reclamation that first established the floodplains continues today. Kakadu's coastal margins are dominated by dense mangrove forests and saline tidal flats. The mangrove communities play a crucial role in trapping large volumes of silt washed along major waterways. In some locations the muddy shoreline can advance seaward by as much as 30 centimetres a year.

Thirty-nine mangrove species are found in the park. They create a surprisingly diverse habitat with abundant marine and bird life, including such redoubtable predators as the White-bellied Sea Eagle, Osprey and Brahminy Kite. While mangrove forests are important fish breeding grounds, nearby beaches are visited by nesting turtles and an array of crabs and other crustaceans.

With tidal flows reaching 80 kilometres upstream, mangroves are a prominent feature along estuary fringes. During the dry months Kakadu's rivers form serpentine channels bounded by backwater swamps, isolated billabongs and bare clay flats. Following torrential monsoon rains, floodwaters spill from the swollen creeks and rivers, immersing hundreds of square kilometres of low-lying plain beneath a shallow freshwater sea.

This rejuvenation triggers riotous growth as lilies, herbs, grasses and sedges rush to take advantage of the annual influx of water and nutrients. Very few trees have the ability to withstand prolonged waterlogging, followed by months of virtual drought. Paperbarks, however, are well adapted for such a life and they are easily the most conspicuous wetland tree, forming large stands in swampy areas and alongside rivers and billabongs.

The rains also refresh isolated pockets of lowland monsoon forest that cling to the edge of Kakadu's floodplains and rivers. These are remnants of the rainforests that once

The rich waters of the Magela floodplain linger well into the dry season.

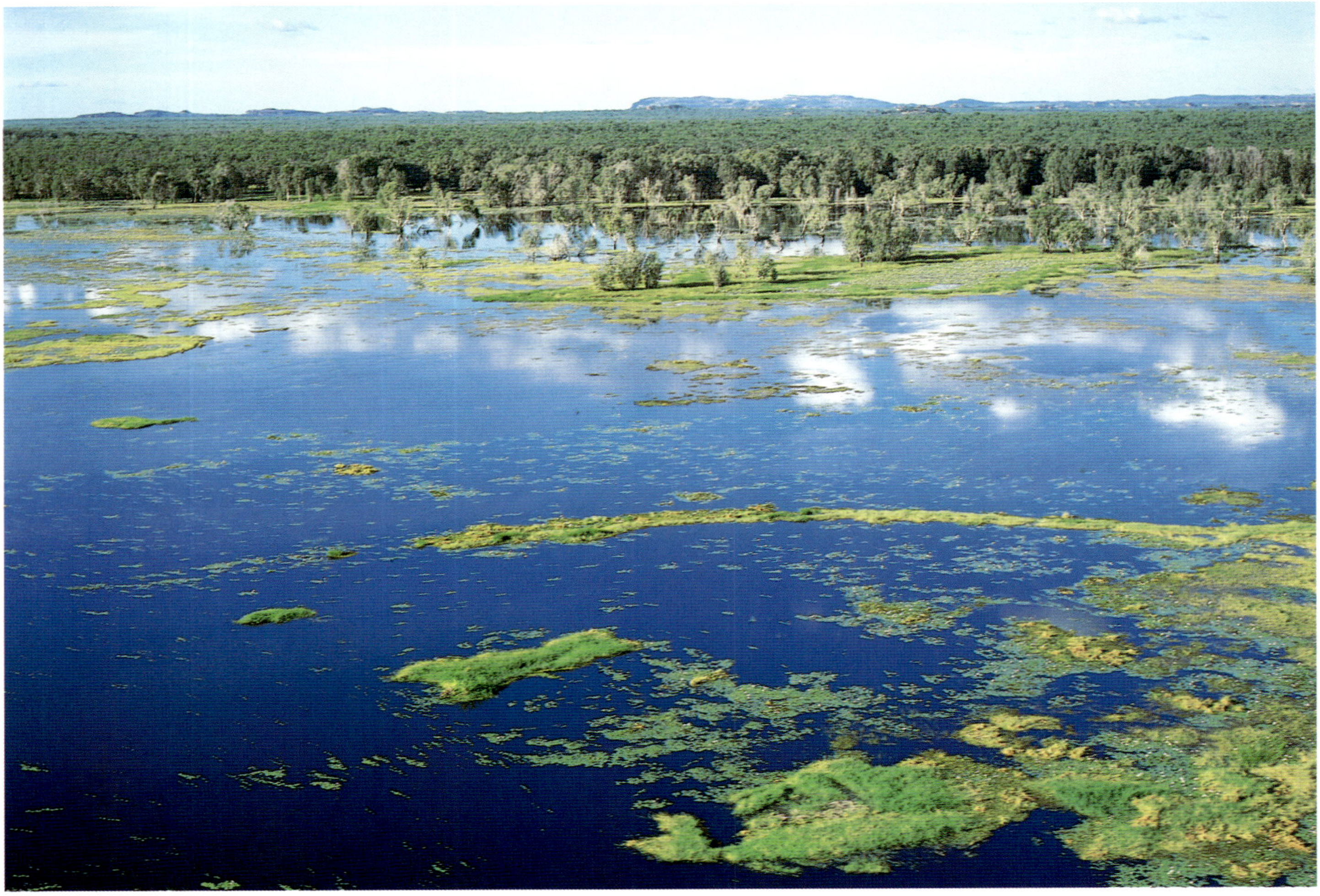

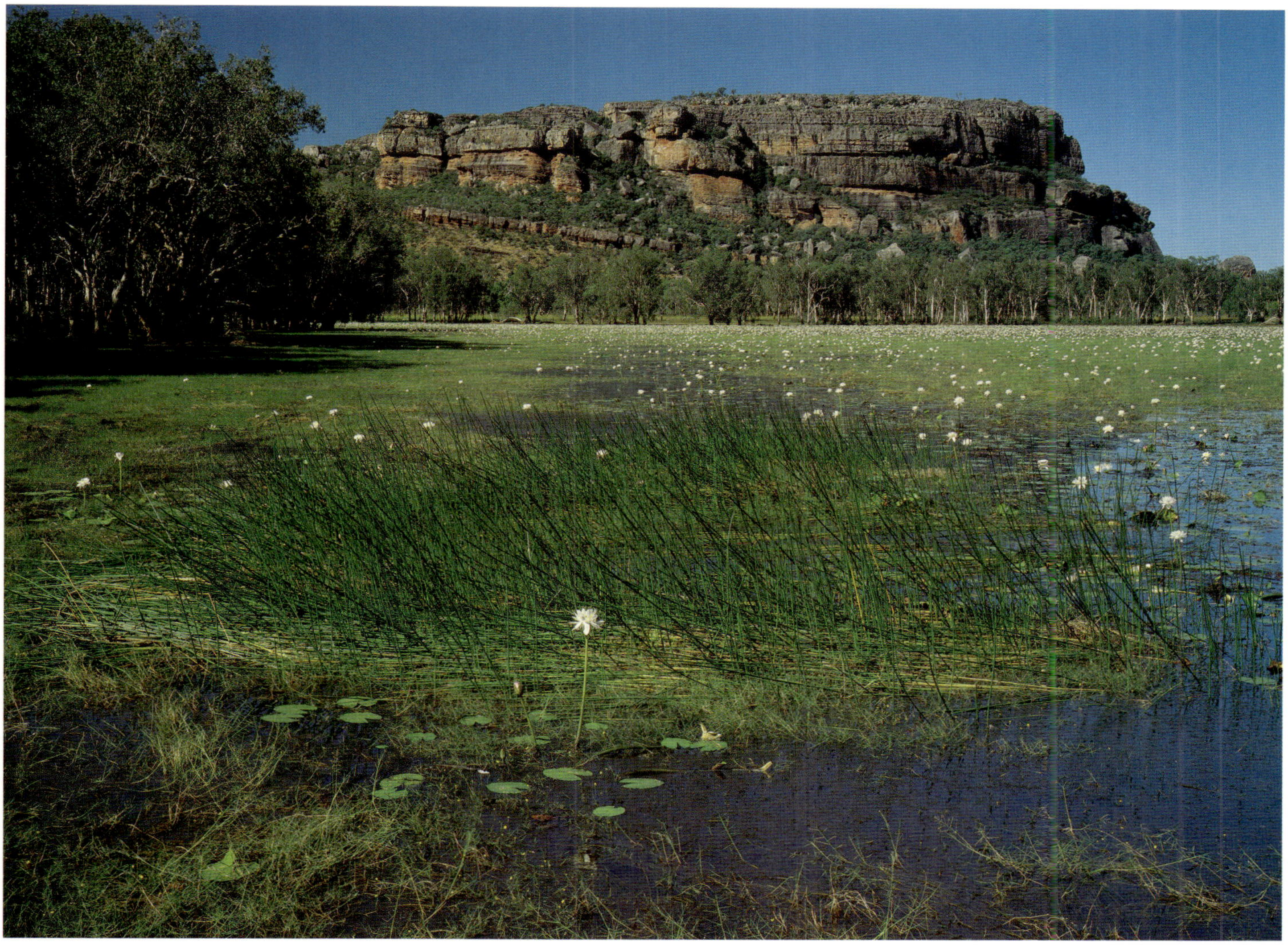

colonised almost the entire Australian continent. Increased aridity and more frequent fire patterns over the past 15 million years have left only these tenuous forest patches. They survive as important havens, especially for a range of birds that are heavily reliant on the small fleshy fruits produced by many species of forest trees.

The monolith of Burrunggui (Nourlangie Rock) provides an imposing backdrop to Anbangbang Billabong.

Beyond the reach of the floodwaters lie the gently undulating plains and rocky ridges of Kakadu's lowlands. For species diversity and sheer abundance this is the park's richest domain. Here the eucalypts and grasses rule. Most widespread are woodland plant communities which support a sparse tree cover and smaller gums, notably Northern Box and Round-leaf Bloodwood. Large areas are also cloaked with open forest where lanky woollybutts and stringybarks rise to form a broken leaf canopy 16 metres or more high. At ground level a variety of tall grasses are interspersed with acacias, shrubs and slender palms.

Casting morning shadows across this botanical splendour is the elevated stone country. The plateau is a complex mosaic of habitats, from stark pavements of exposed rock and sandy heaths dotted with spinifex, to moist gullies where rainforest giants soar overhead. Over thousands of years the plateau has become a natural citadel with a host of ecological niches providing refuge to most of the park's endemic species.

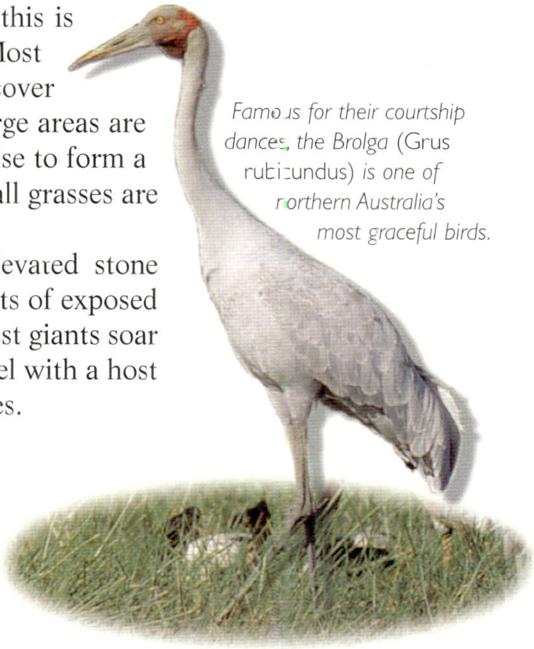

Famous for their courtship dances, the Brolga (Grus rubicundus) is one of northern Australia's most graceful birds.

HABITATS OF KAKADU

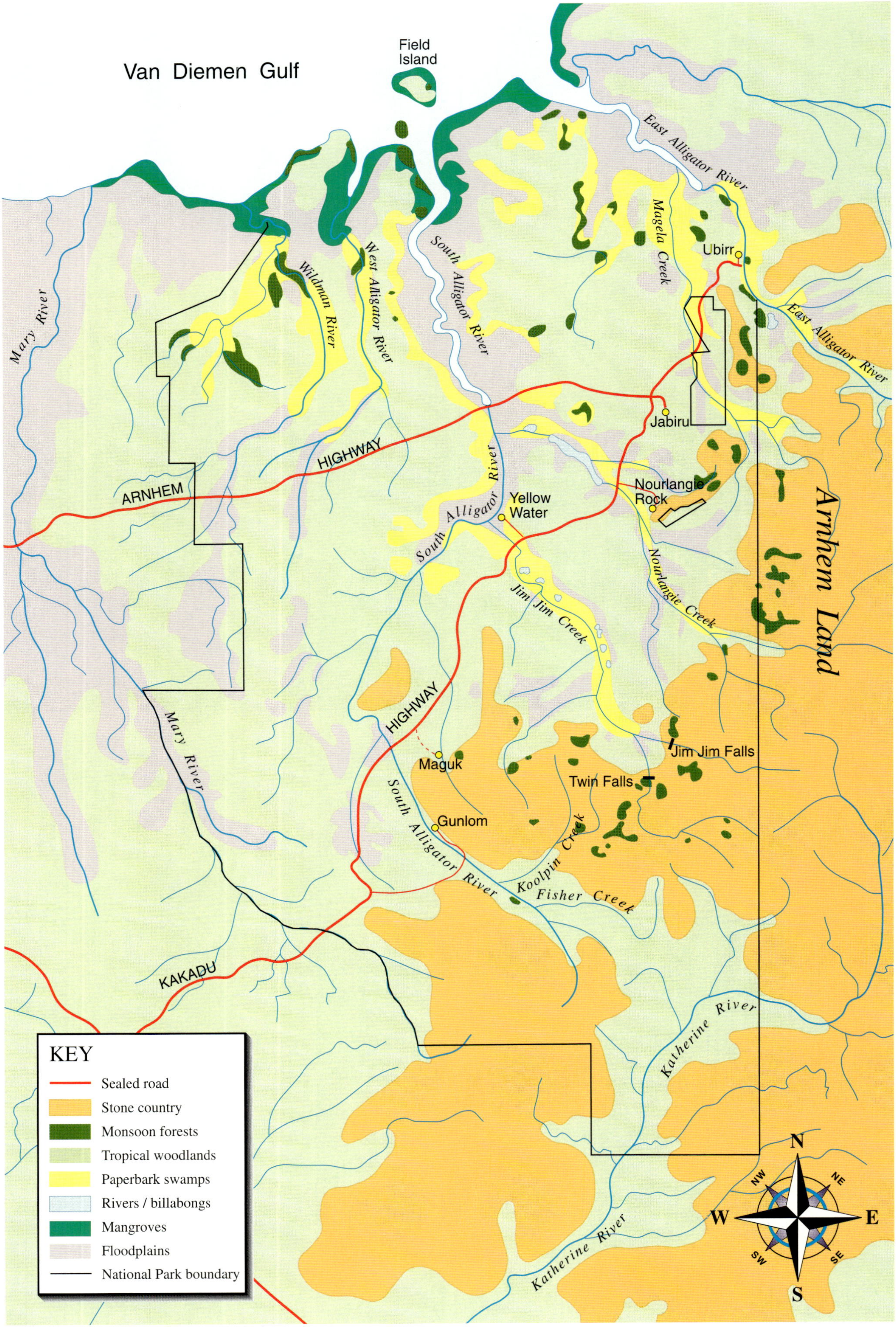

FOREST SURVIVOR

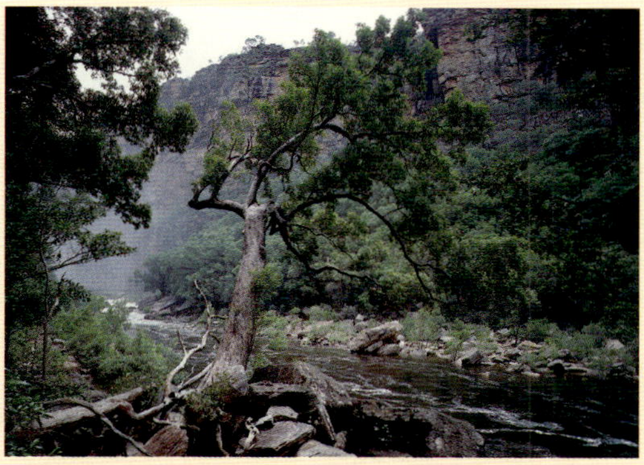

Although escarpment gorges provide shelter for Anbinik and other tree species, these forests also bear the brunt of raging wet season stormwater and debris.

The Anbinik tree *(Allosyncarpia ternata)* is found nowhere else but on the Arnhem Land Escarpment. It is the signature species of the plateau's remaining pockets of monsoon forest. In well-watered locations some specimens can grow to heights of 40 metres, forming a dense, spreading canopy, below which a lush underworld of palms, vines and other rainforest trees can flourish.

A member of the Myrtacae family, the Anbinik tree is a hardy evergreen relative of the ancestors that evolved to form Australia's all-conquering eucalypts. Thus it endures as a fascinating link to the ancient forests that once cloaked most of Gondwana. When Antarctica parted company from Australia around 50 million years ago Australia drifted northward and conditions became increasingly arid and cool. This climate shift caused a dramatic dwindling of the tropical Gondwanan forests. The decline was accelerated during later glacial periods as lower sea levels made it possible for competing species of Asian forest trees to spread into northern Australia.

Yet, despite these changes, isolated refuges of Gondwana's inheritance have hung on in northern Australia. A survivor of these struggles, Anbinik thrives in moist ravines and at sheltered sites at the foot of the escarpment. Travellers visiting the waterfalls and gorges in the south-eastern corner of the park have ample opportunity to appreciate the outstanding character of these forests.

Surprisingly, Anbinik trees are by no means confined to these protected nooks. Shady clusters are also found scattered inland from the escarpment on high sandstone terraces and rocky slopes. Even though these Anbiniks are often less than half the height of those in better watered sites, it is testimony to this tree's resilient character that it can survive at all in such exposed outposts.

Coping with the debilitating effects of seasonal drought is one thing, but these outlying patches of Anbinik forest have few defenses against wild dry season fires that can spread into the park from Arnhem Land. Such savage blazes threaten a variety of smaller trees dependant on the Anbinik's protection, as well as other fire sensitive species such as the Northern Cypress Pine.

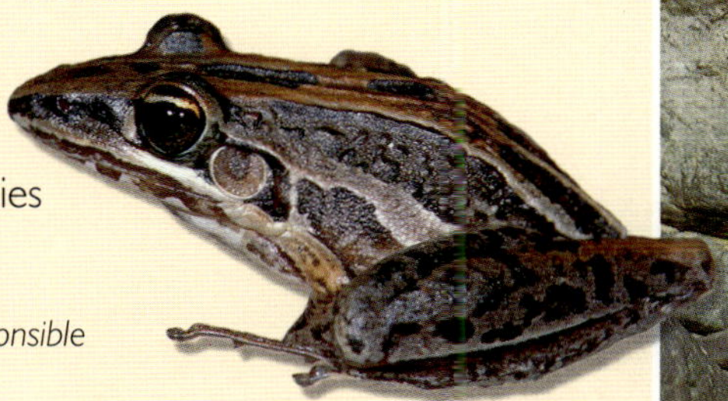

A Rocket Frog (Litoria nasuta), *just one of the many thousand frogs responsible for the deafening chorus of calls during Gudjewg.*

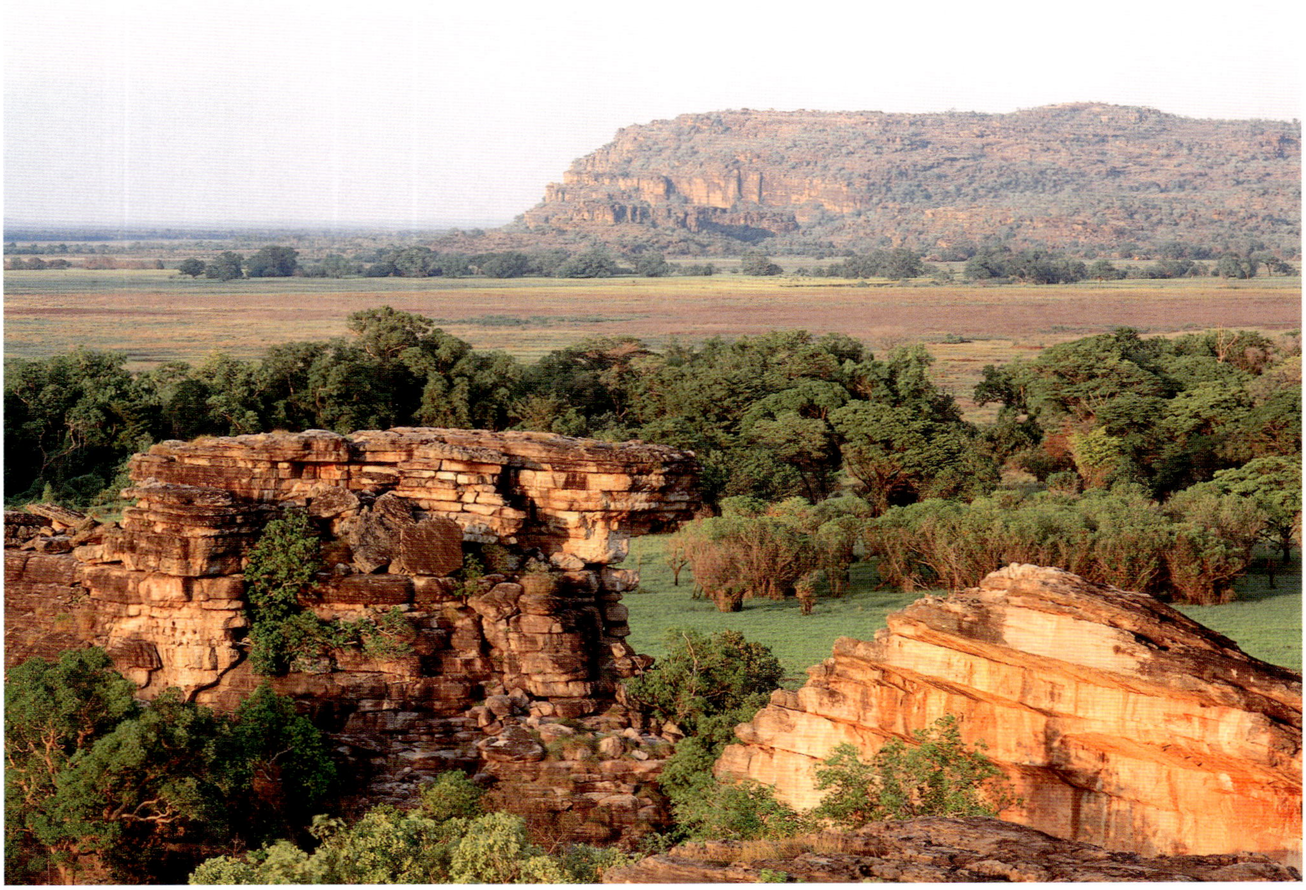

Evening light catches the rock outcrops of Ubirr. Beyond the East Alligator River and its floodplain rises another northern outlier of the escarpment..

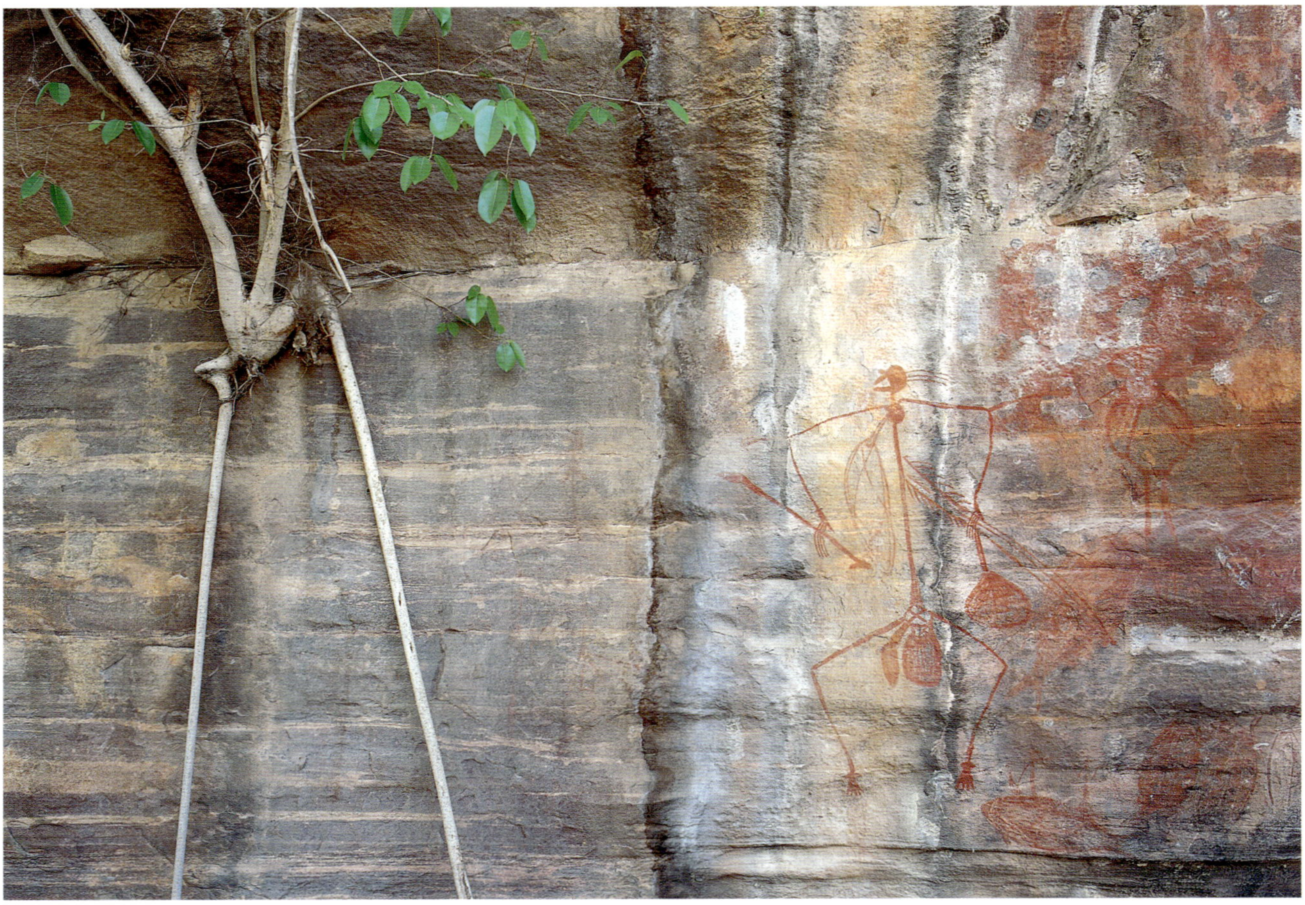

Ubirr is famous for its art sites. Here the roots of a Rock Fig offer a curious counterpoint to a finely drawn hunting figure wielding the tools of his trade.

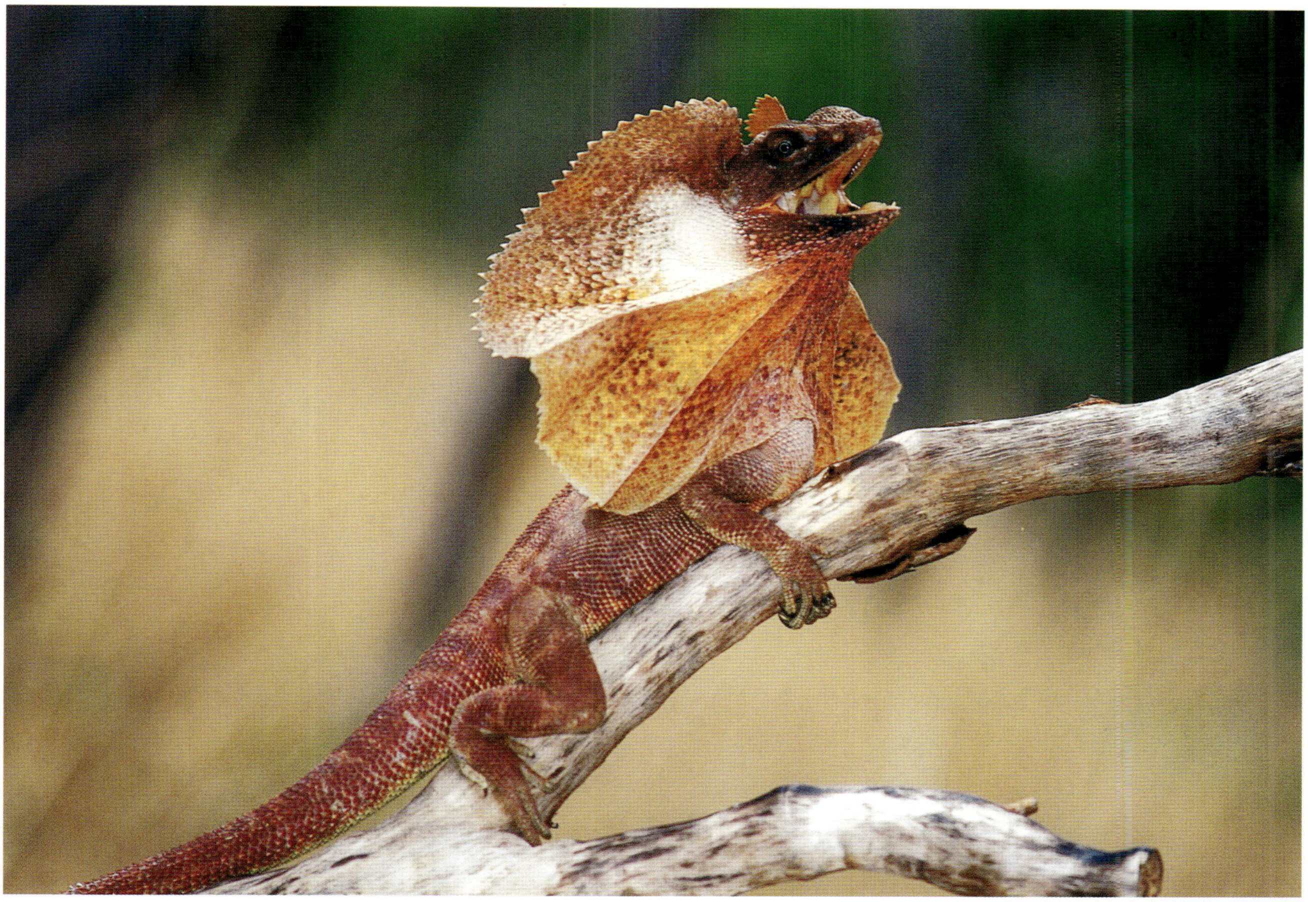

The Frilled Lizard, an habitual tree-dweller, is most active and visible during the wetter months of the year.

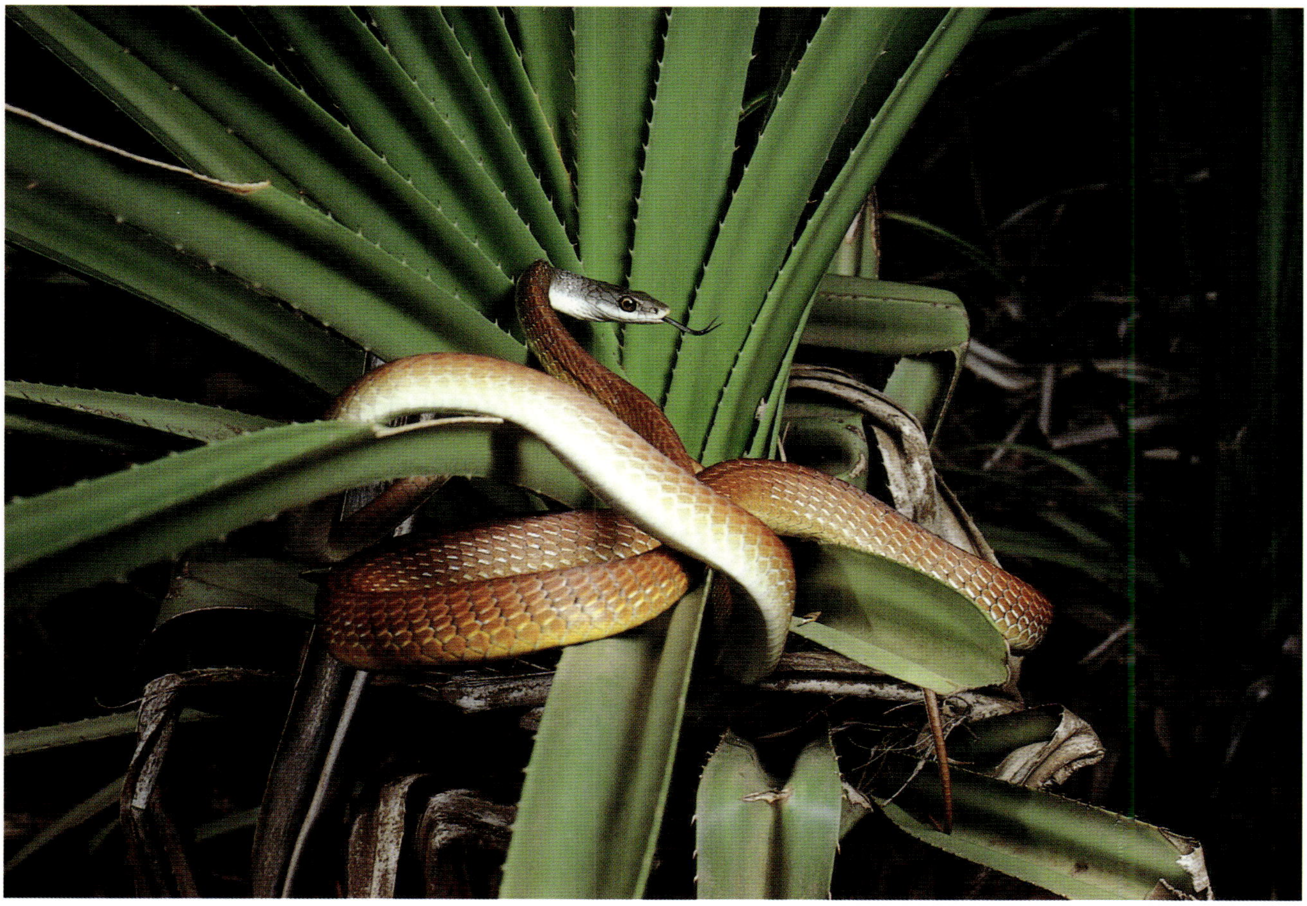

A Common-tree or Green-tree Snake (Dendrelaphis punctulatus) *embraces the barbed leaves of a pandanus.*

CATARACTS & CASCADES

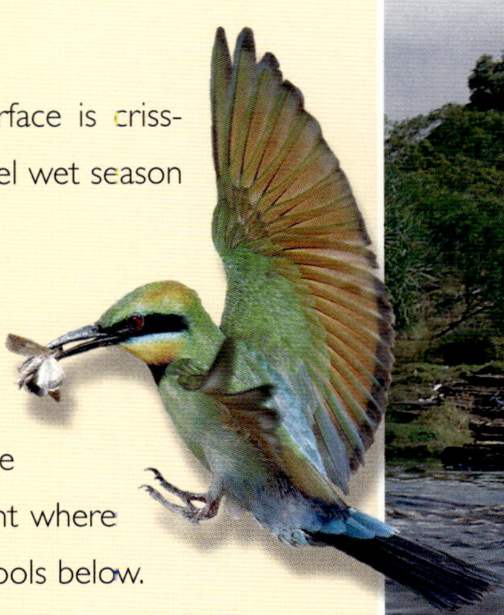

The Arnhem Land Plateau shows its age. Its weather-worn stone surface is criss-crossed by fissures and scoured fault lines. These ravine networks channel wet season runoff into the major watercourses.

Many of these creeks ease off the plateau in gradual stages. They enter secluded gorges where the waters drop down a succession of small cascades under the cover of a leafy canopy. Other creeks, however, lose little elevation in their passage across the plateau's horizontal stone terraces - that is until the waters converge at the rim of the escarpment where they topple headlong into space, plunging hundreds of metres to dark pools below.

The most celebrated of these locations is Jim Jim Falls or Barrkmalam. Nevertheless, few visitors get close to this icon in its most thunderous moods. Road access to the area is limited to the dry season, by which time the monsoon run-off has all but dispersed. Just a few kilometres further south on the escarpment stands Twin Falls (Gungkurdul). Here floodwaters crash over rocky tiers into one of the park's most imposing gorges. This backdrop and a year-round flow from springs on the plateau make this feature no less spectacular than its near neighbour.

Including its gorges and promontories the Arnhem Land Escarpment extends for nearly 600 kilometres. Along this ragged perimeter there are many hundreds of waterfalls. They are special places, not just for the drama of wet season cataracts, but for their sheltered pools and sanctuary of the surrounding forests.

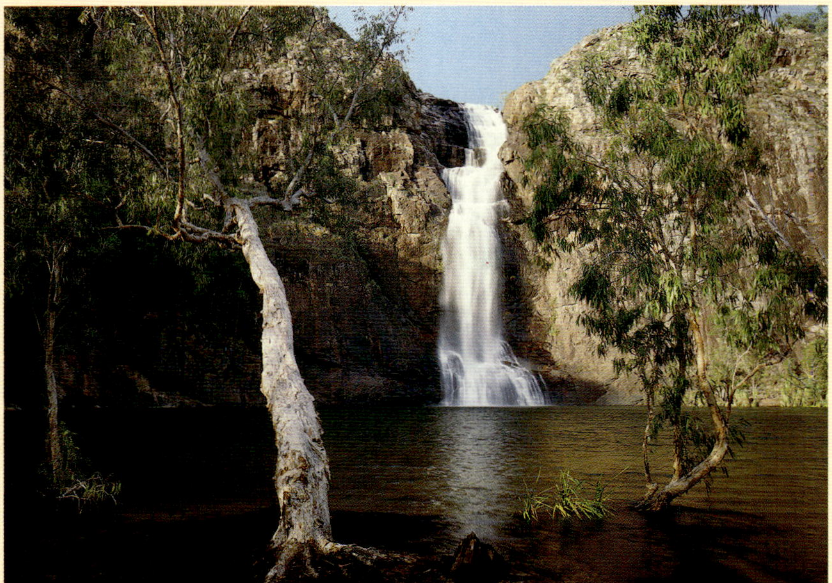

Gunlom is one of the many waterfalls and inviting pools found along the southern outcrops of the escarpment.

ABOVE *The Rainbow Bee-eater, a proficient hunter of insect life.*

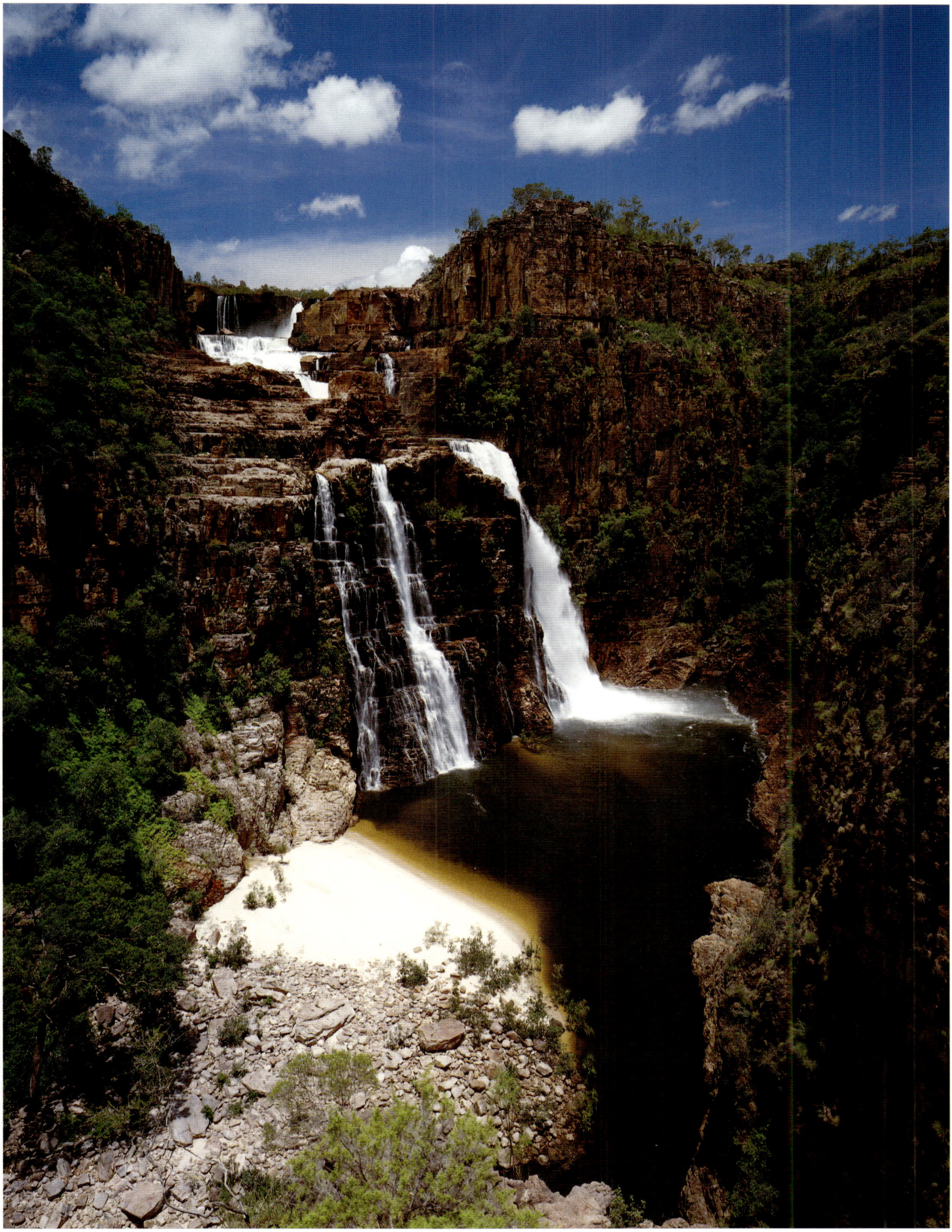

Wet season rains on the plateau feed the dramatic tiered cascades at Twin Falls.

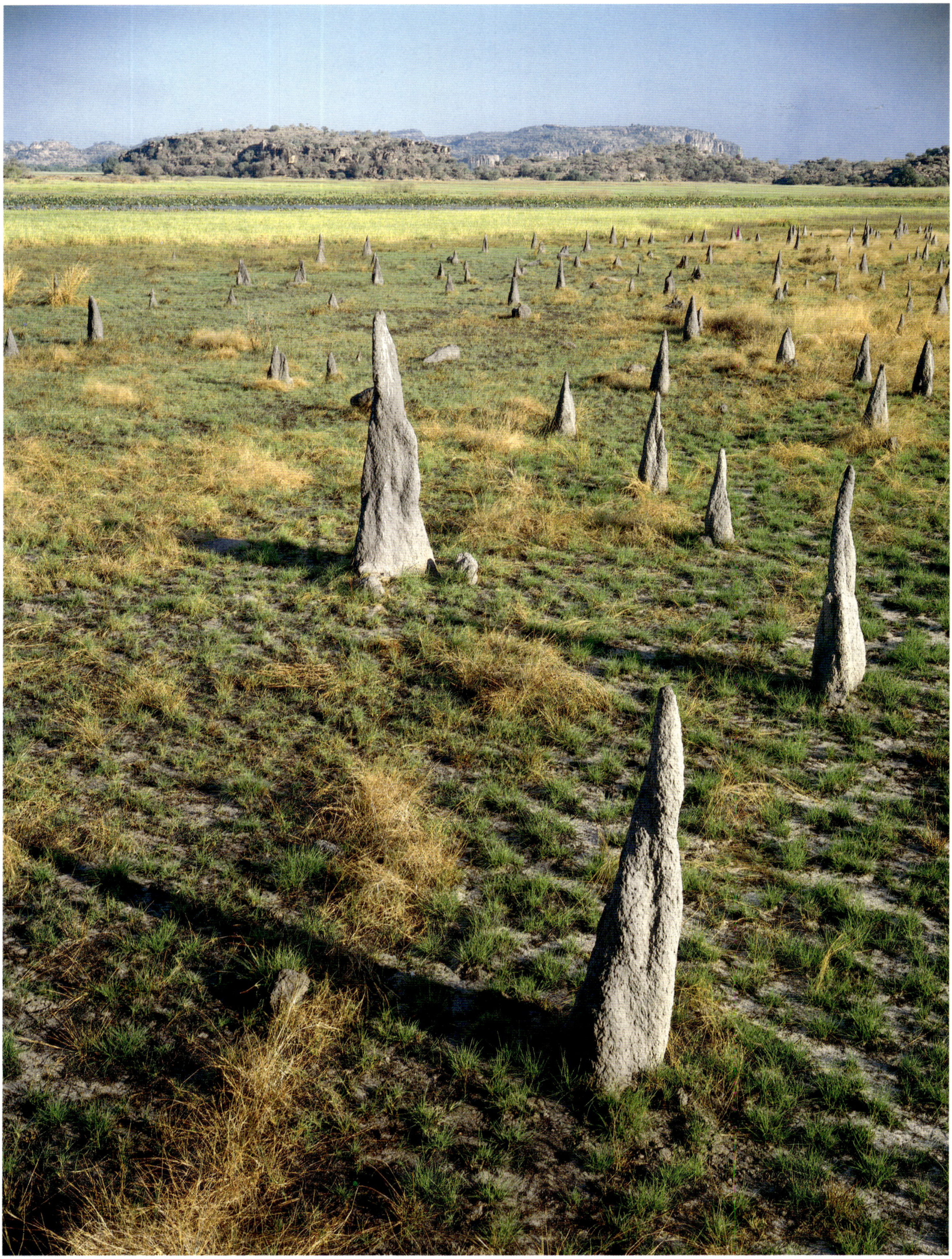

Unsung heroes of the lowlands, termites play a vital role in recycling plant material. Here their mounds dot the Magela floodplain like giant discarded crocodile teeth.

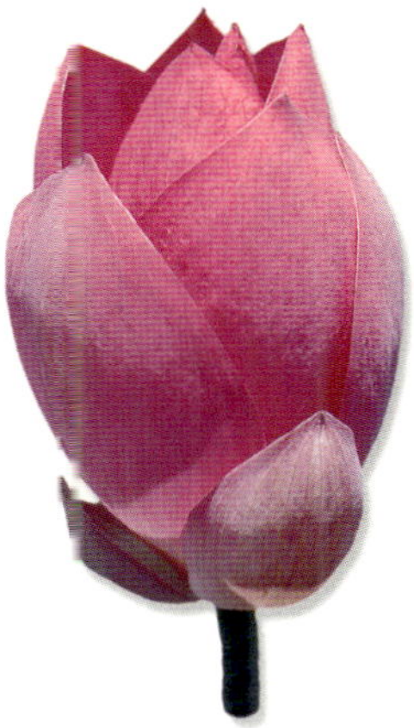

The flower of the Lotus Lily, (Nelumbo nucifera).

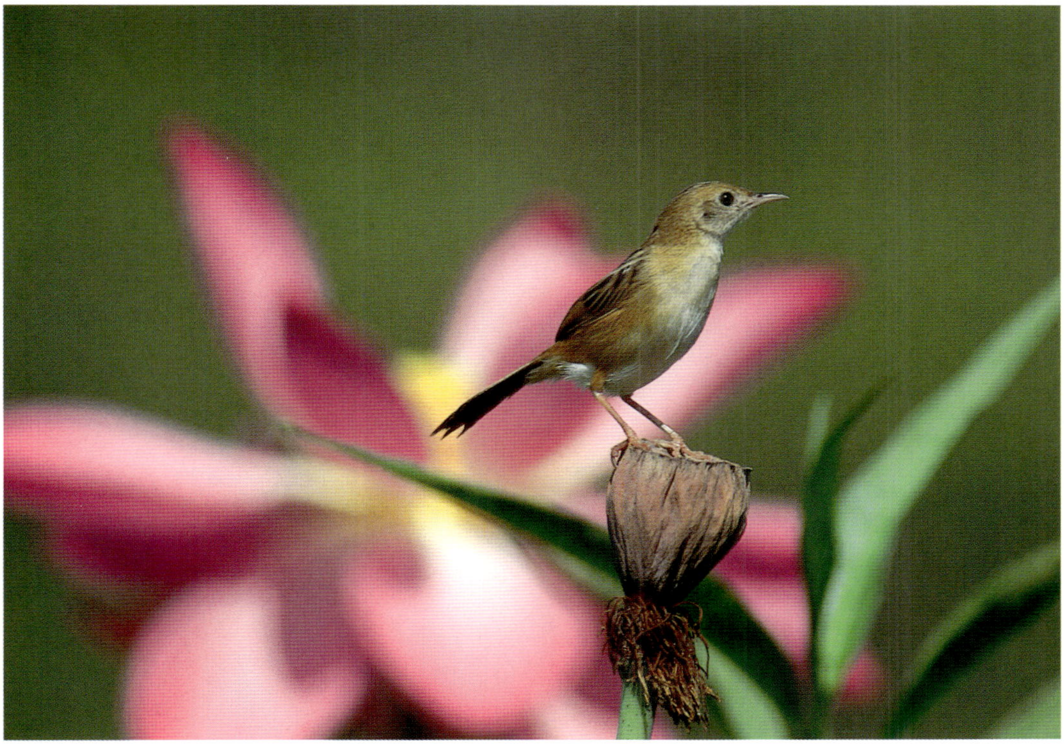

The flower stalk of a lily provides an elevated vantage point for a Golden-headed Cisticola (Cisticola exilis).

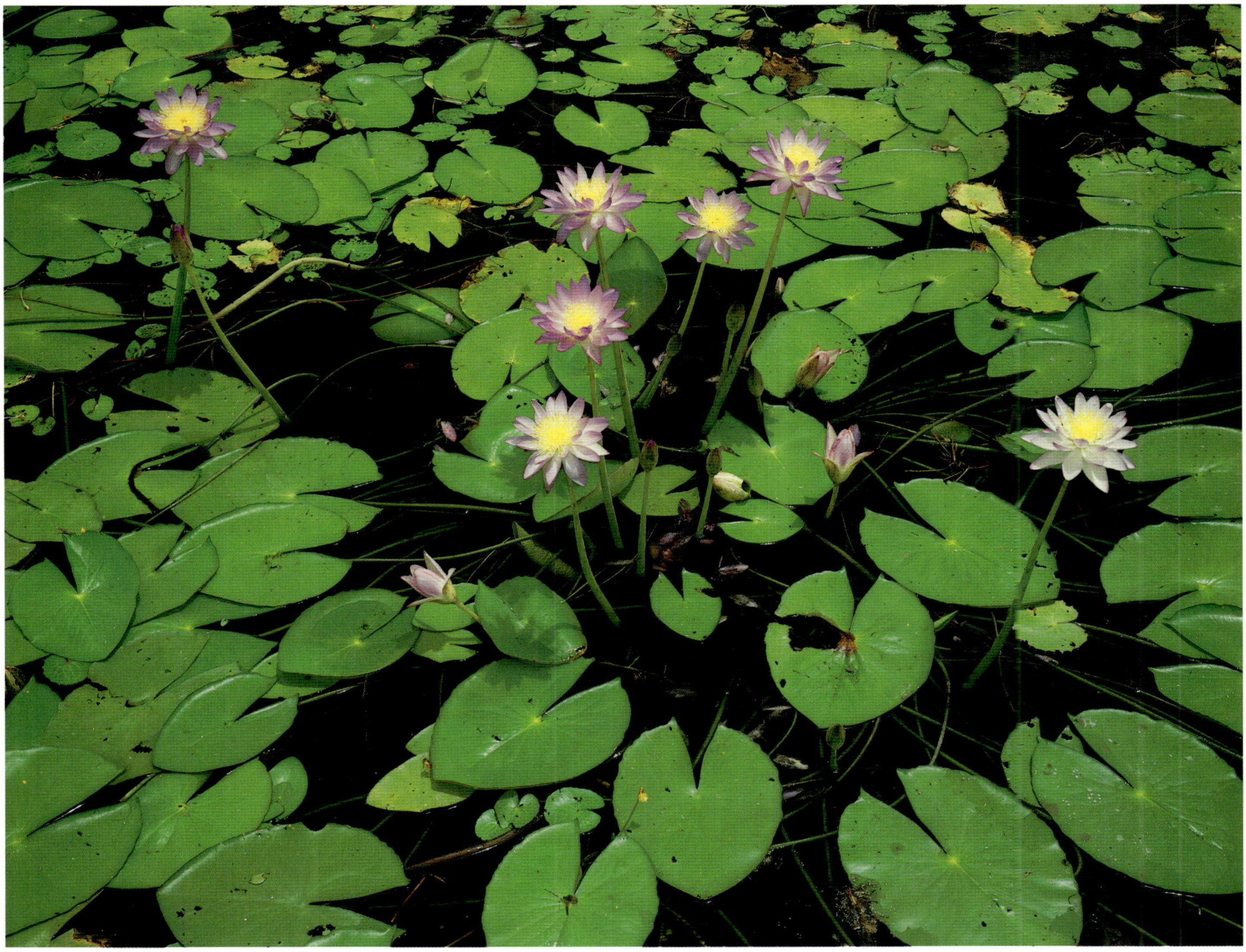

Kakadu's billabongs are dominated by lilies, including the common Blue Waterlily (Nymphaea violaceae).

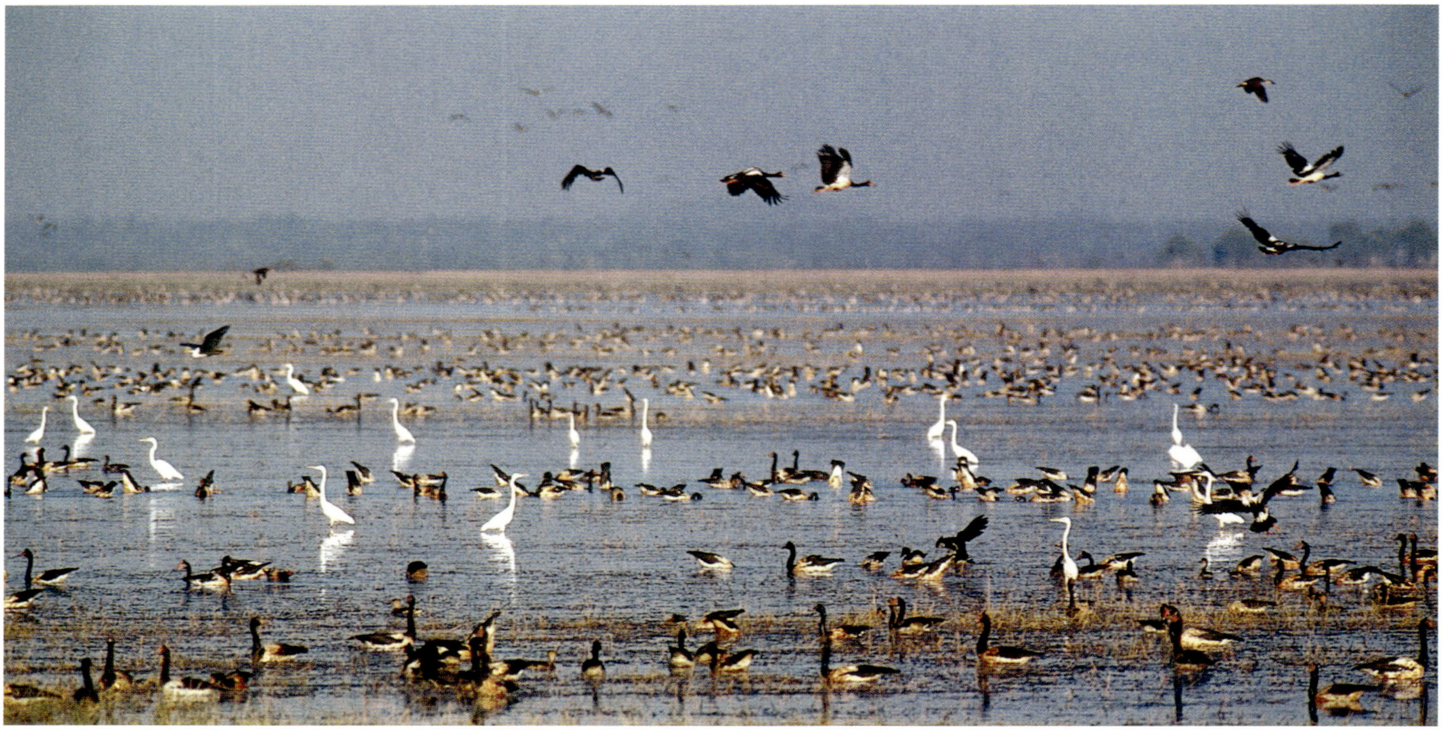

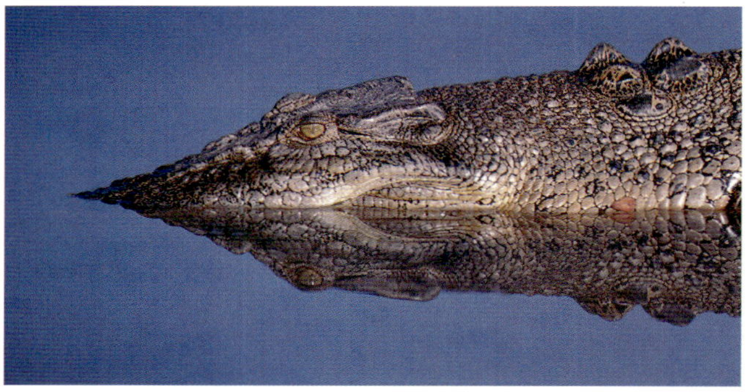

The all-seeing, all-powerful saltwater or Estuarine Crocodile (Crocodylus porosus) *roams widely from the coast and rivers to the floodplains and billabongs.*

TOP *By late August any remaining expanse of water teems with birdlife, such as this section of the Nourlangie foodplain.*

RIGHT *A Pied Heron* (Ardea picata), *one of the many deft fish feeders of Kakadu's wetlands.*

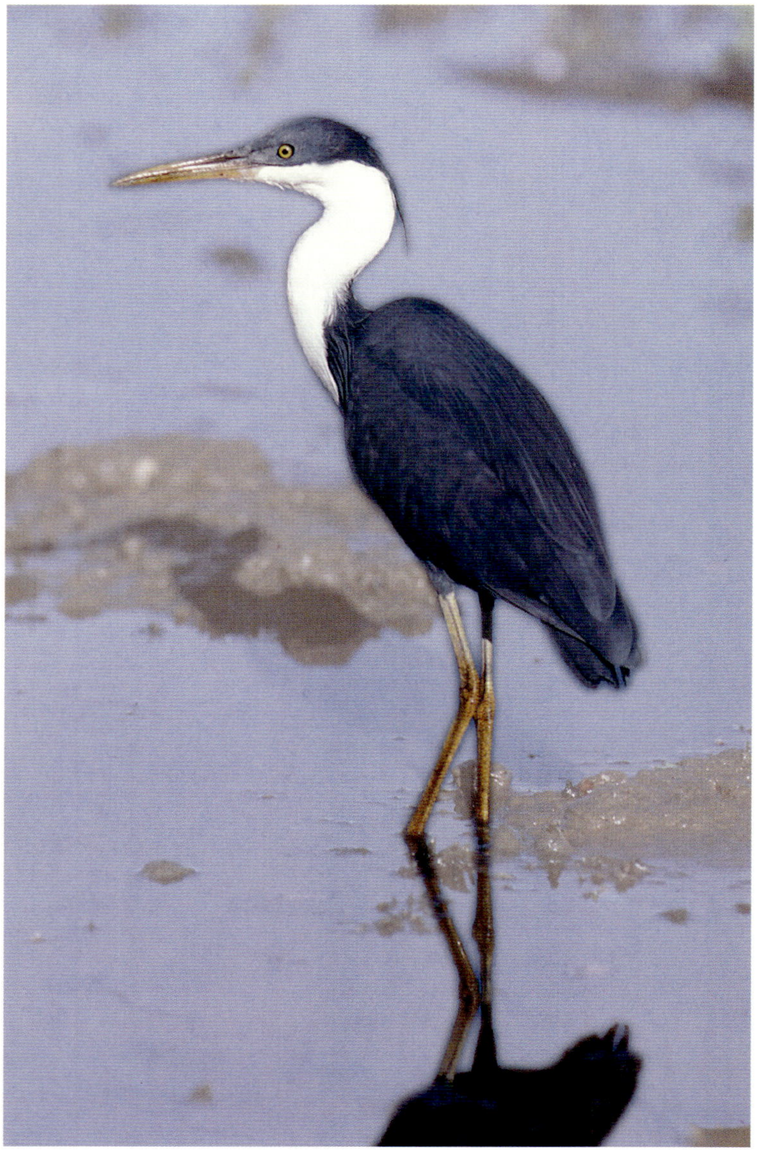

WET & WILD

A billabong at dusk. The water is smooth, the air still. Hundreds of Plumed Whistling Ducks are quietly gathered on a grassy bank. Late afternoon light catches the water lilies, their large floating leaves crinkled at the edges like the ruff of a Frilled Lizard. The only movement is a Comb-crested Jacana, silently prancing from lily to lily. All appears tranquil. But appearances can be misleading and with the stab of a beak or the thrash of a tail everything can change.

When visiting a billabong it pays to be prepared for the unexpected. As the dry months drag on these last remaining deep pools become crowded stages for life and death struggles. The surrounding floodplains are now virtual deserts, as dormant as a tundra in winter. For any animal reliant on water and the life it supports, there is no choice but to join the throng. During brief lulls a billabong might look like a calm oasis, yet it can also turn into a frantic, congested battleground.

As the food chain tightens the hunter becomes the hunted. So a file snake surfacing for air finds itself plucked from the shallow water by the powerful beak of a Jabiru. Or a Barramundi cruising the surface in search of a meal is itself suddenly caught in the crush of a crocodile's jaws. There is food, but there is also intense competition for territory and prey. Fierce rivalries develop.

Down at water level the vulnerability of smaller inhabitants to sudden attack is strikingly apparent. All around the billabong in the branches of the pandanus and paperbarks there loiter dagger-beak onlookers, from compact Azure Kingfishers to much larger predators like herons, Darters and egrets.

As dusk closes in many creatures settle, while others begin their nocturnal routines. The cooling air resounds with a chorus of frog calls and the fizzing hum of insect life. Bats appear, seemingly from out of nowhere, swooping in low, silent passes across the surface of the billabong.

For many animals darkness brings a reprieve from threat of ambush, but the scene is rarely peaceful for long. All through the night there are squabbles in the trees and thrashing skirmishes in the water as tenants continue their restless wait for the rains to return.

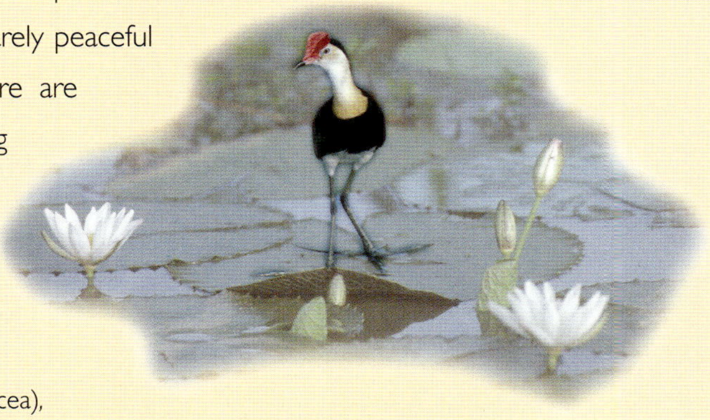

The Comb-crested Jacana (Irediparra gallinacea), *one of the most distinctive and engaging of all wetland birds.*

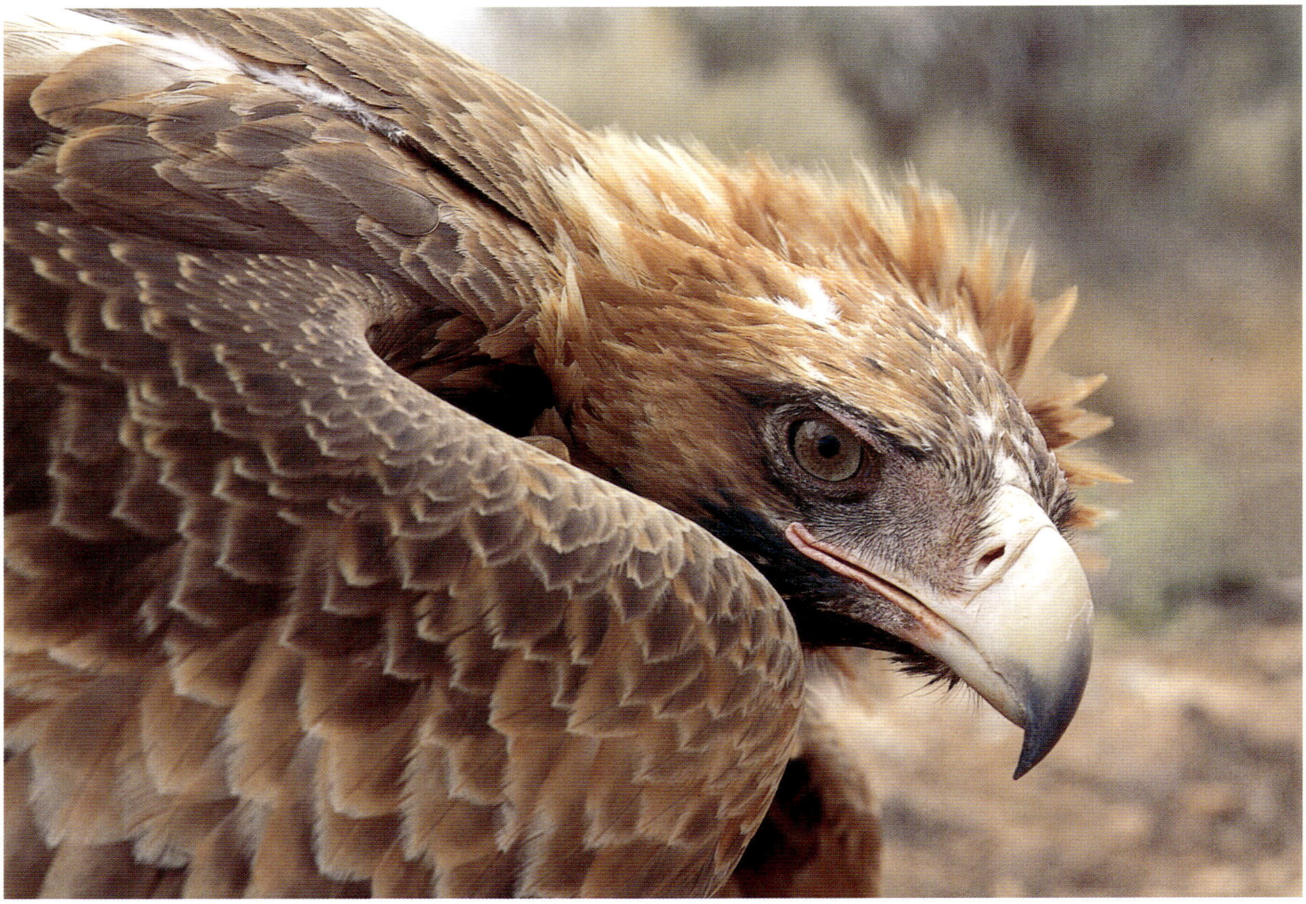

In the rocky eyries of the escarpment nests the Wedge-tailed Eagle (Aquila audax), *Australia's largest bird of prey.*

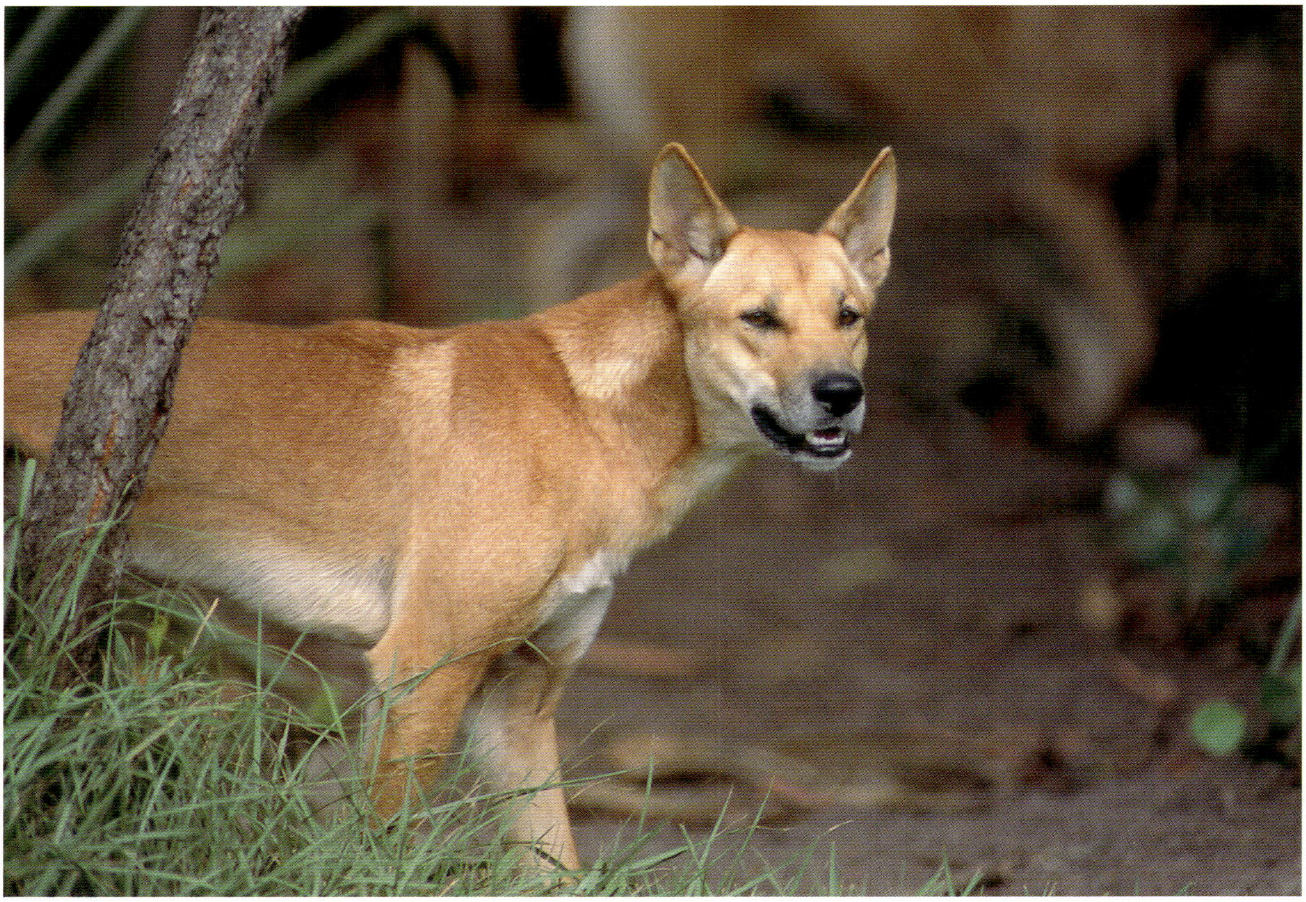

The Dingo (Canis familiarus dingo) *is the dominant carnivore of Kakadu's vast lowlands.*

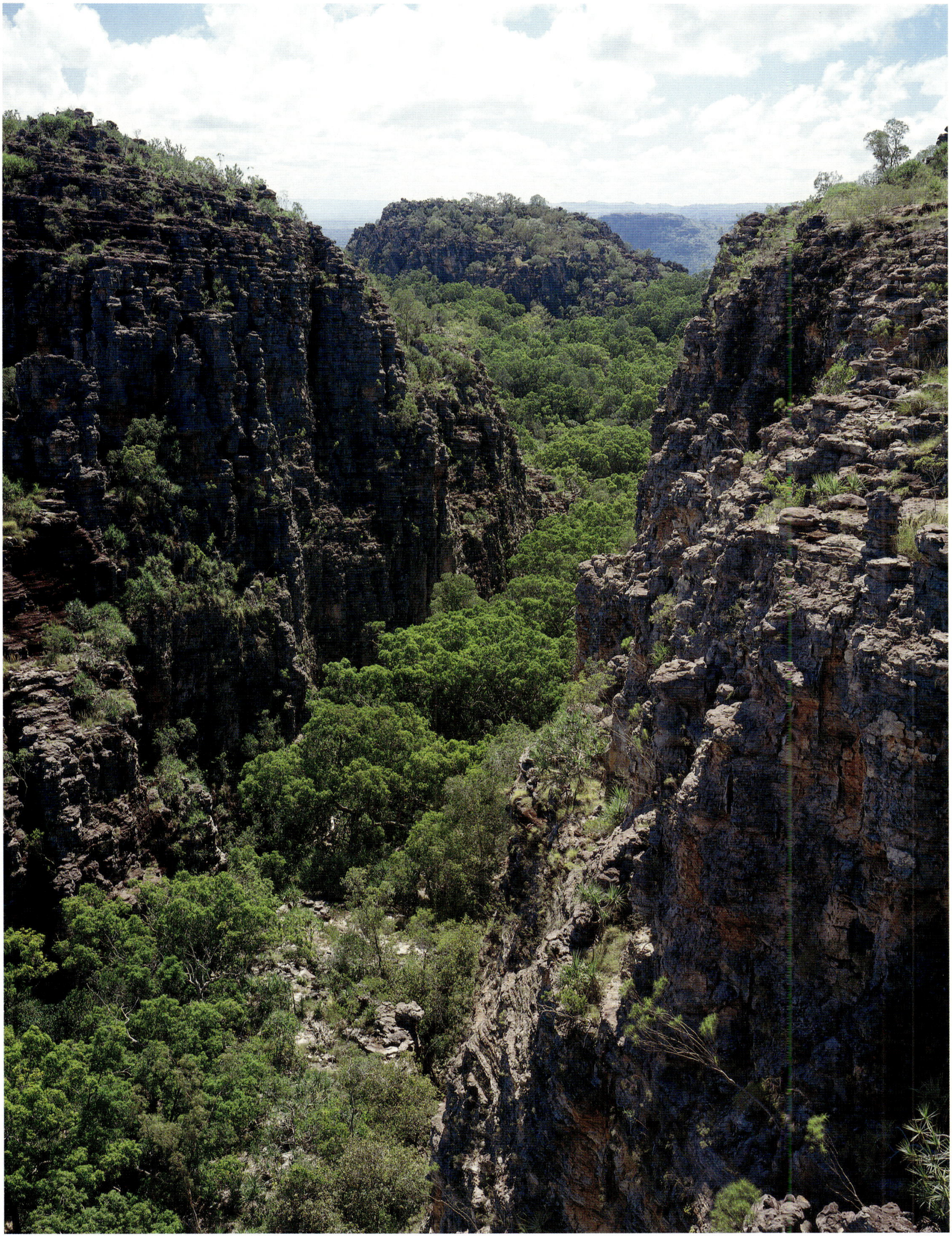

The broken terrain of the northern escarpment is a baffling complex of gorges, forested slopes and craggy outliers.

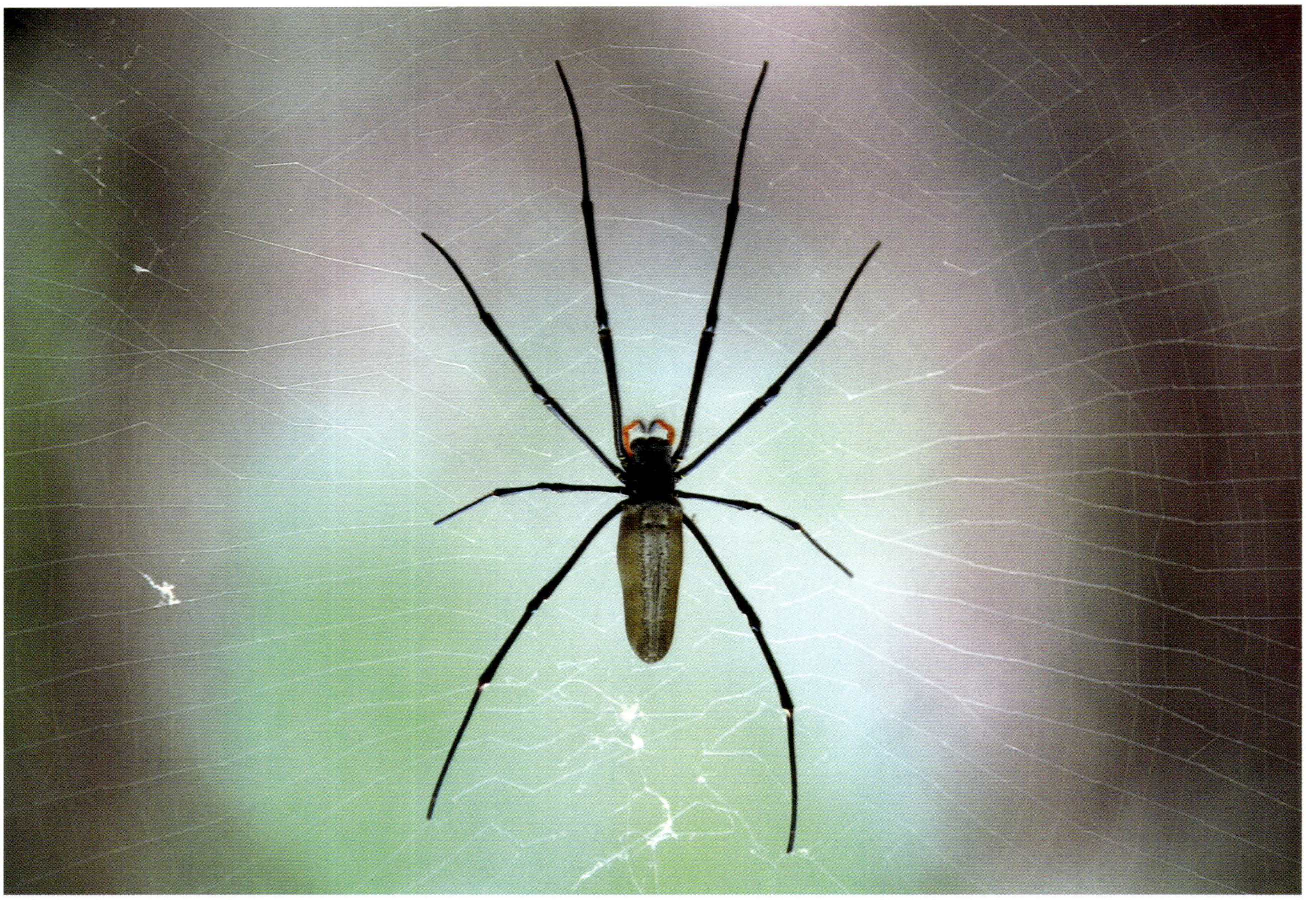

The spectacular female Golden Orb Spider spins her impressive web to snare large insects as they pass through the forest interior.

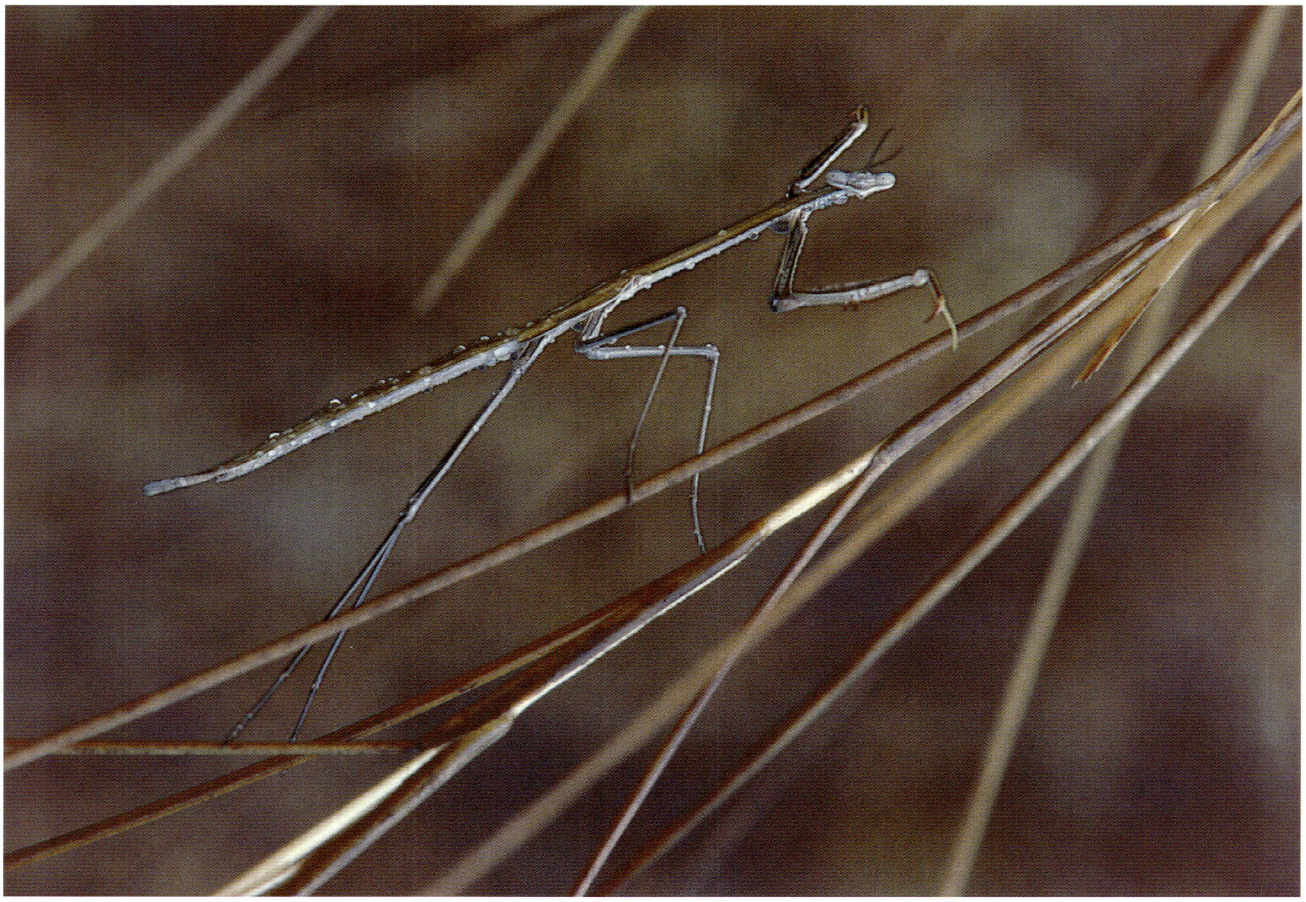

Kakadu's abundance of spear grass provides stick insects with ample opportunities for concealment and ambush.

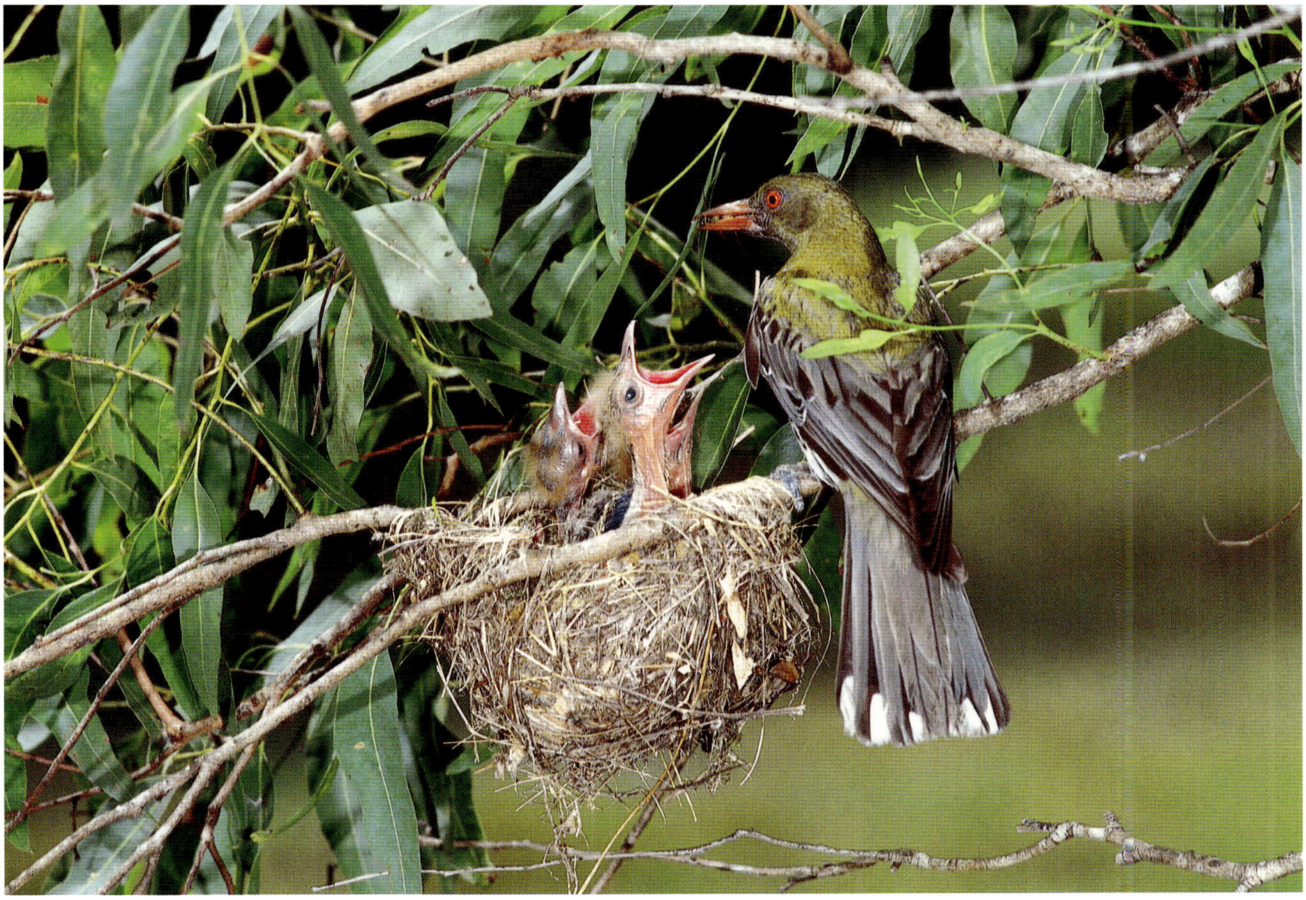

The Olive-backed Oriole (Oriolus sagittatus) *feeds in the canopy of the forest and woodland.*

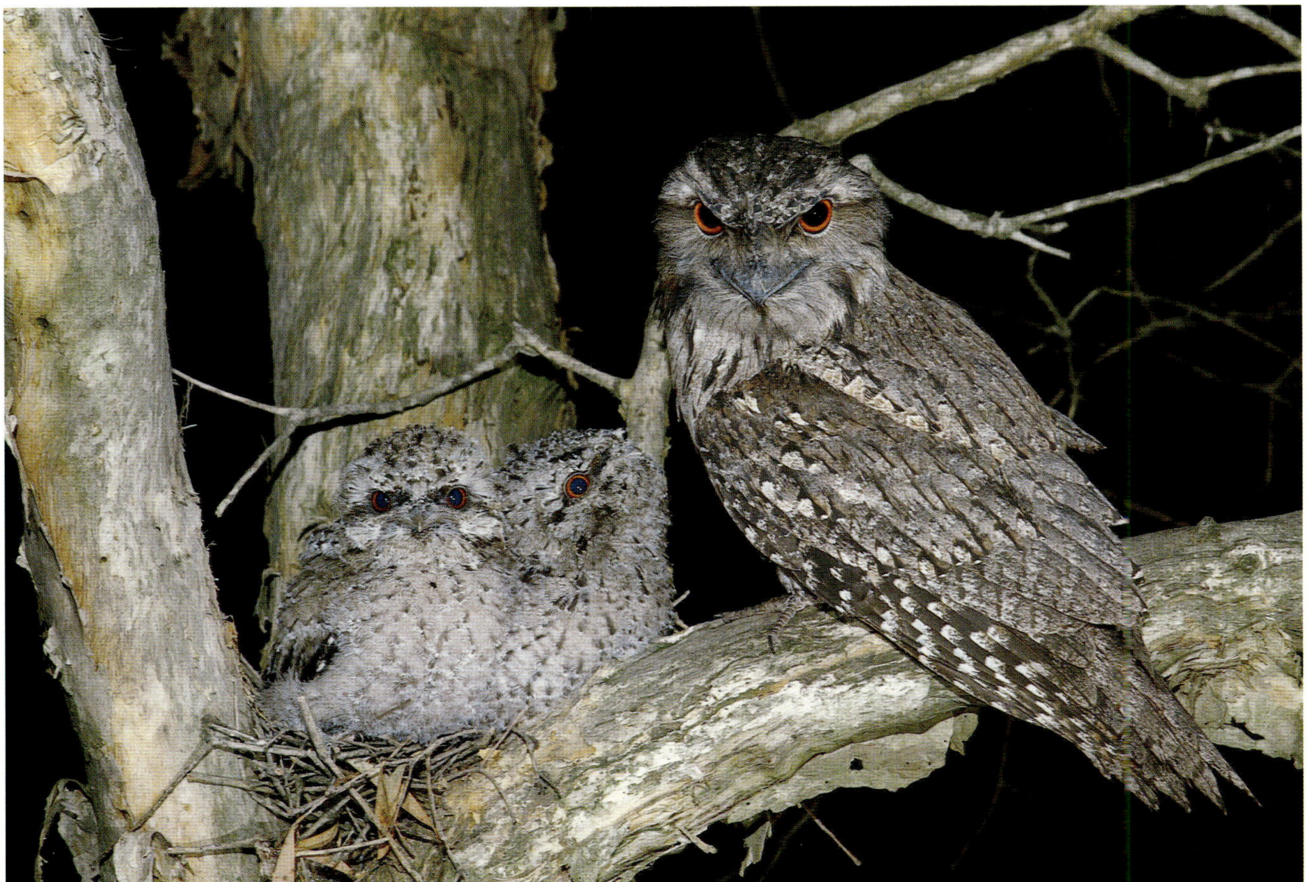

A silent night-time hunter, the Tawny Frogmouth (Podargus strigoides) *is widespread throughout Australian woodland habitats.*

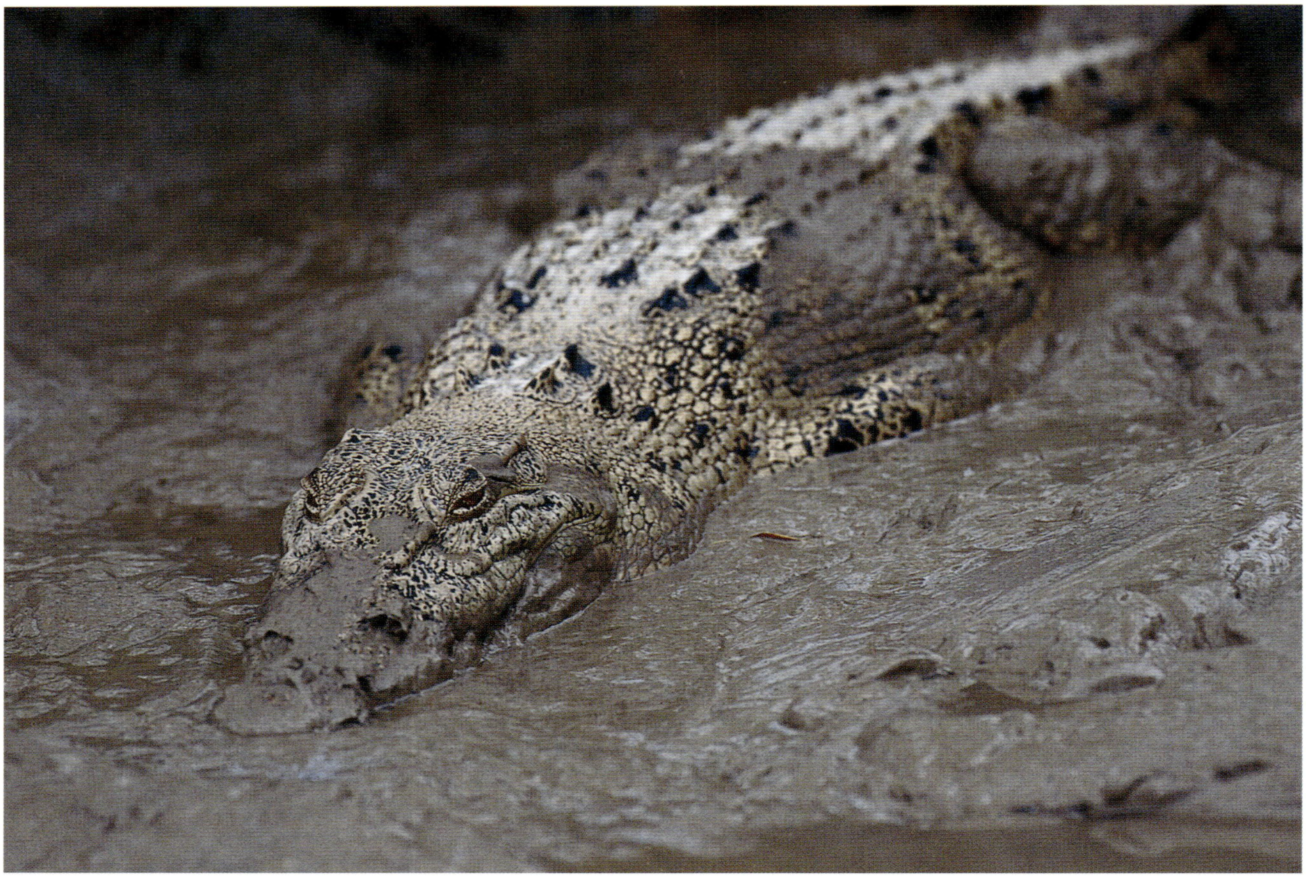

Wallowing at the top of the food chain, 'salties' enjoy lazing in cool mud during the heat of the day.

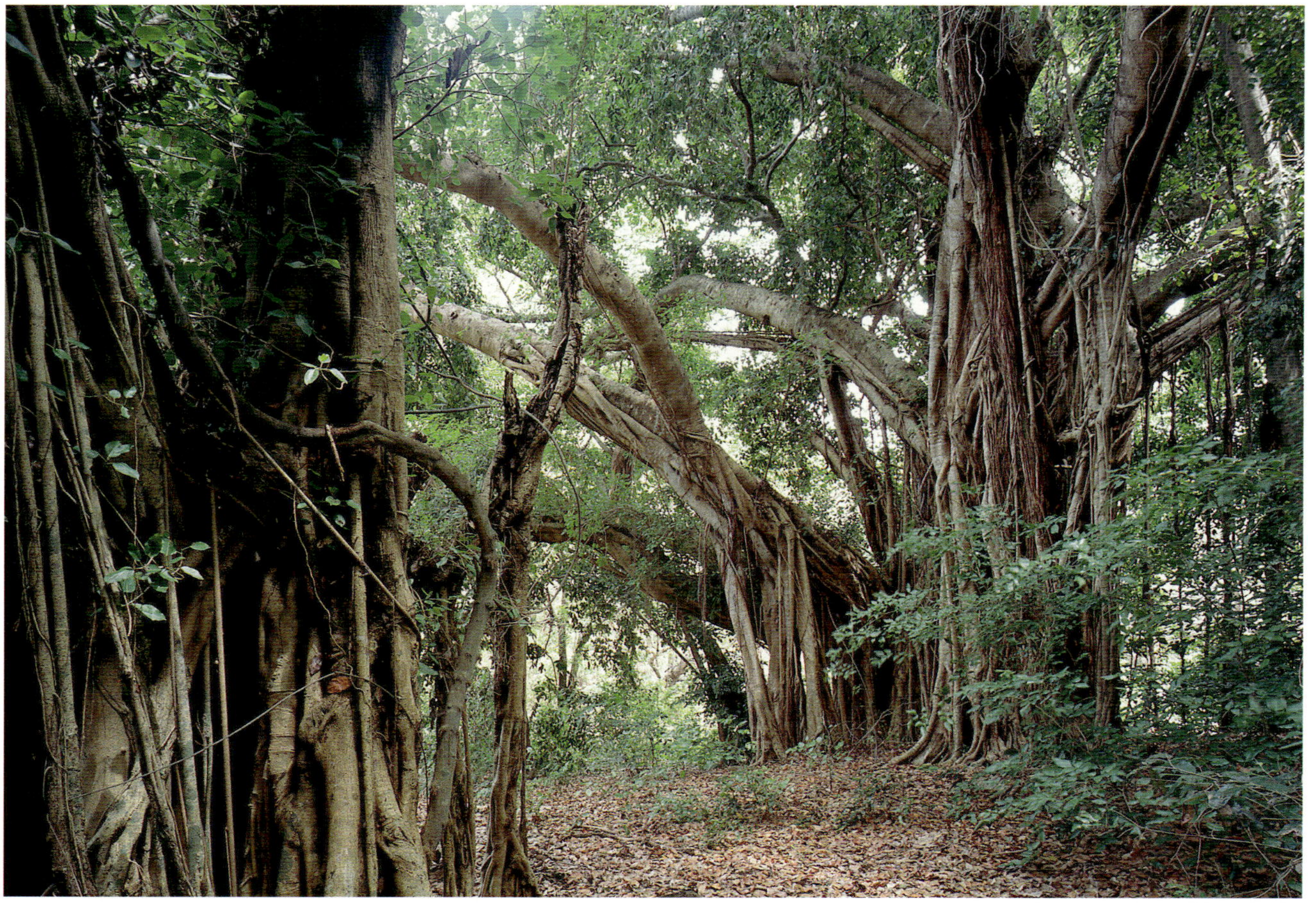

Small plots of coastal monsoon forest surviving on ancient dune-rises, include trees such as the majestic Banyan Tree (Ficus virens).

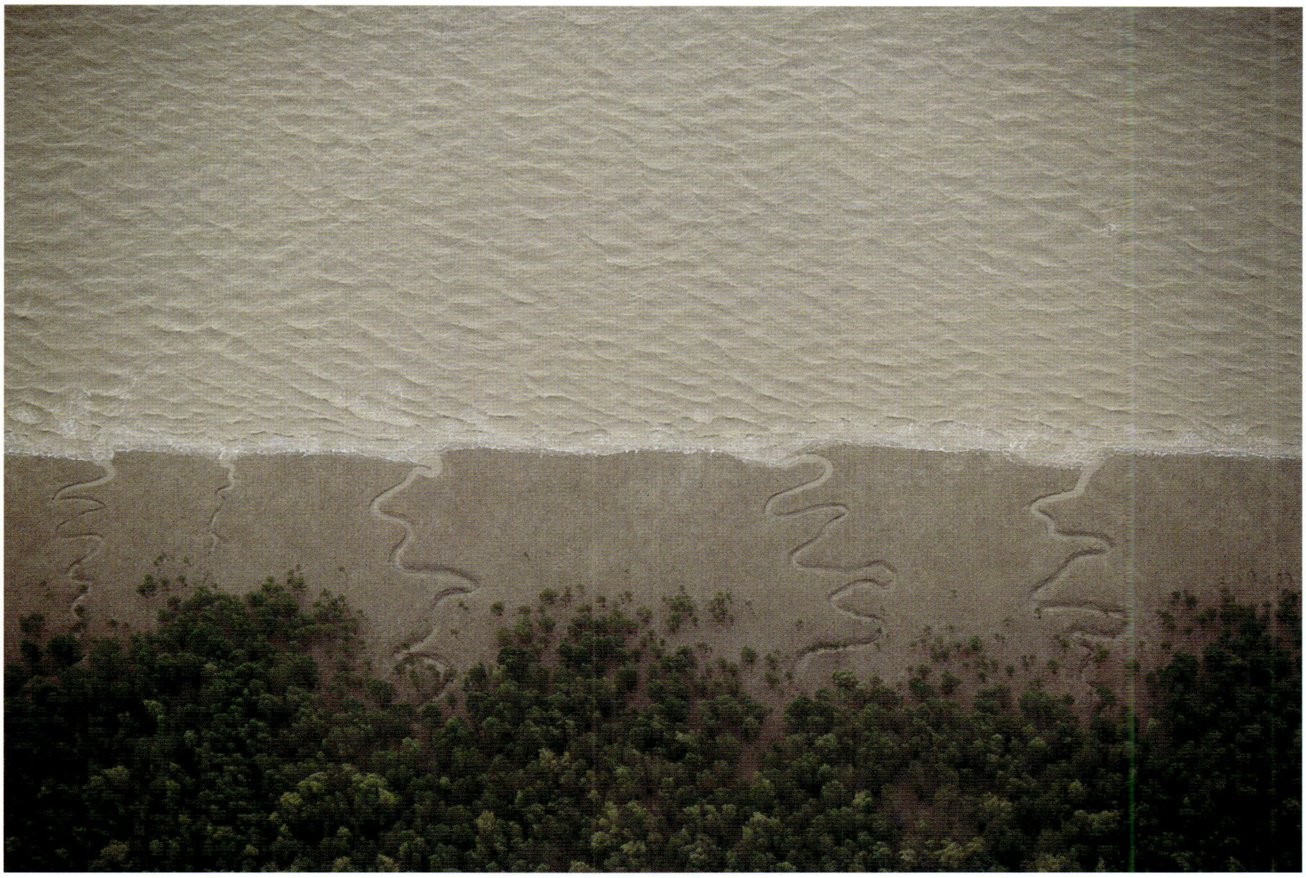

Ebbing tides expose the natural calligraphy of channels draining coastal mangrove communities.

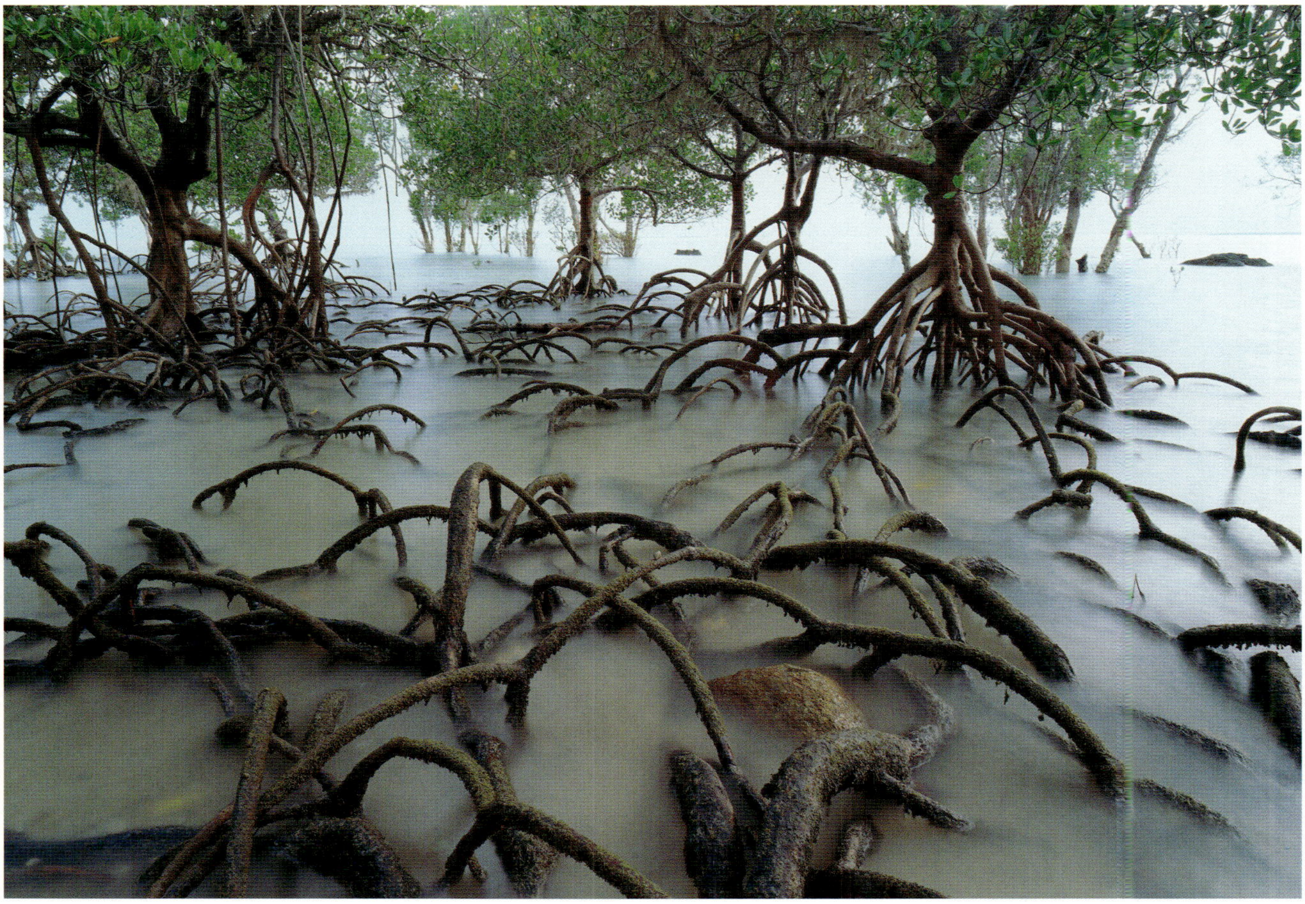

Anchored in suffocating mud, the roots of the Spider Mangrove (Rhizophora stylosa) *draw life-giving oxygen from their elevated arches.*

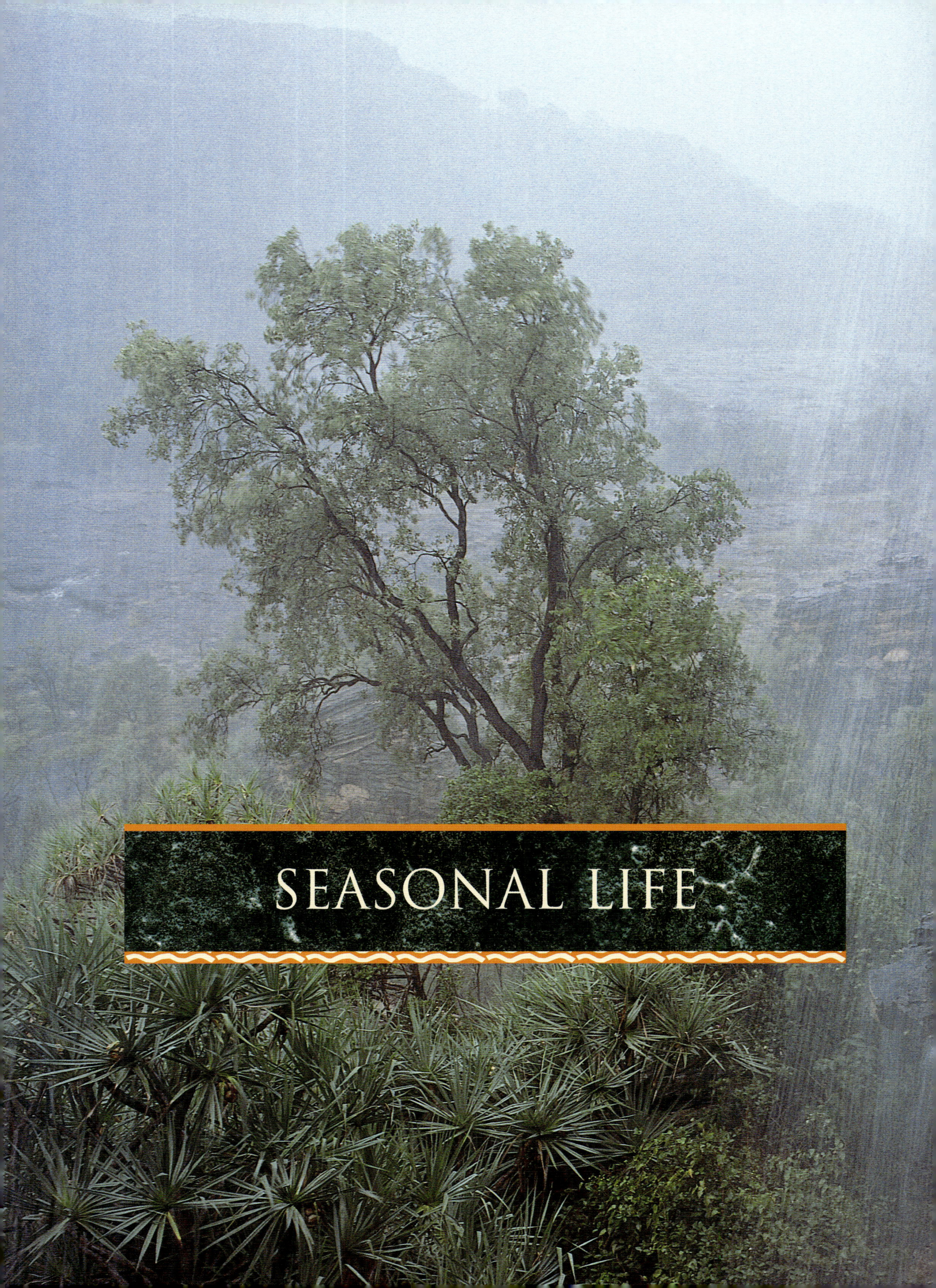

SEASONAL LIFE

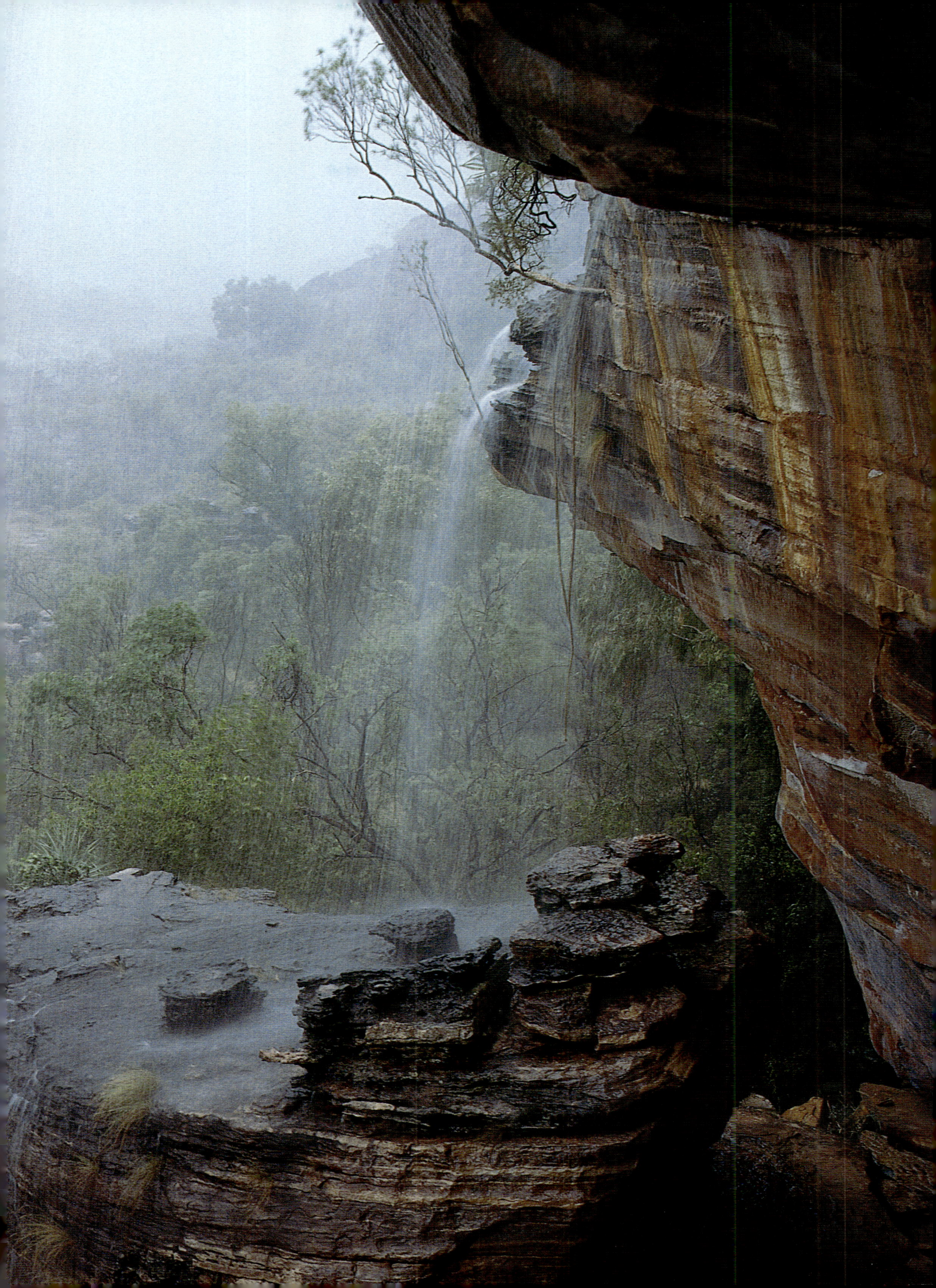

SEASONAL LIFE

PREVIOUS PAGE At the height of the Gudjewg storms, cliffs and overhangs along the escarpment form a continuous waterfall.

The pulse of life is different in Kakadu. The region falls within what is broadly defined as the wet-dry tropics. According to this description the climate has two main cycles, with warm, dry weather extending from May to October, while wet, humid conditions predominate between November and April.

Around 80 per cent of visitors travel to Kakadu in the dry months. During this phase of the year the days are warm and for long periods a hazy calm prevails. To anyone accustomed to the restless pattern of events in southern temperate regions, these dry spells might give the impression that Kakadu's climate is subdued and listless. As the end of the year approaches, however, the temper of the place undergoes a dramatic transformation.

Kakadu's average annual rainfall is around 1400 millimetres. Close to 90 per cent of this falls between November and March. Through October and November temperatures and moisture levels rise, feeding afternoon thunderstorms which gather in frequency. By January and February - the wettest months in the calendar - the entire region is in the sway of monsoonal depressions, as powerful tropical convection currents draw moisture-laden air from South East Asia, bringing intense humidity and drenching rains.

The monsoon can be an erratic beast. Its timing and intensity vary markedly from year to year according to atmospheric conditions and fluctuations in the global climate. In some years the monsoon pattern is weak with patchy, localised rainfall. At the other extreme, Kakadu is also besieged by tropical cyclones, with lashing winds and torrential rain. Over the past century around 20 of these events have affected the region.

Kakadu is truly a land of extremes. While temperatures remain relatively high year round, with maximums in the low to high 30's, the annual regime of scorching droughts and rampant rains dictates the patterns of life. Over countless millennia, plants and animals have had to adapt to the climate's wild pendulum swings.

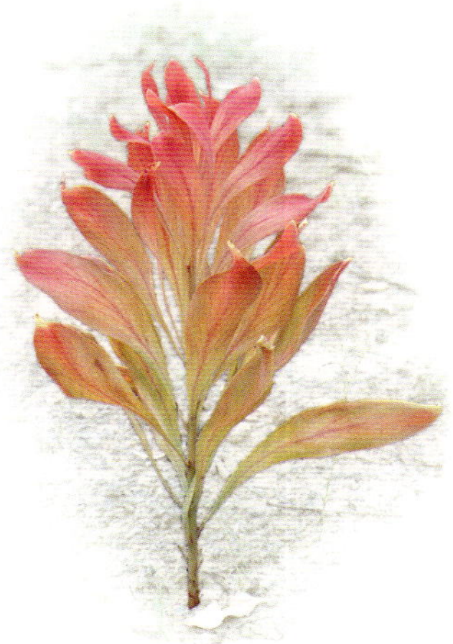

With nature reinvigorated by life-giving rains, lush new plant growth emerges in profusion.

Lightning blasts the Jim Jim escarpment as torrential rain transforms the road into a temporary river.

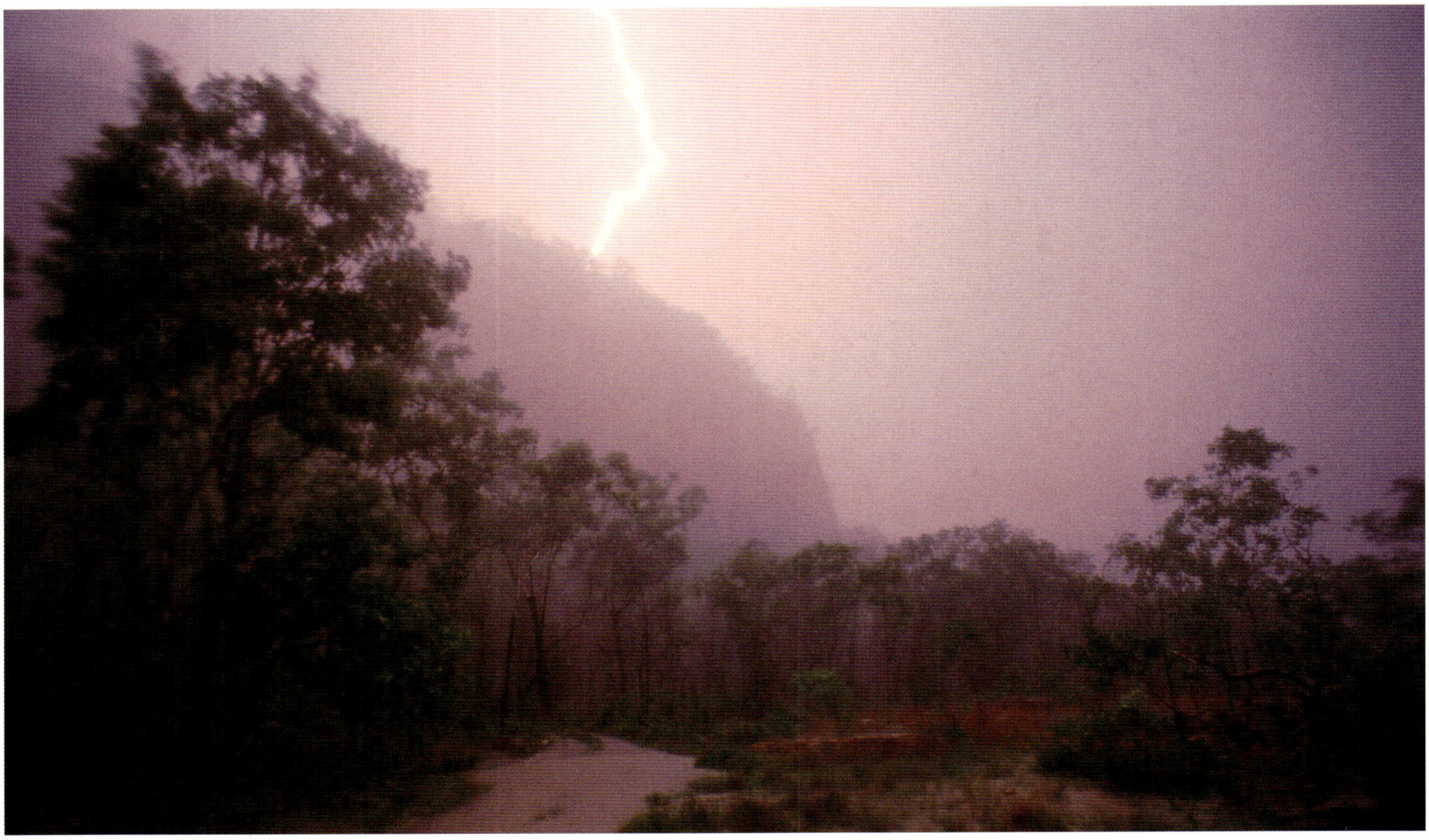

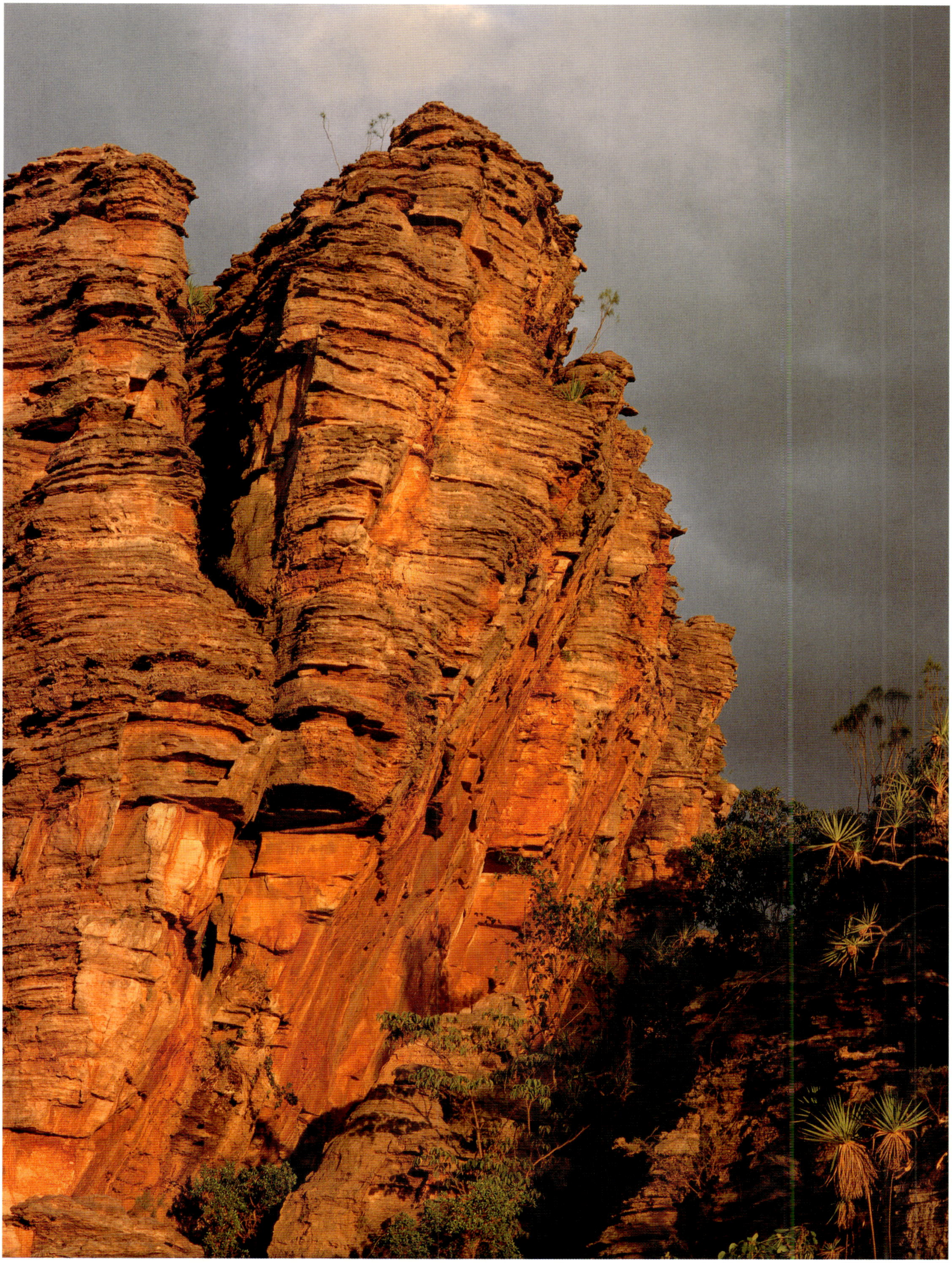

An escarpment bastion catches the sun's last rays under a sky of threatening cloud.

WILD DIVERSITY

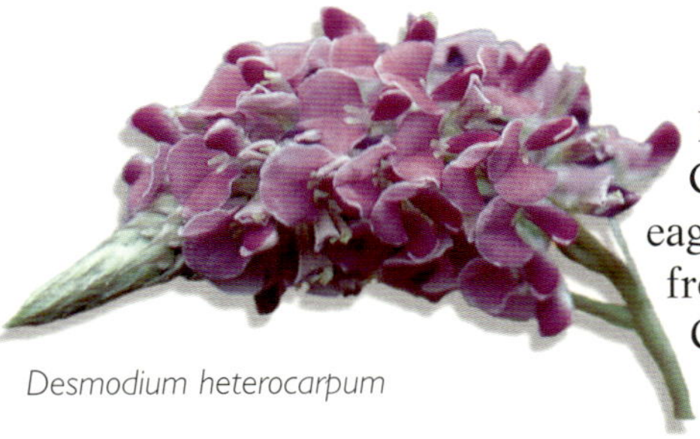

Desmodium heterocarpum

Nowhere is this more apparent than on the floodplains. Rising waterlevels during Gudjewg brings a chaotic time. As a prelude to breeding, Magpie Geese feed eagerly on the flush of new aquatic plantlife. Meanwhile a host of animals including frogs, freshwater fish and turtles disperse across the inundated landscape. Crocodiles and snakes, such as the Water Python and Arafura File Snake, also join in the moveable feast. These opportunists prey upon a range of hapless small lizards and mammals, marooned by the swirling waters.

Six months later the same floodplains are turning to a cracked desert of baking clay and grasses. Dwindling waterholes attract congregations of birds lured by the promise of fresh vegetation, fish, frogs and insects exposed in concentrated numbers by the retreating water. The total seasonal population of waterbirds can reach two and half million, the majority of which are Magpie Geese and Wandering Whistling Ducks. Others to partake of the smorgasbord include some 15 species of migratory wading birds, such as plovers and dotterels, together with larger resident waterbirds like ibis, spoonbills, herons and egrets. Prominent in the throng is the Jabiru or Black-necked Stork whose stately air belies a lethal skill at catching fish, eels and water snakes.

In many ways the annual changes in the park's grassy open forests and woodlands are no less striking. While several larger trees have energy reserves to actively flower and fruit through the dry season, by the beginning of Gunumeleng these habitats are hungry for moisture. At ground level the red sandy soils are powder dry, the grass is bleached and large areas have a charred, gaunt appearance.

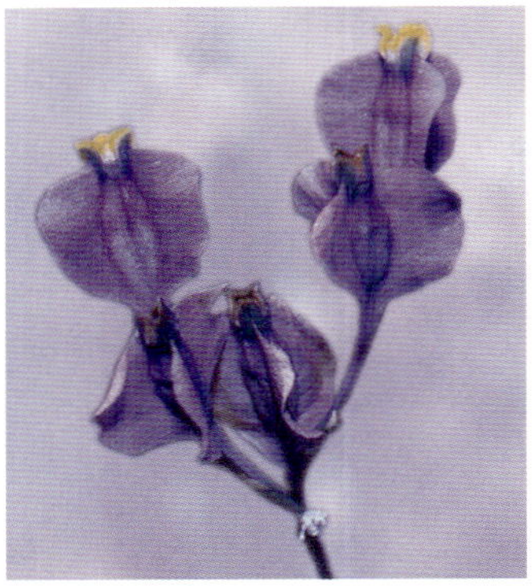

Burmannia juucea

Looking from the top of Ubirr at the end of the wet season everything is brimming - from tiny sandstone basins to the vast floodplains.

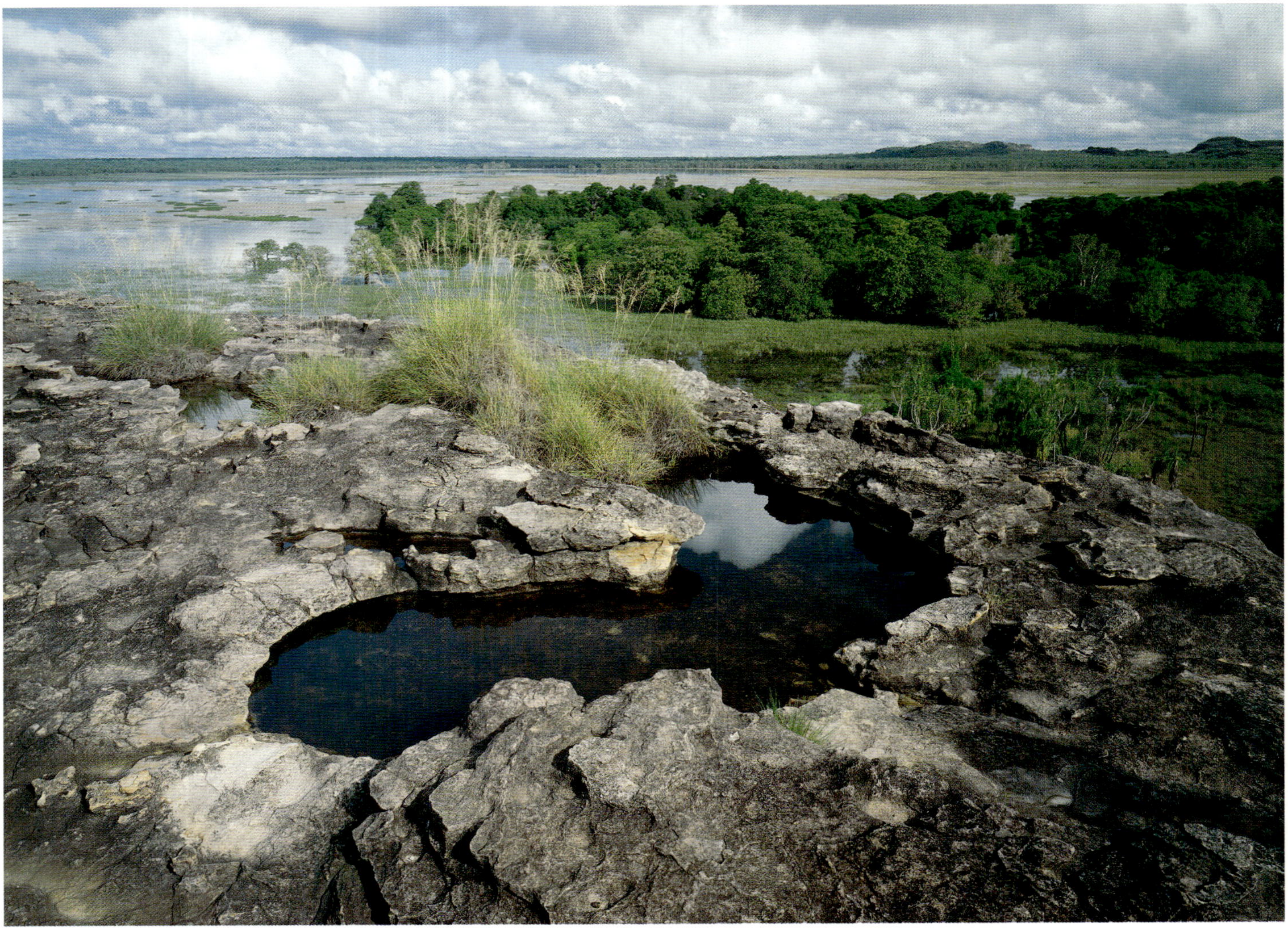

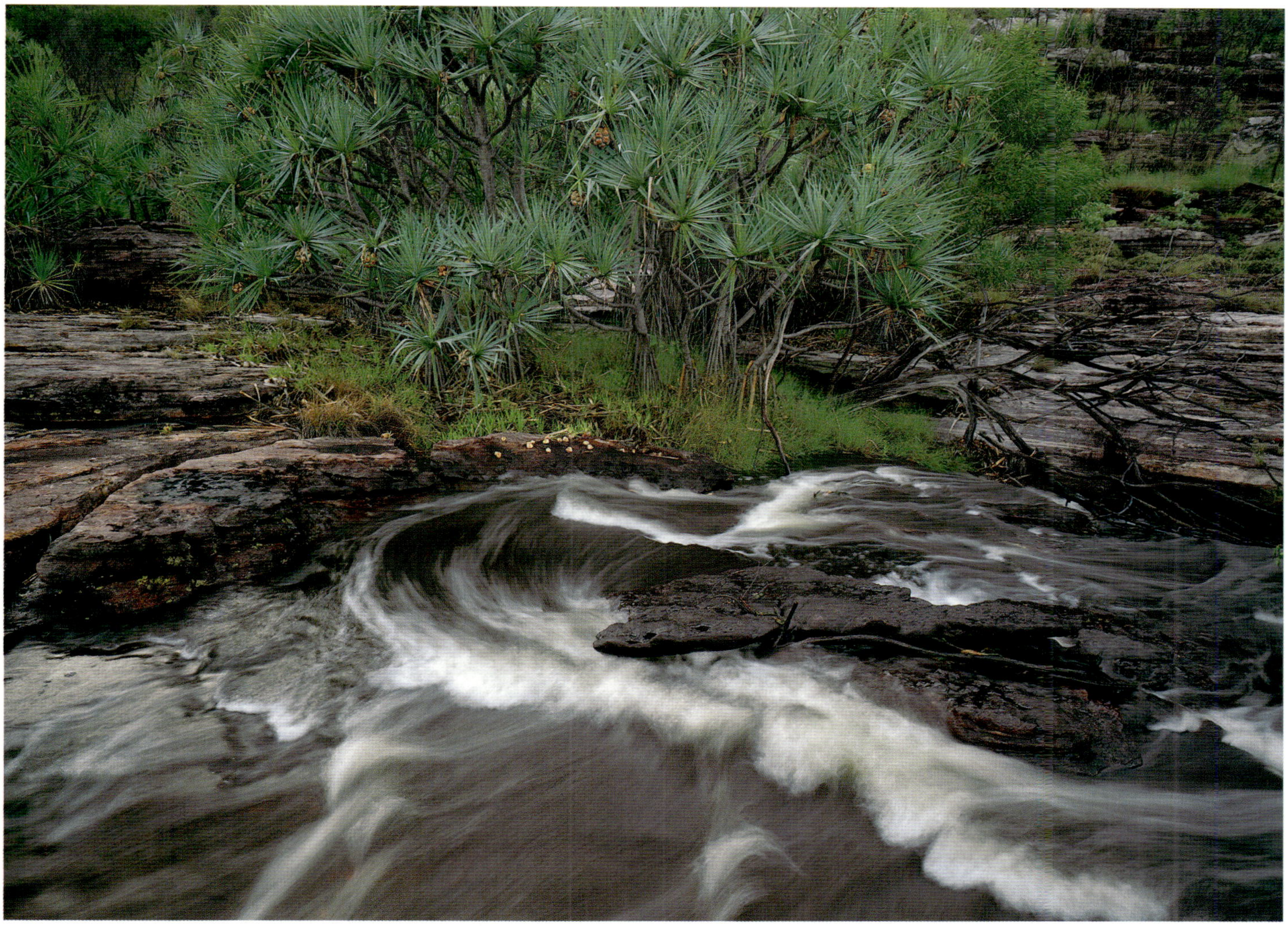

Within days of the early rains everything changes. Most obvious is the initial growth of spear grass which surges to heights of two metres or more through the monsoon months. Animal life takes advantage of this rejuvenation in the lowlands. Agile Wallabies and Antilopine Wallaroos revel in the tasty grass shoots. Many birds begin their breeding season and at night the forest erupts with frog calls and a riot of insect noise

Birds are easily the most prominent inhabitants of the wooded lowlands. Larger birds such as lorikeets, cockatoos, parrots and honeyeaters are colourful, often noisy and always on the move. During the burning season raptors like Whistling Kites, Black Kites and Brown Falcons patrol the fire lines, picking off smaller wildlife flushed out by the smoke and flames. Finches, quails and a host of other small birds occupy the understorey, feeding on scattered seeds. One of the most significant of the ground dwelling species is the scarce Partridge Pigeon. Other rare birds to find refuge in Kakadu include the Gouldian Finch and Hooded Parrot.

During Gudjewg every plateau creek is awash and vegetation such as the hardy Sandstone Pandanus (Pandanus basedowii) *is refreshed.*

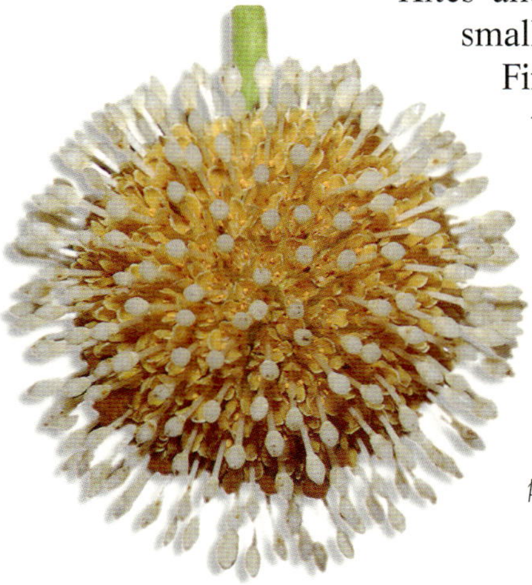

The large Leichhardt Tree (Nauclea orientalis) *produces distinctive flowers.*

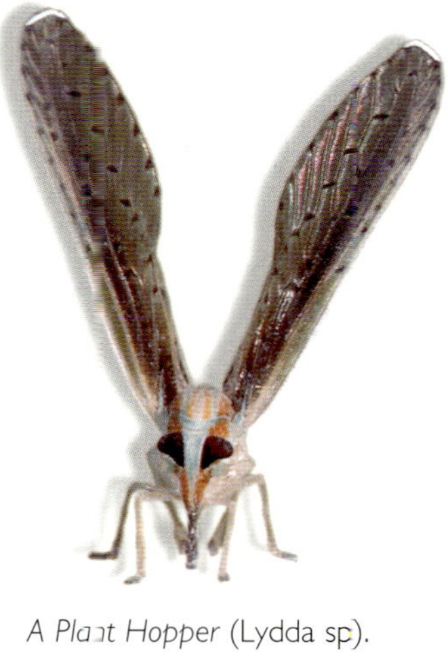

A Plant Hopper (Lydda sp).

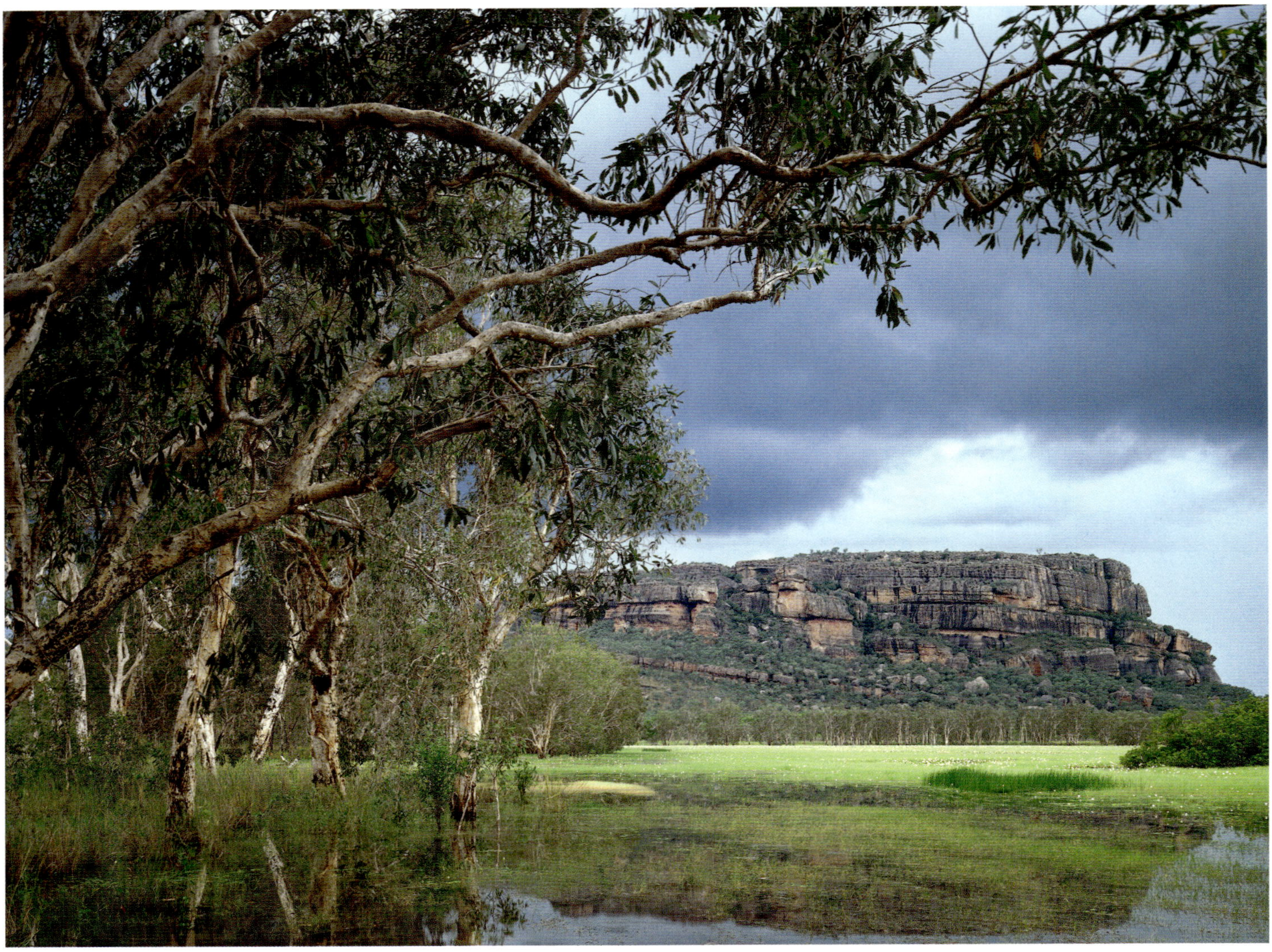

Stands of large paperbarks border the Anbangbang Billabong, a short walk from Burrunggui.

During daylight hours lizards, including dragons, skinks and the impressive Sand Monitors are another animating presence in wooded country. With the onset of wet season rains the spectacular Frilled Lizard becomes a regular sight.

Some of the most important creatures in the woodlands are also the smallest. One of the Frilled Lizard's favourite foods is termites. In response to early storms these insects emerge in vast numbers to mate and establish new colonies. Kakadu is home to at least 50 termite species. As well as constructing huge mounds – some rising to seven metres – termites play a pivotal role in recycling nutrients by eating wood and plant material another species cannot digest. At the same time, their mounds and the hollows they create in trees provide cosy accommodation for birds, reptiles and small mammals.

While Agile Wallabies may be the most visible mammals in the woodlands, a variety of more diminutive species are common here. The Northern Brown Bandicoot, Fawn Antechinus, Northern Quoll, Brushtail Possum and Sugar Glider are all widespread, though usually active only under the cover of darkness. Of all mammals, bats are the best represented, with 28 species recorded in the park. Flying-foxes are the most prevalent, dispersing across a wide area at night to forage on fruits and nectar. By day they roost in large colonies among the canopy of the riverine monsoon forest.

Other important bat habitats include caves and fissures in the stone country where the unusual Ghost Bat and Orange Horseshoe Bat find sanctuary. One of the most enthralling aspects of Kakadu's wildlife is the importance of the escarpment and plateau as a refuge for creatures found nowhere else and others whose numbers and range are limited.

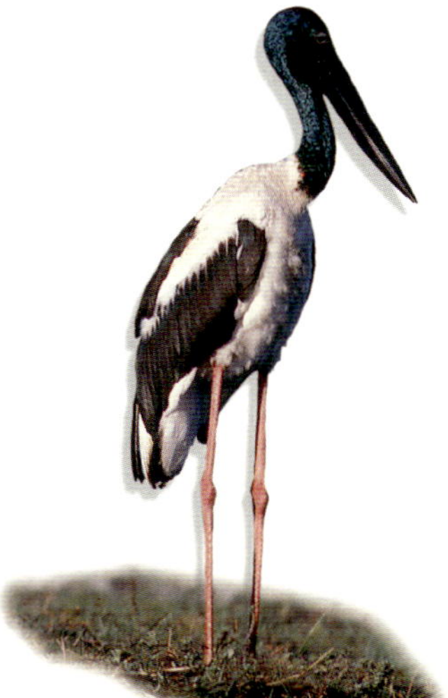

The Jabiru or Black-necked Stork (Ephippiorhynchus asiaticus) *is a formidable hunter throughout the wetlands.*

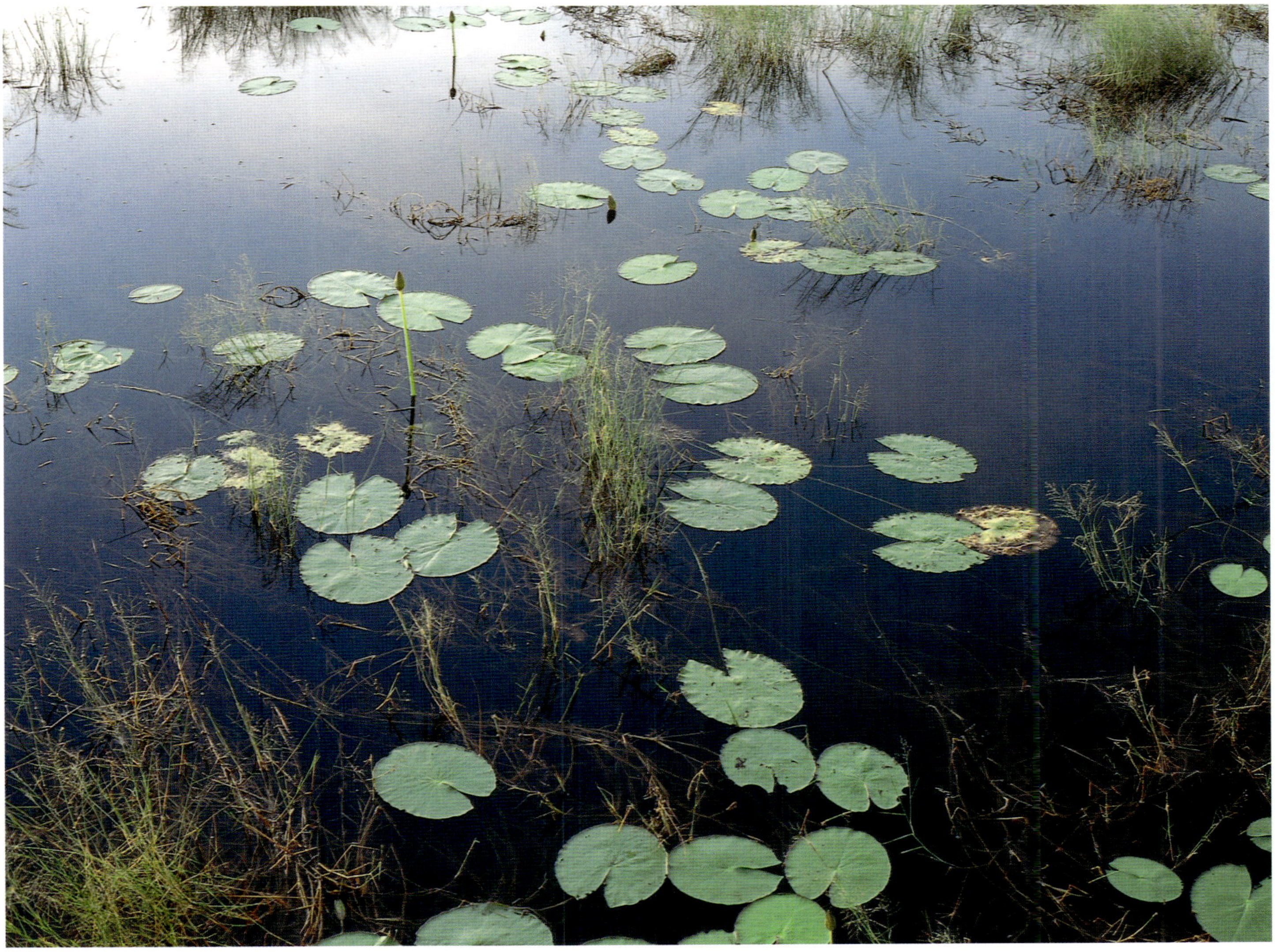

The permanent water of the billabongs is a focus for life as the dry season unfolds.

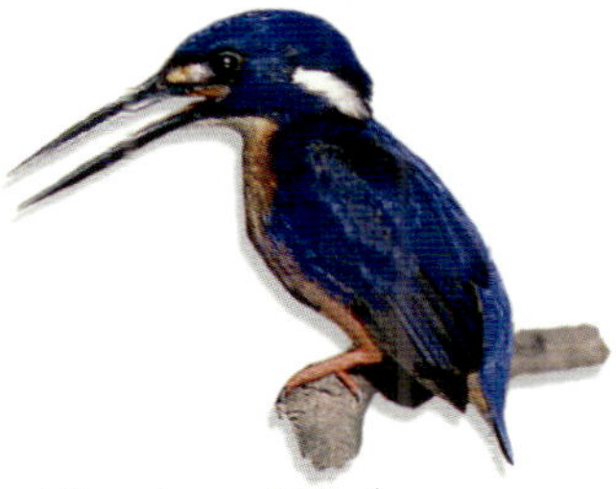

Although small, the Azure Kingfisher (Alcedo azurea) is a striking presence on the river and billabong fringes.

Scattered among this vast maze of gorges, creeks and rocky terraces are such exquisite creatures as the White-throated Grass Wren, the Rock Ringtail Possum and the Sandstone Antechinus. Here there dwells the wary hunter Nawaran – the Oenpelli Rock Python – who grows to more than four metres in length. Plateau creeks are home to the spectacular rainbowfish and in moist nooks nearby there lives the Carpenter Frog and Copland's Rock Frog. Shelter outcrops provide daytime shelter for the small, shy Narbarlek and their much larger, but equally retiring relation, Barrk, the Black Wallaroo.

Several of these fascinating stone country recluses have only become known to western science in the past three decades. Bininj have known about these and many other creatures for thousands of years. This knowledge is more than just names and places for interesting animals: it embraces complete life histories, how each species relates to its surroundings, with the unfolding events in the passage of the seasons and with Bininj beliefs.

Take Aldjurr, for example, another stone country specialist. In the text books this is Leichhardt's Grasshopper. To Bininj the maturing of Aldjurr into its vivid adult hues of deep orange, black and bright blue has always heralded the advent of Gunumeleng storms. Indeed, in Bininj mythology these grasshoppers are the children of Namarrgon – the Lightning Man.

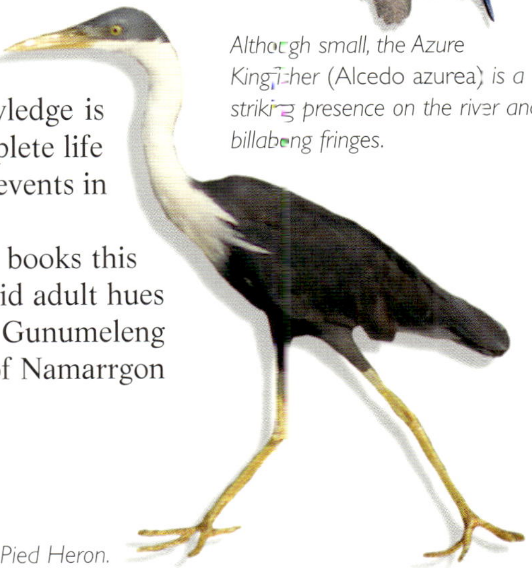

The Pied Heron.

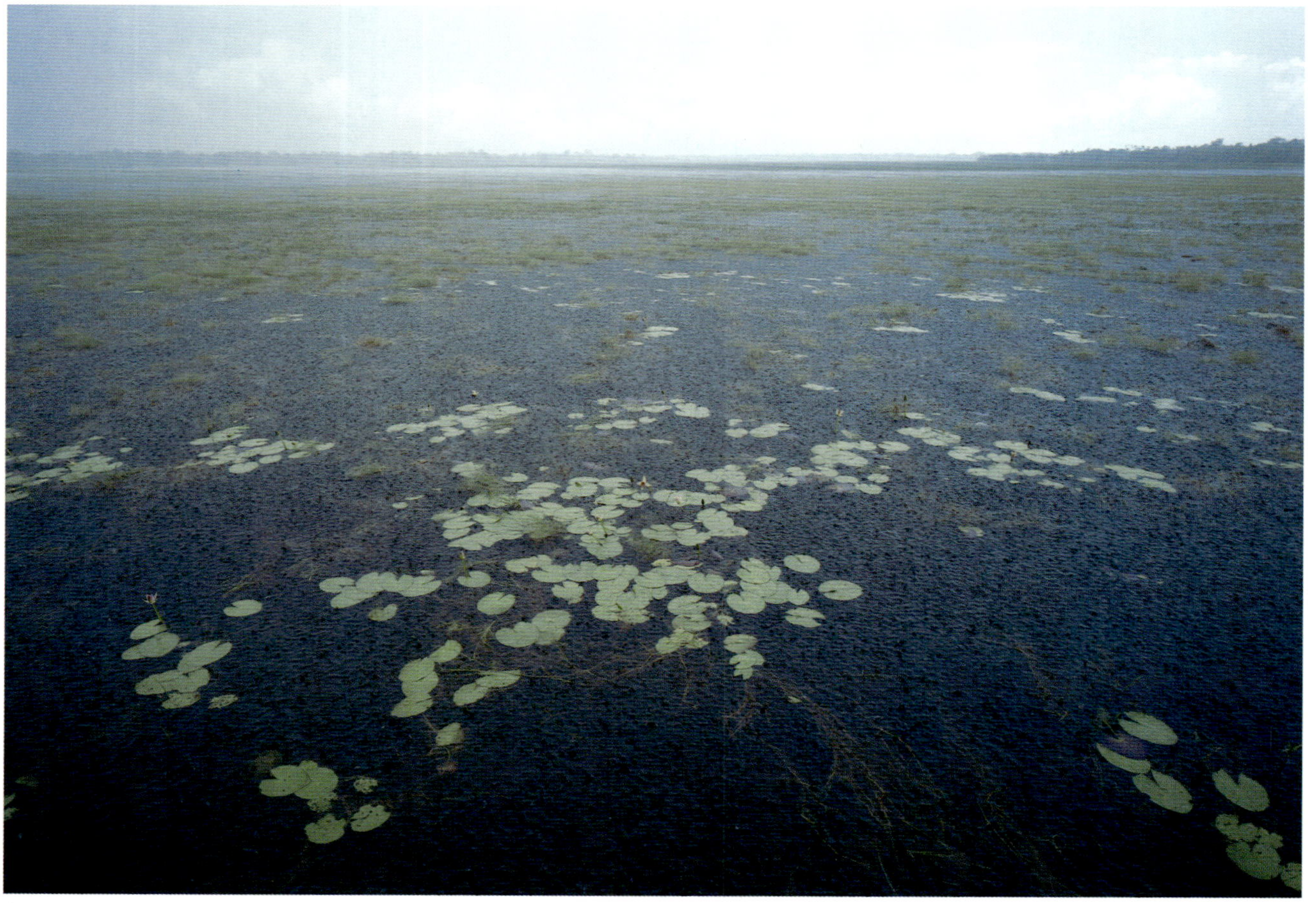

Same place, different season. In the wake of the monsoon the Mamukala wetland is a sea of aquatic life.

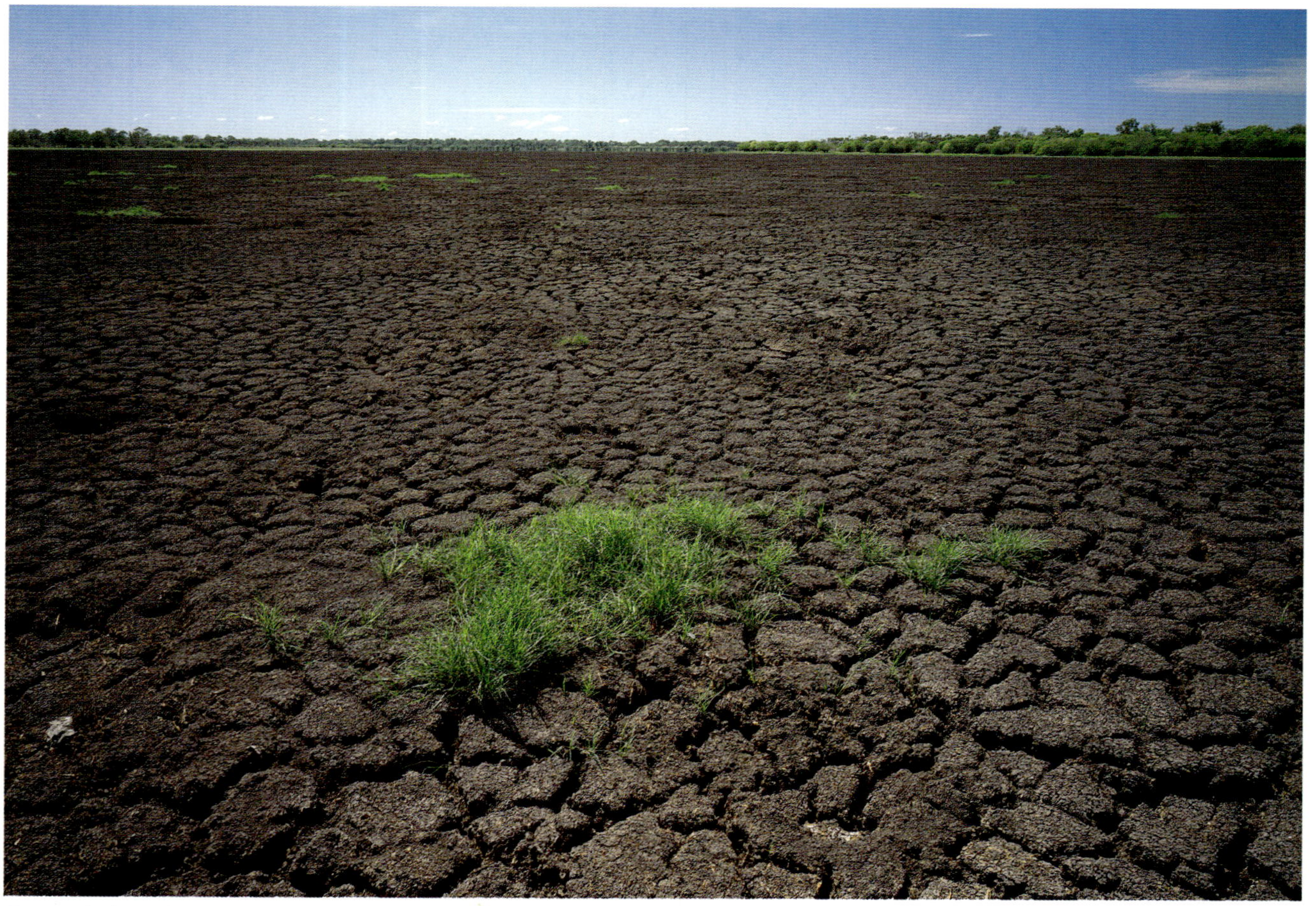

Six months later the identical scene has been reduced to a cracking black-soil plain.

SIX SEASONS

From a Bininj perspective Kakadu has six seasons. This cycle is not simply dictated by changes in weather but also reflects annual events in the lives of plants and animals – a vividly detailed natural calendar gleaned from living close to the land for hundreds of generations. In the Gun-djeihmi/Mayali language the Kakadu year unfolds as follows:

Gudjewg is the torrid monsoon time from late December through to early March when the winds blow from the north and north-west bringing a soupy mass of tropical cloud, storms and prolonged bouts of soaking rain. Widespread flooding spurs a hectic resurgence of plant life in all habitats, with bird populations, especially Magpie Geese, beginning an active nesting phase.

Banggerreng is a briefer interval characterised by blustery 'knock 'em down' storms moving in from the south-east to flatten the high spear grass. For Bininj this is a rich time of harvest and plenty. Receding floodwaters allow for easier access in lowland areas and the gathering of yams and other staple food plants. Insect and frog activity is high.

Yegge extends from around late April to mid June and marks the initial onset of the dry months. Daybreak often reveals swathes of woodland blanketed by morning mists. Drier winds rolling in from the east usher in another phase of Bininj life as clans are on the move and traditional burning is underway.

Wurrgeng is the time of 'cold weather'. Many wetland areas dry out, exposing the swampland and permanent billabongs where birdlife congregate. Patchwork burning continues and for Bininj this is the flowering season of the woollybutt and many important fruit trees.

Gurrung covers the austere weeks from mid August to early October. Continued dry breezes from the south-east parch the landscape. Resources are limited and life is subdued as animals seek refuge in the searing heat of the day. Fruits begin to ripen.

Gunumeleng is the surly overture to the monsoon. Unforgiving heat and rising humidity are accompanied by spectacular skies as billowing afternoon storm clouds roam in over the plateau. These threatening formations bring erratic downpours – the catalyst for the rapid germination of grasses and sudden bursts of new growth on deciduous trees.

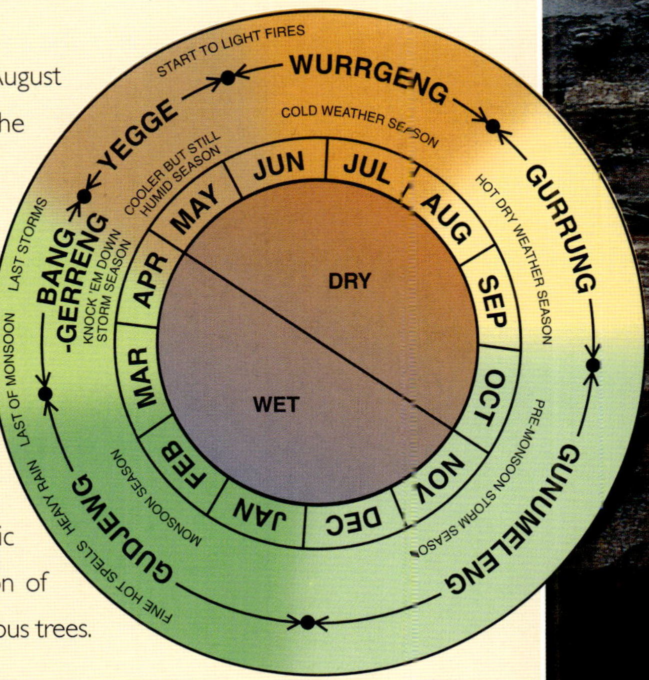

Seasonal calendar for the Kakadu Region in Gun-djeihmi language.

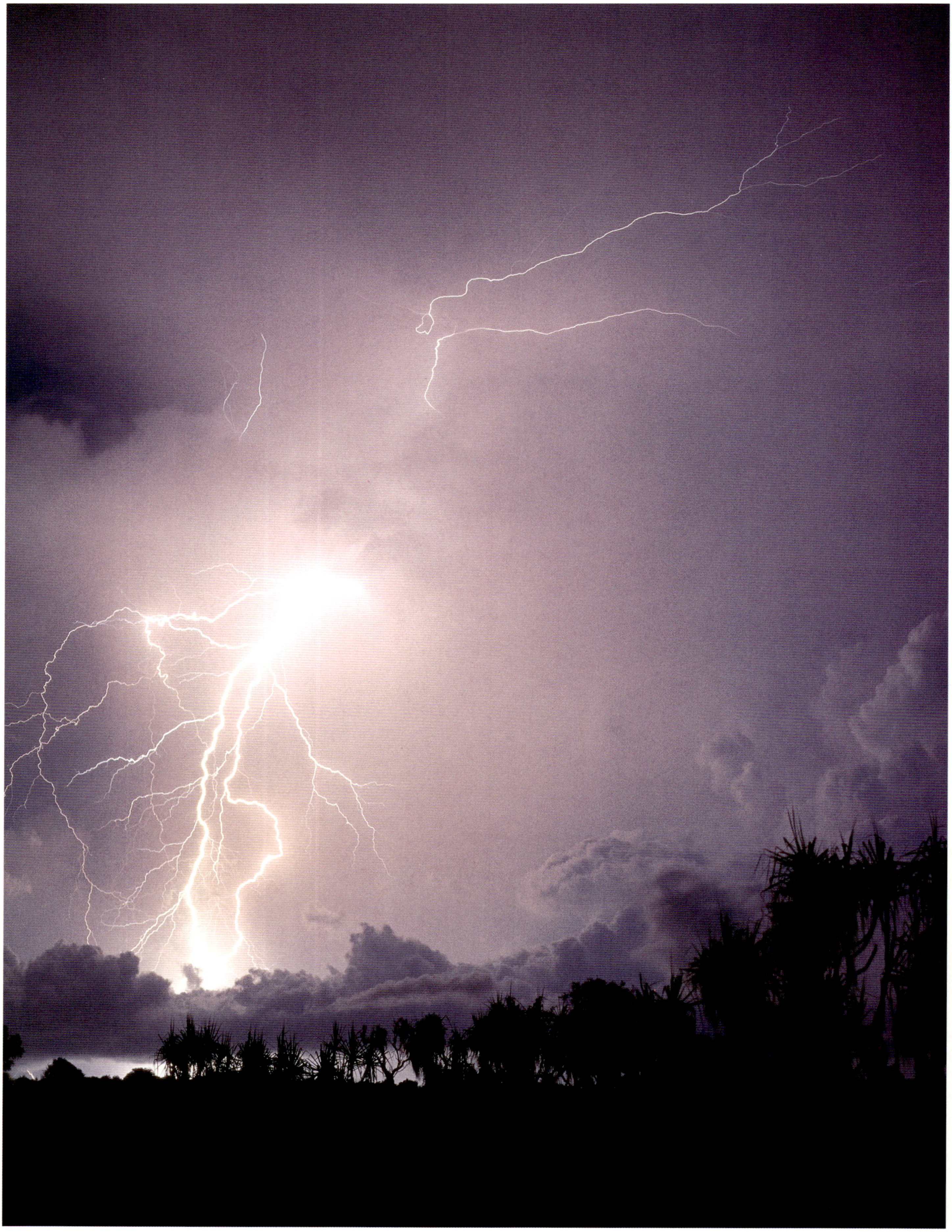

Gunumeleng storms generate astonishing electrical displays that gather in frequency during November and December.

NAMARRGON

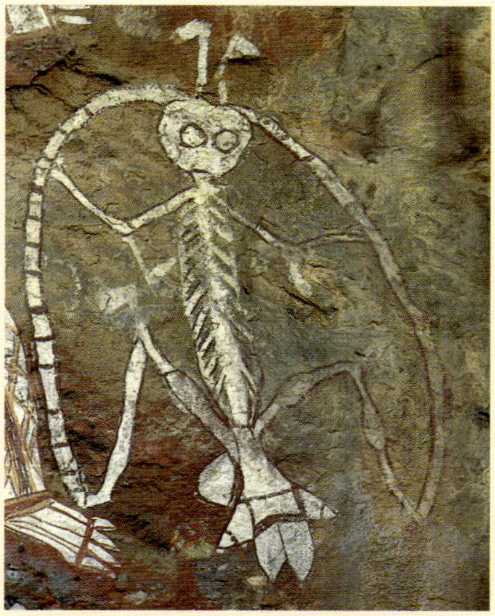

Namarrgon - the Lightning Man asserts his power with the approaching storms.

Australia's Top End is host to some of the world's most potent storms. Through Gunumeleng, seething masses of cumulus cloud traverse the region. They advance under blackening skies with distant, bellowing rumbles. As a storm closes in the heavens erupt. Thunder cracks through the dank air. Spectral flashes burst within the cauldron of cloud and jagged veins of light streak earthwards.

These storms are not one-off events. Nor are they mere spectacles. Violent wind gusts flatten vegetation. Lightning strikes turn 20-metre-tall trees into splinters and shattered stumps. And pelting rains flood the land, transforming dry creekbeds into swirling torrents.

It's hardly surprising that such seasonal convulsions figure prominently in Bininj stories and beliefs. According to their cosmology the storms are the work of Namarrgon the Lightning Man. In the creation time Namarrgon travelled across the sea from the north. Together with his wife Barrginj and their children he crossed the coast on the Coburg Peninsula and headed south-east, leaving his power at many places. He then turned to the west passing through the stone country.

There are many paintings of Namarrgon in Kakadu. The best known is at Burrungui's Anbangbang Gallery. Here he is depicted with stone axes attached to his head, elbows and knees. The lines joining his head and feet represent lightning while the bands on his body belong to the thunder. By striking his axes against the clouds or ground he makes thunder and lightning. Other figures in this gallery include Namarrgon's wife Barrginj and the imposing spirit being Namondjok.

A short walk from the gallery leads to Gunwarrdehwarrde Lookout. From here you can look east to the escarpment and Namarrgondjahdjam – Lightning Dreaming. Here Namarrgon removed one of his eyes and placed it on the cliffs where it sits waiting for Gunumeleng. He then backtracked to a rock shelter at Bolkngok. Though he remains in this rock shelter, the great progenitor of Kakadu's storms continues to exert his power, and his children, in the form of the grasshopper Aldjurr, are a vivid reminder of his influence.

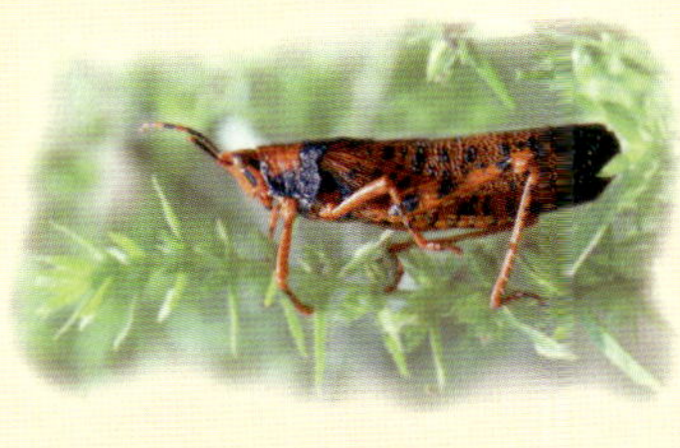

Aldjurr, the children of Namarrgon.

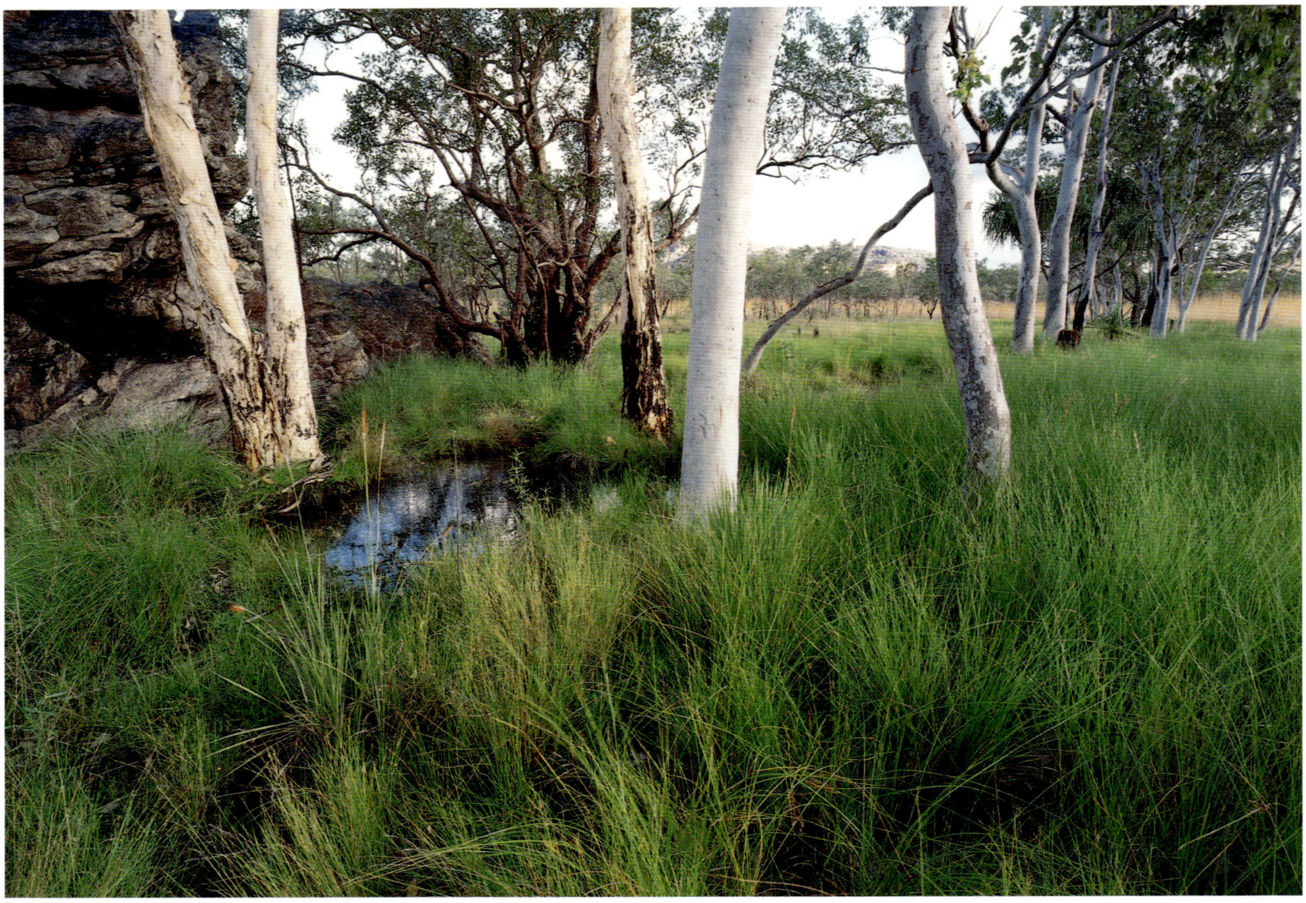

The white trunks of paperbarks and Ghost Gums emerge from the lush grasses of a moist hollow.

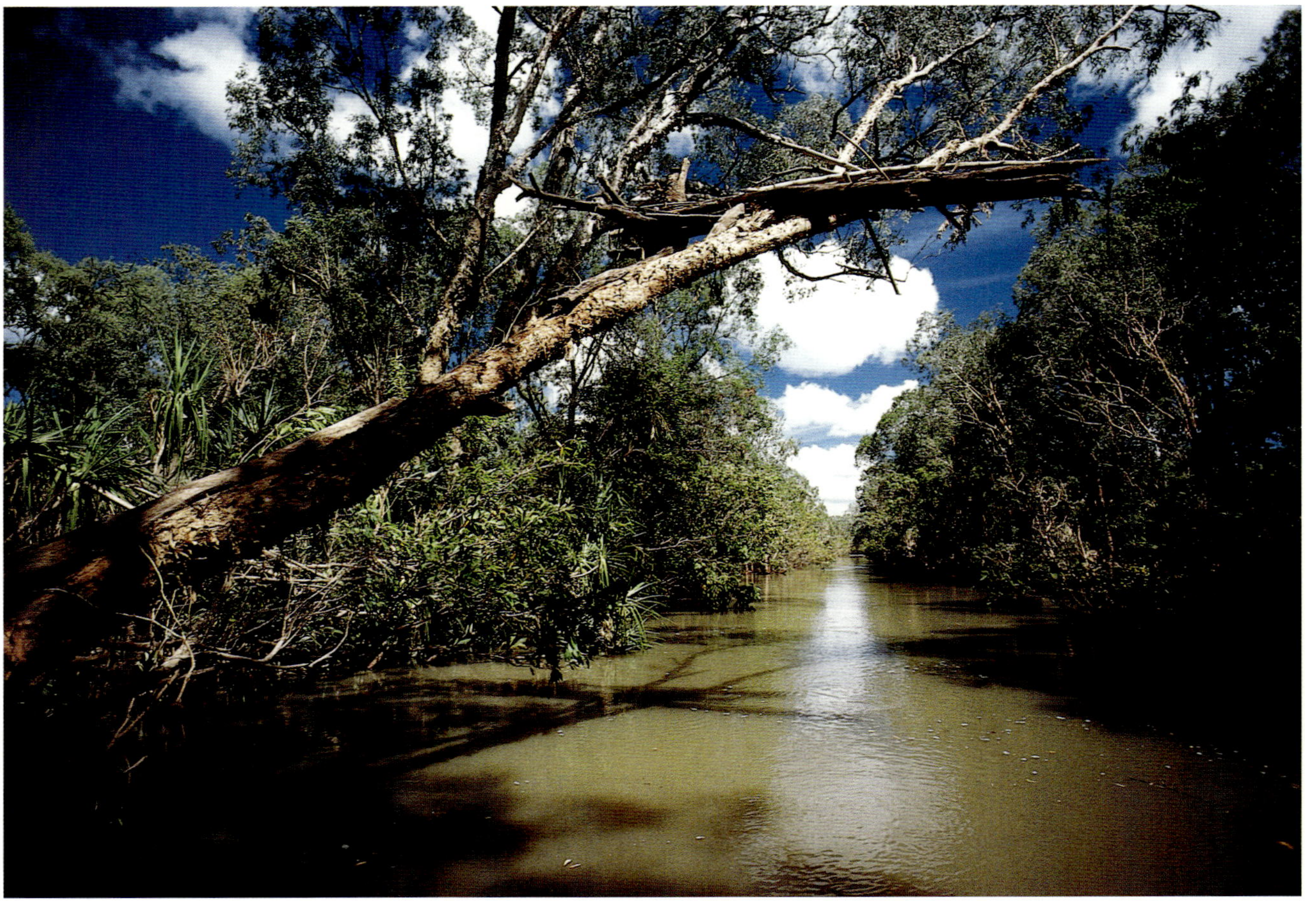

Flood debris is balanced in the high branches of a paperbark leaning over the South Alligator River - a graphic reminder of the wet season's power.

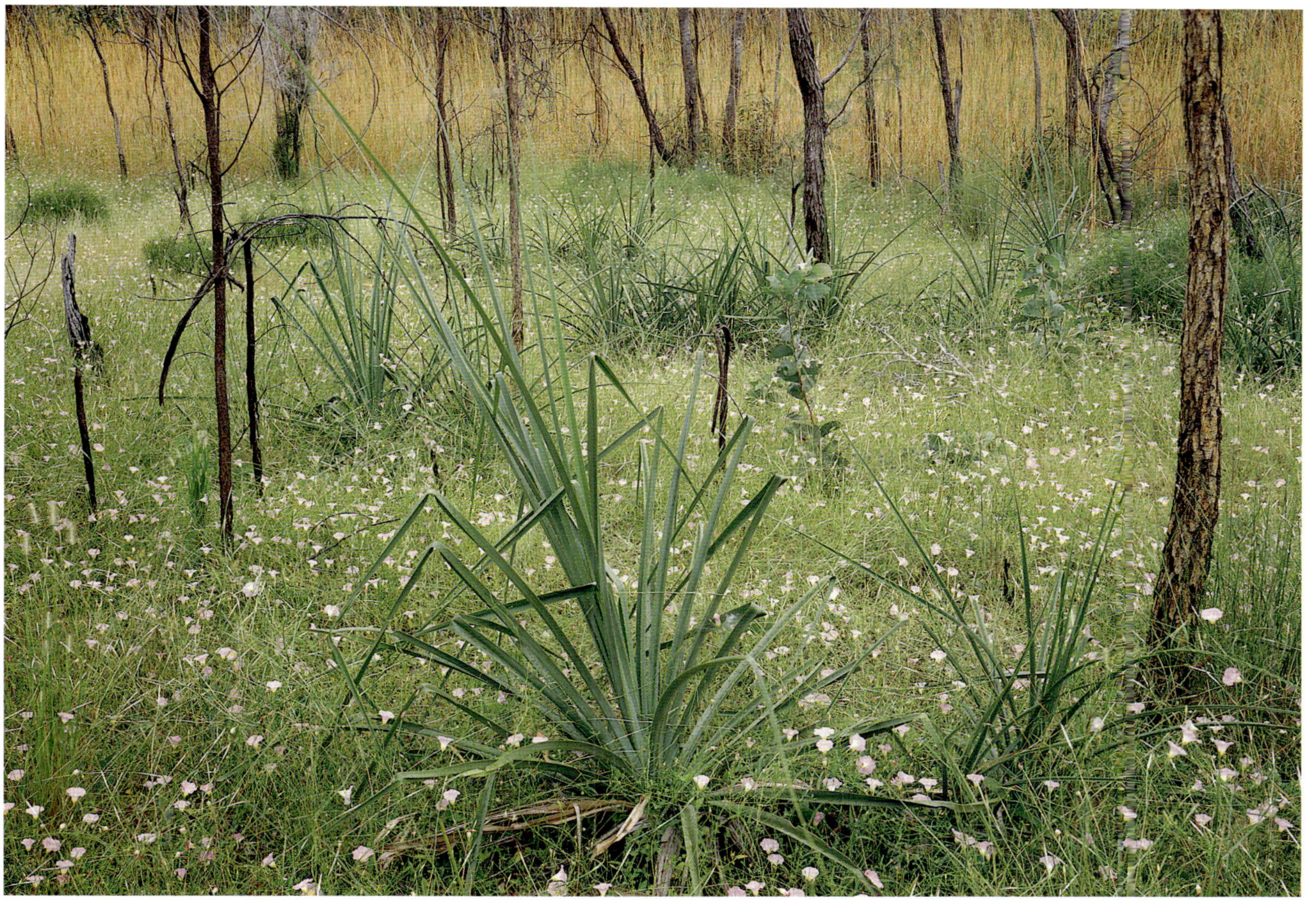

Pandanus and late-maturing grasses in a moist depression contrast with the tall spear grass beyond.

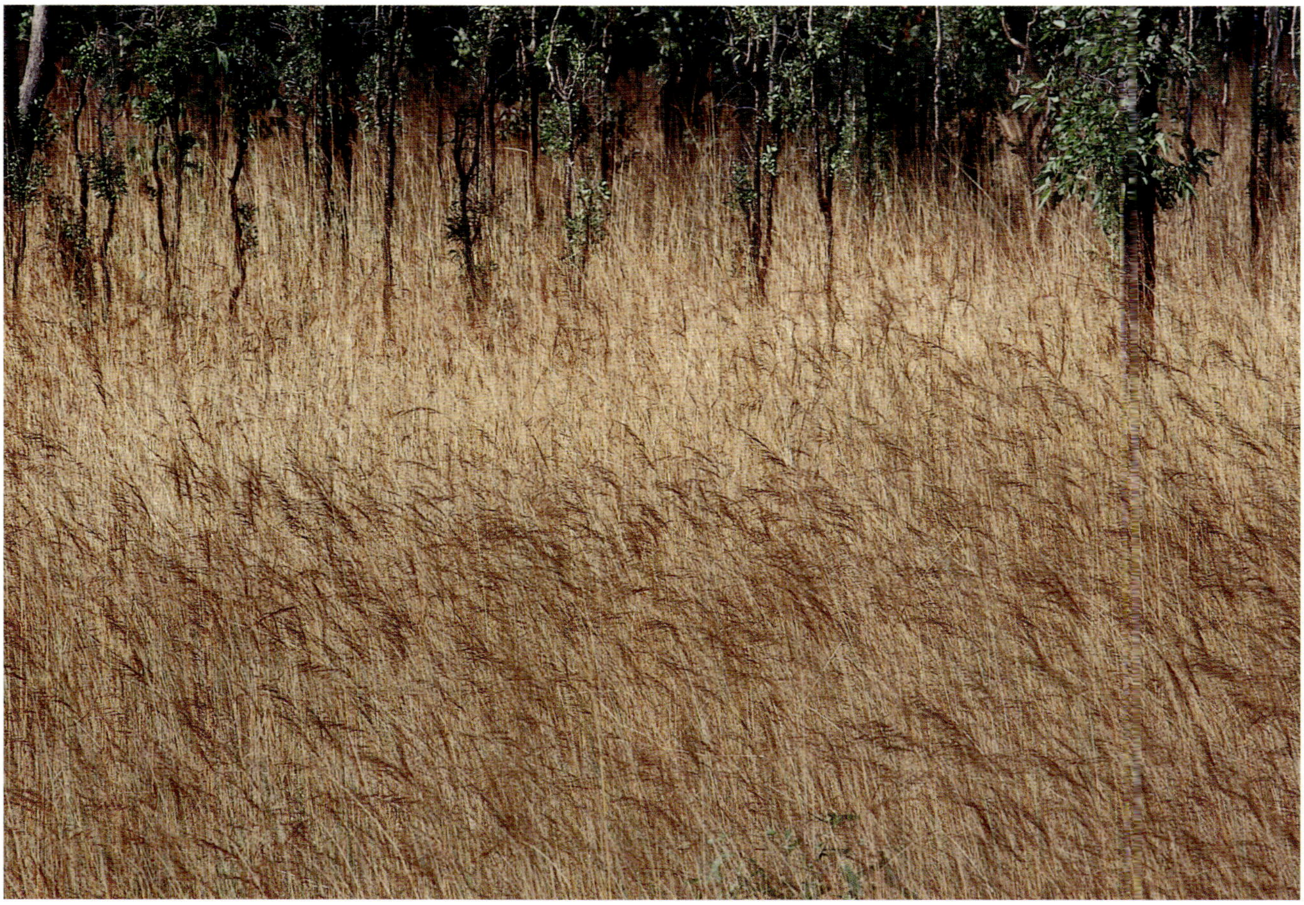

The long stalks of spear grass dominate clearings throughout Kakadu's extensive woodlands.

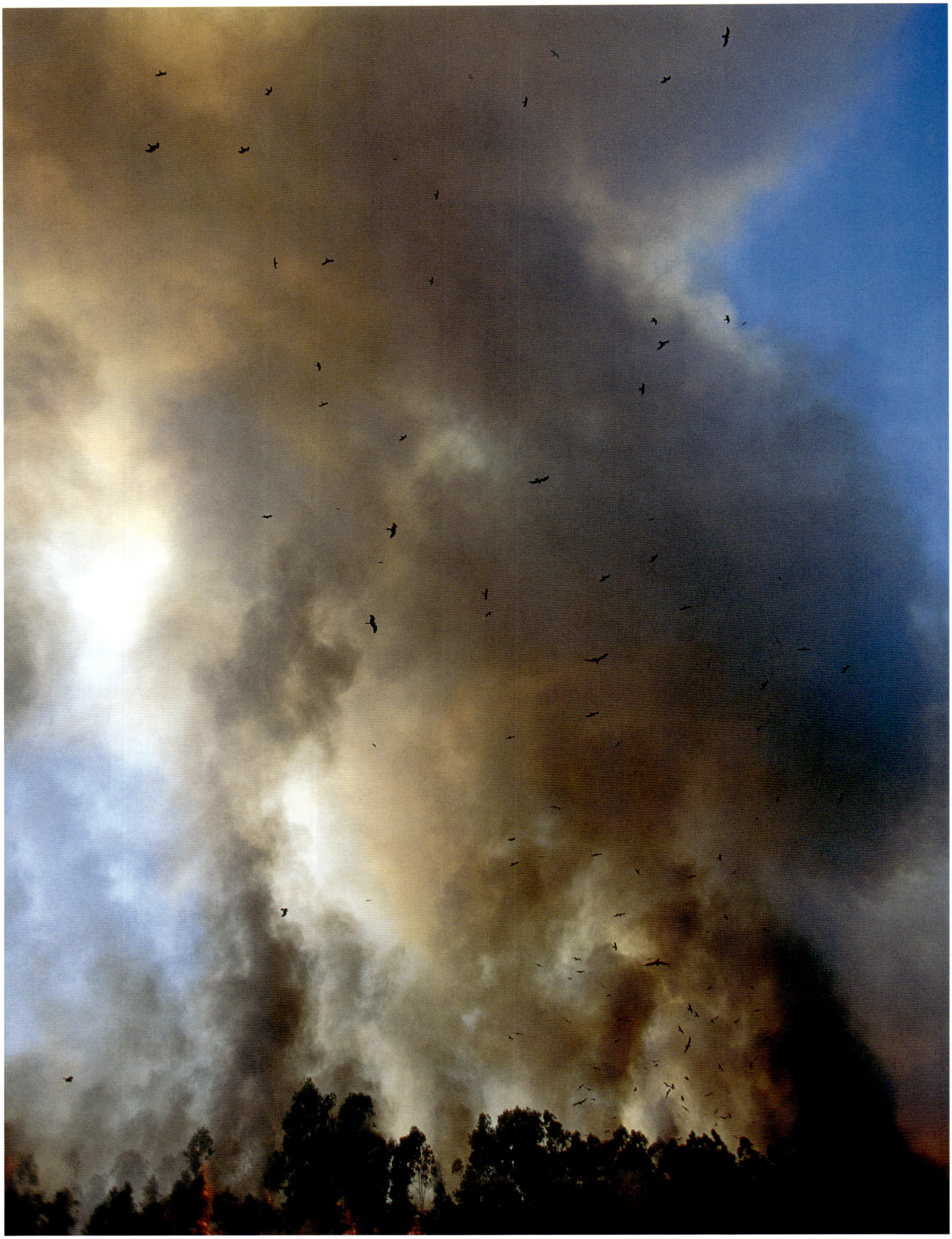

Great columns of smoke surge upward into an otherwise clear sky, a signal to squadrons of Whistling Kites (Haliastur sphenurus) *that a feast is at hand, as small mammals, insects and reptiles are flushed out by the flames.*

BURNING ISSUES

Fire has long been a fact of life in Kakadu. For countless millennia naturally occurring fires have been sparked by lightning strikes. The great majority of these blazes have accompanied the electrical storms that sweep the region during the months from October to December. With vegetation having been exposed to several months of dry heat, the potential for fierce, widespread fires is high.

Fire has always been one of the most important aspects in the relationship of Bininj to the land. Their patterns of burning clan estates at particular times of the year are not just integral to hunting and harvesting practices, they also have strong spiritual significance. For Bininj, the controlled use of fire is a demonstration of their responsibility to look after country.

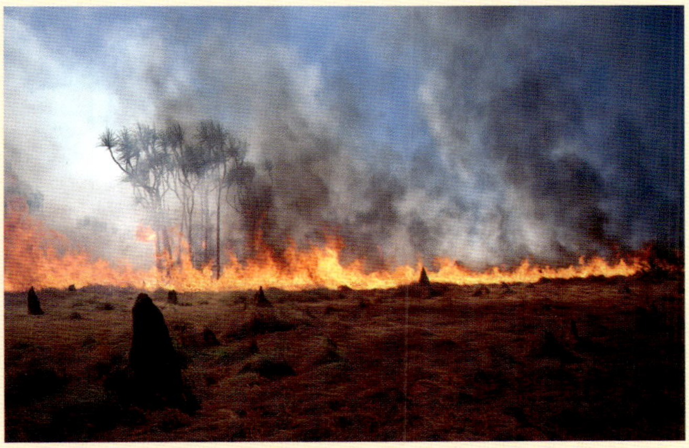

Low-intensity fires, such as this one raking the South Alligator floodplain, are integral to the ecology of the region.

Traditional patterns of burning were part of the life of extended family groups as they moved among habitats. Fire was carefully managed with most burns initiated early in the dry season, principally to clear the build up of grass in localised patches of woodland and other areas. Over thousands of years this practice has had a profound effect on the ecology of the region, not just in reducing the impact of destructive late dry season fires but encouraging species adapted to regular low-intensity burns.

While Bininj fire management was severely disrupted in the decades following European settlement, recent years have seen efforts to return to more traditional approaches. Opportunistic wet season burns, combined with early dry season fires are now being used to try to re-create a patchwork of burnt and unburnt vegetation in a variety of habitats. The aim is to restore the botanic diversity, reduce fuel loads, protect vulnerable areas such as rainforests and maintain the cultural ties associated with 'cleaning the country'.

However, for all this, fire remains one of Kakadu's most emotive and challenging issues, for locals and visitors alike.

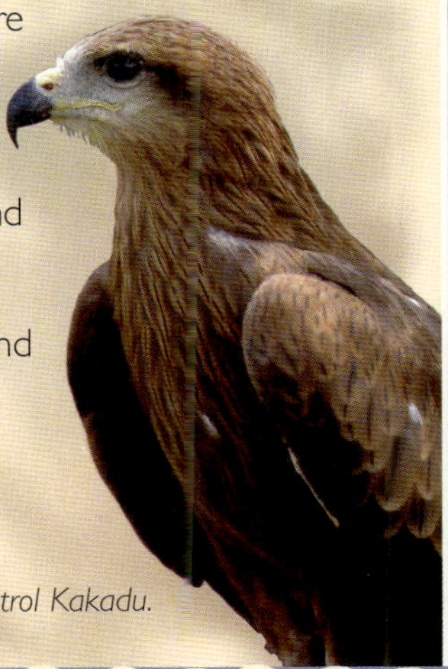

*The Black Kite (*Milvus migrans*) is one of 25 raptors that patrol Kakadu.*

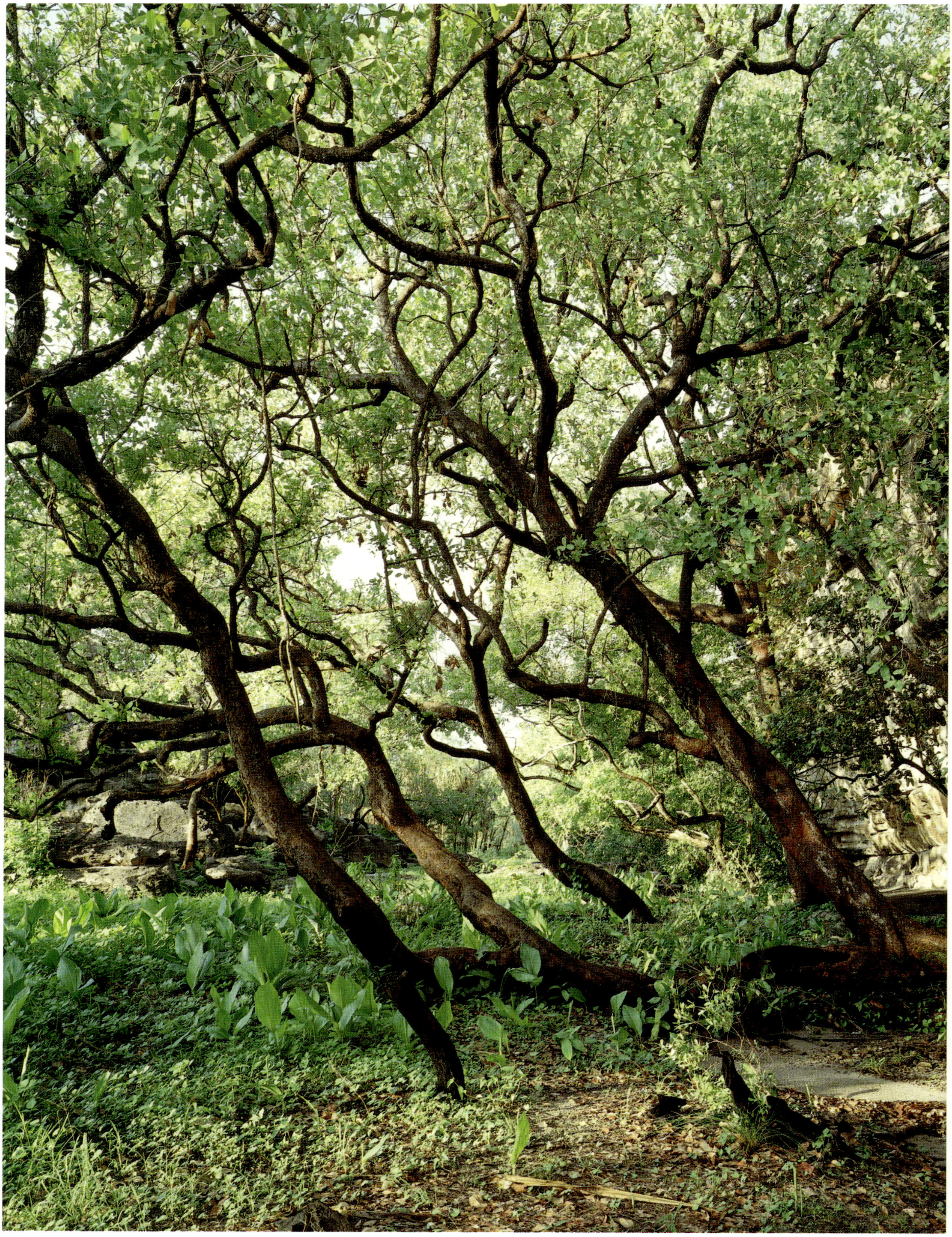

A spreading canopy shades emerging Native Ginger Plants in a sheltered grove at Ubirr.

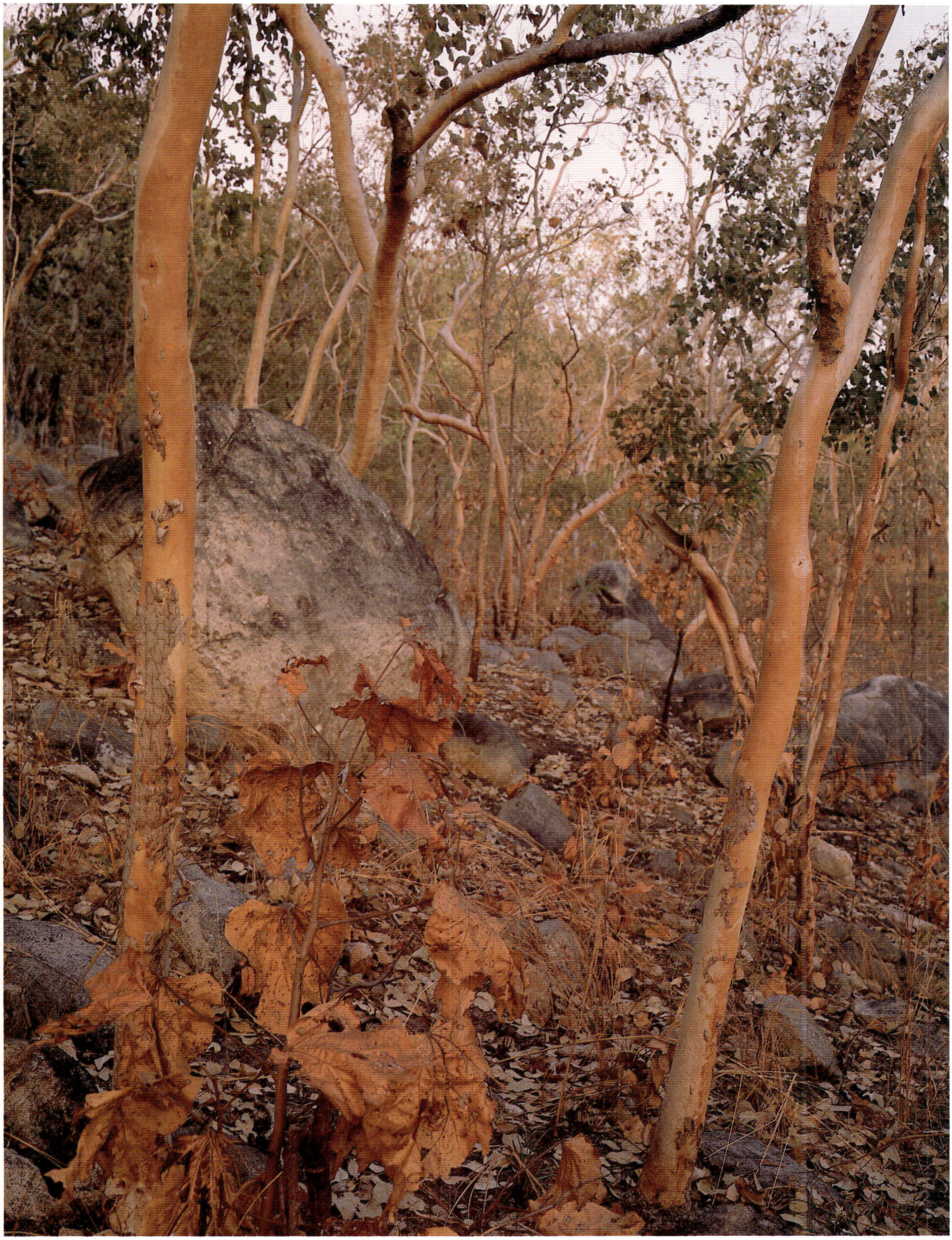

Through Gurrung many forest and woodland trees drop their leaves as a survival strategy against the parching heat.

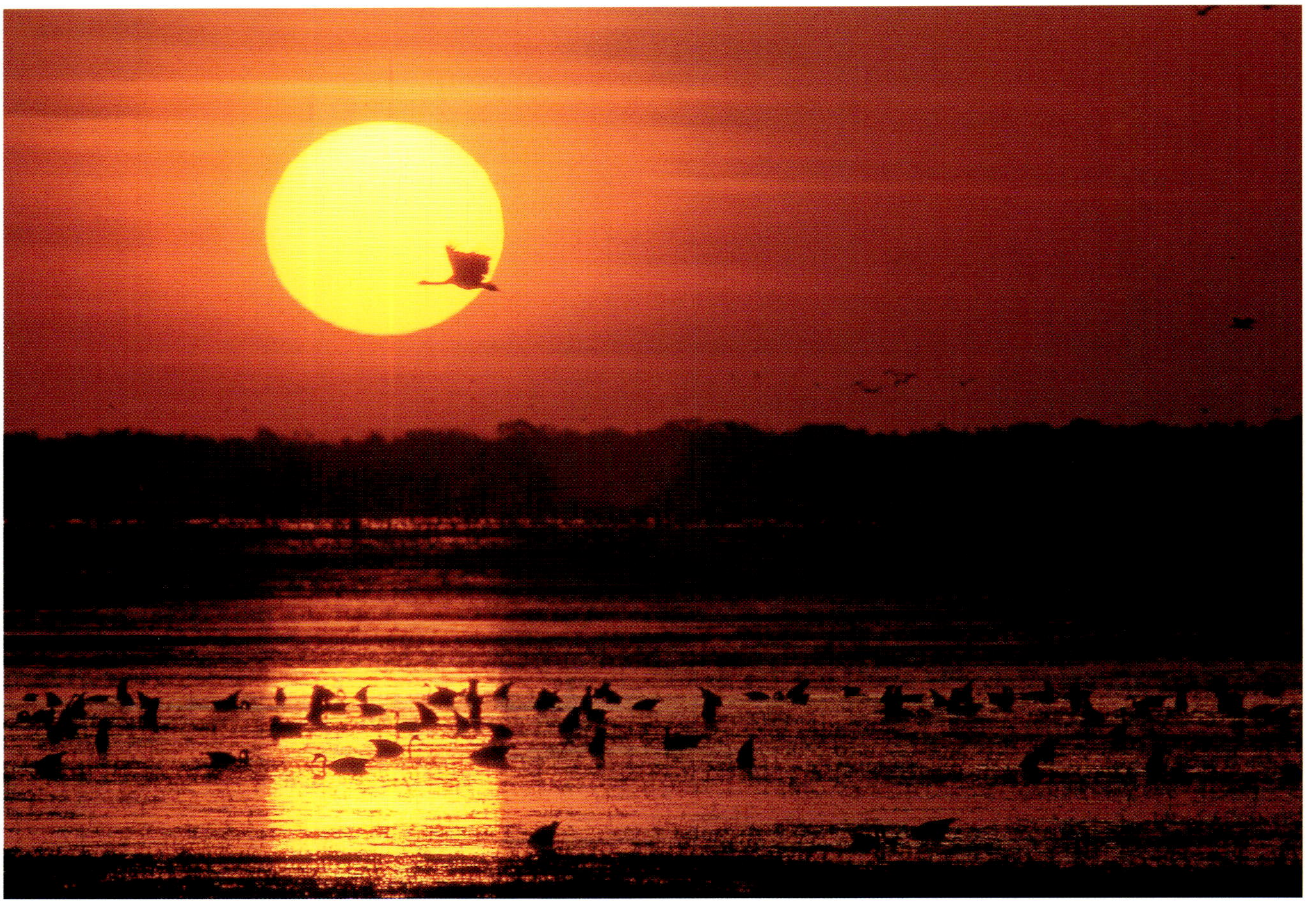

Sunset over the expansive wetlands of the Nourlangie floodplain.

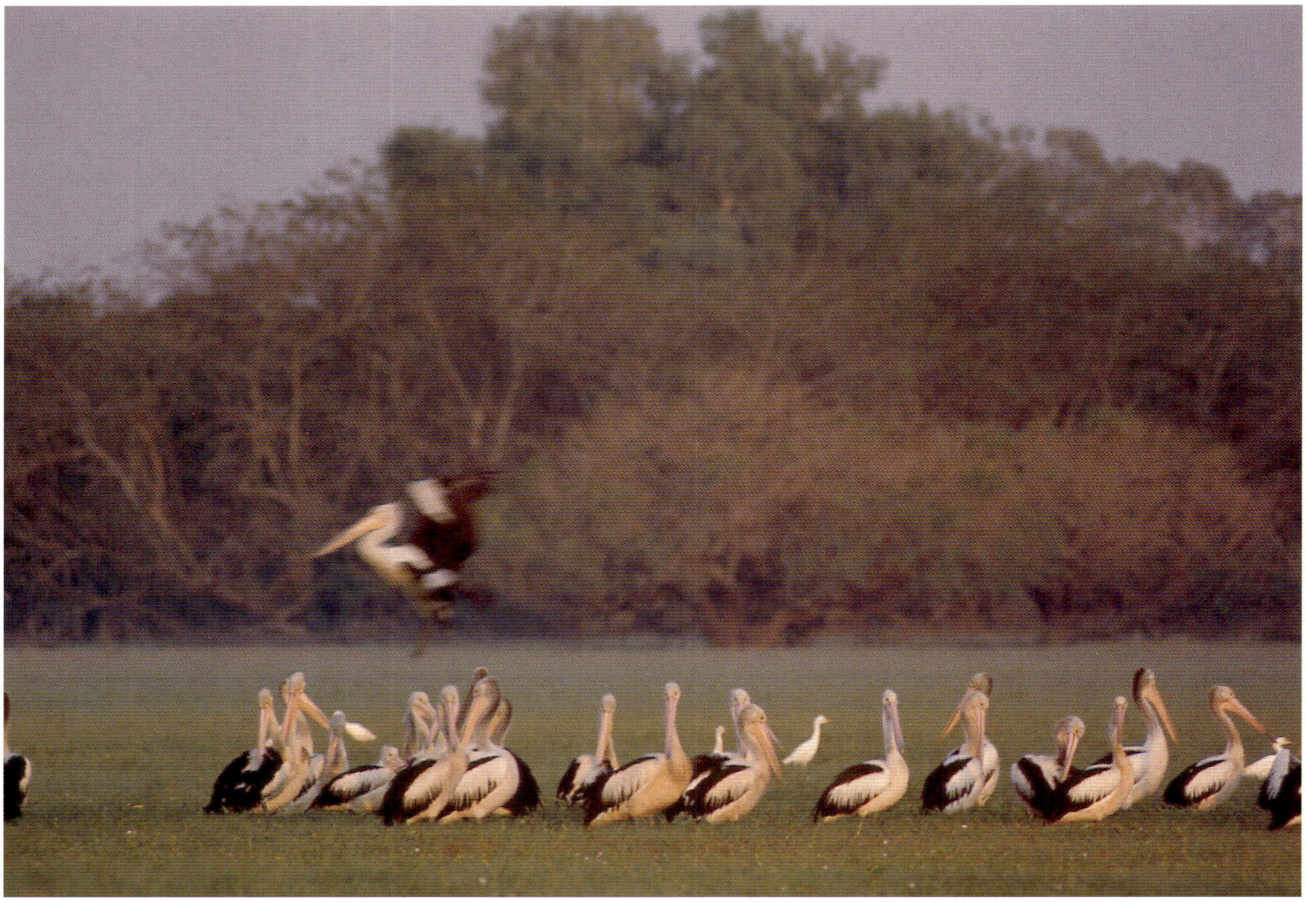

A flock of Australian Pelicans (Pelecanus conspicullatus) *settles in for the night as a latecomer approaches to land in the last remaining vacancy.*

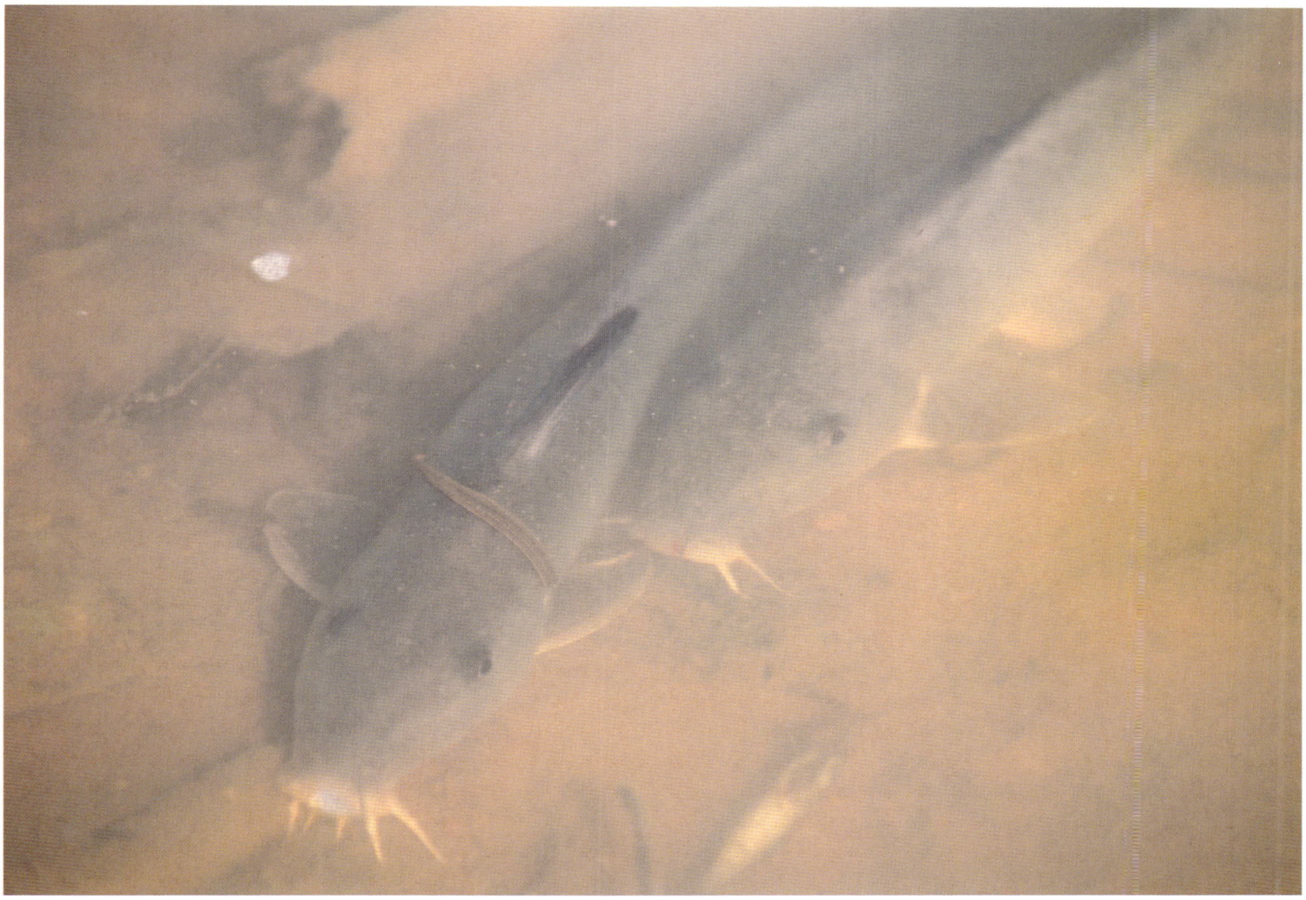
A catfish awaits judgement day as a shallow pool evaporates.

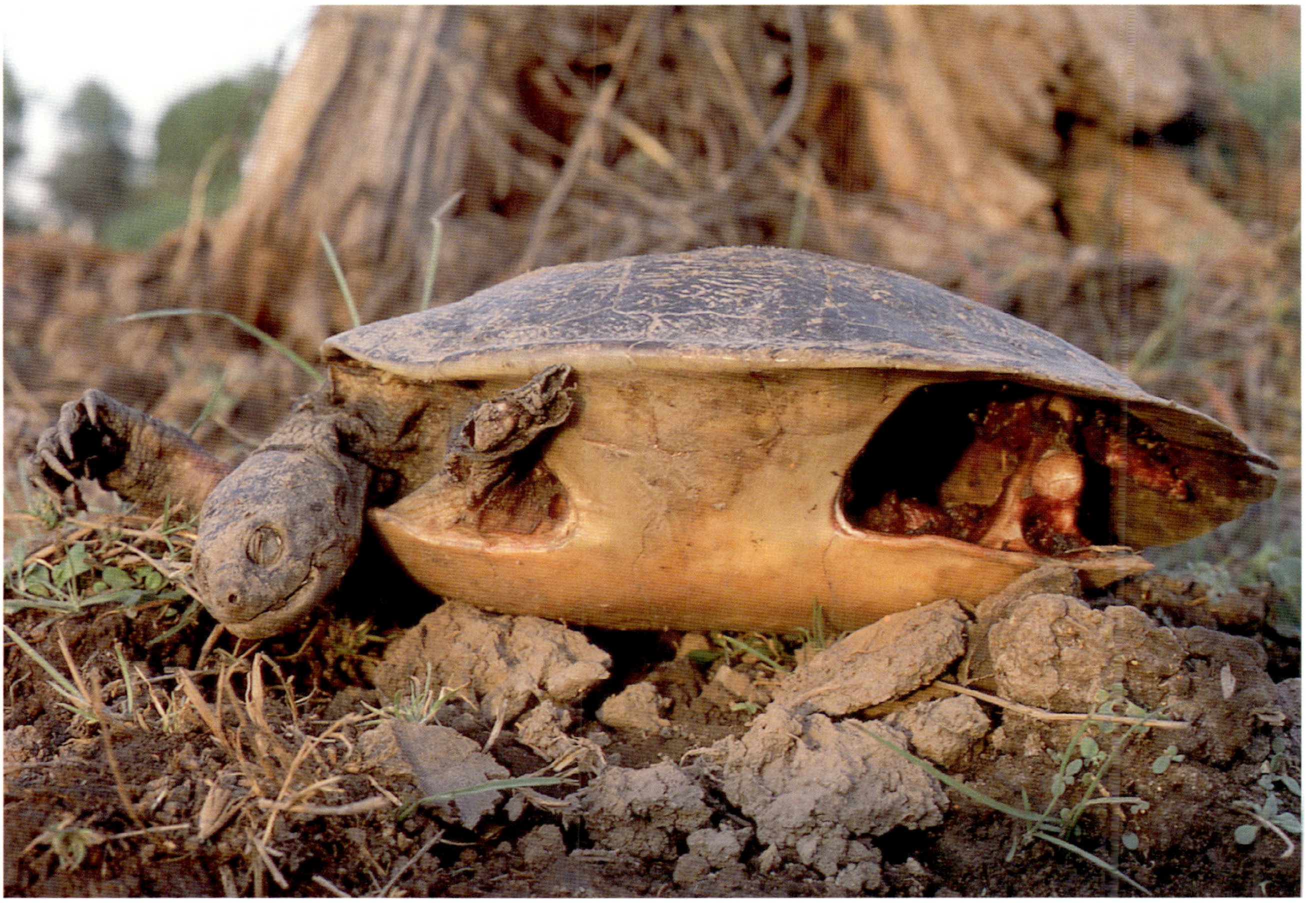
The remains of a freshwater turtle lying at the foot of a large paperbark - home to a White-bellied Sea Eagle (Haliaeetus leucogaster).

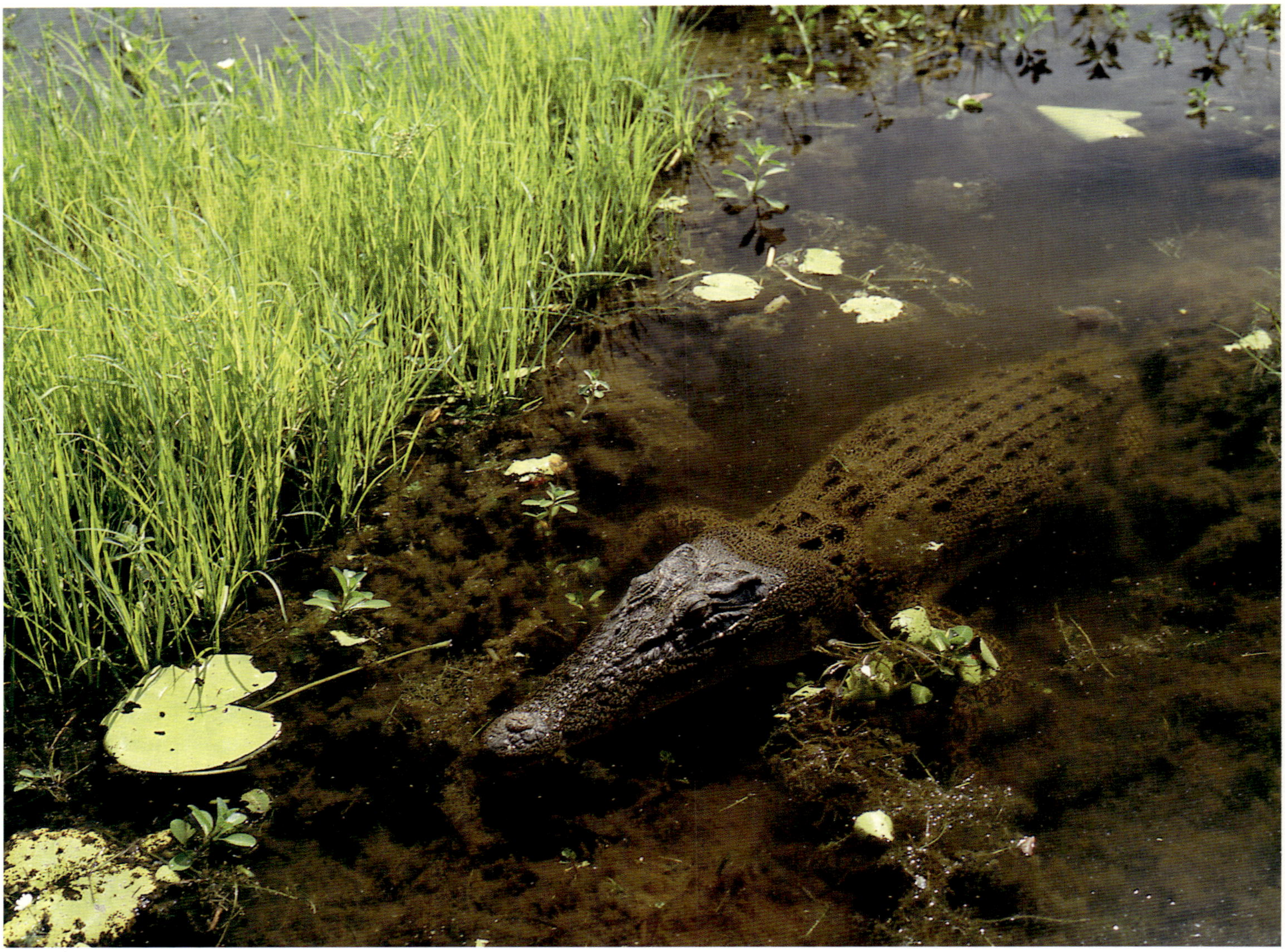

The rich billabongs at Yellow Water are a favourite lair of the saltwater crocodile.

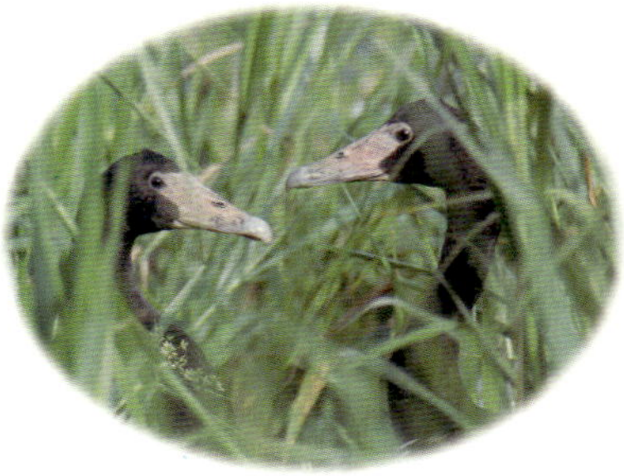

*One of Kakadu's most prolific birds, the Magpie Goose (*Anseranas semipalmata*) is a popular item on the extensive crocodile menu.*

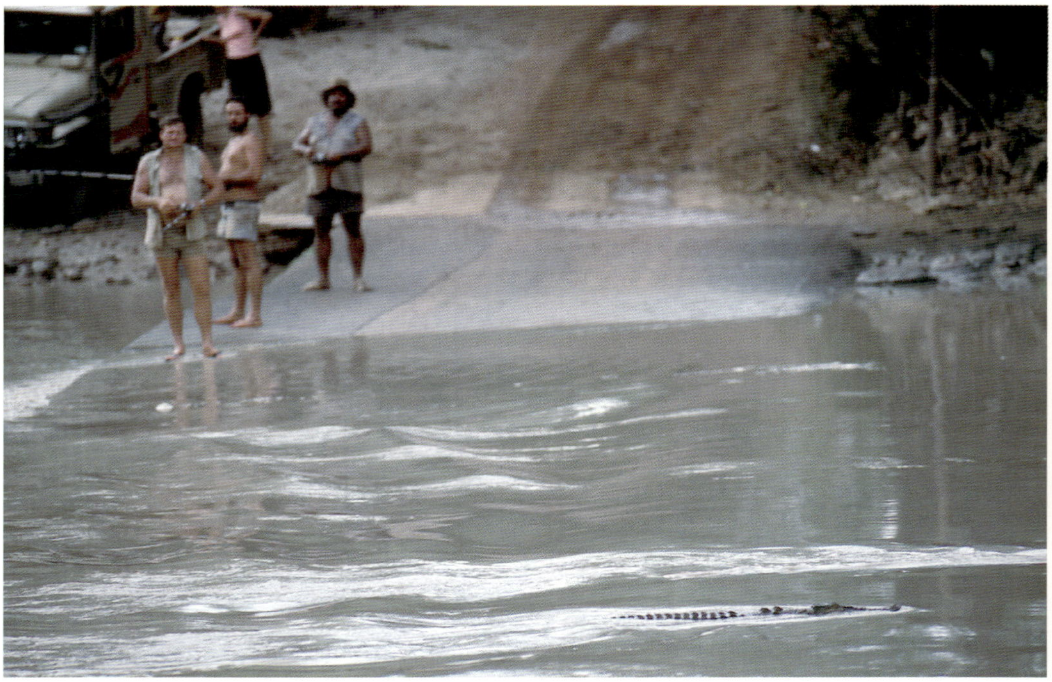

Fishermen look on undaunted as a saltwater crocodile cruises upstream past Cahills Crossing on the East Alligator River.

SALTIES AND FRESHIES

Kakadu's most notorious and feared residents are also great survivors from the age of dinosaurs. The saltwater or Estuarine Crocodile *(Crocodylus porosus)* is the world's largest living reptile with some adult males growing to six metres or more in length and living in excess of 70 years.

These fearsome predators are found throughout South East Asia and along Australia's northern tropical shores and waterways. In Kakadu they range widely from the coast to the escarpment, lurking in a great variety of habitats, including river estuaries, freshwater billabongs and seasonal wetlands.

'Salties' are superbly adapted to life in these domains where they feed on fish, birds and large mammals. Camouflage, stealth and speed make them a formidable predator with the ability to erupt from concealed positions and strike at prey on land and water with deadly force.

This species generally breeds during the wet season with eggs laid in nests on mounds or floating rafts of vegetation near permanent water. The sex of the embryos is determined by incubation temperatures. Eggs and hatchlings are, however, acutely vulnerable to sudden environmental changes such as floods, as well as predation by goannas, birds and other species – less than 10 per cent survive the first year of life.

Kakadu is also home to the smaller Freshwater Crocodile *(Crocodylus johnstonii)*. Unlike its larger cousin, the 'freshie' breeds during the dry months of the year and prefers to bury its eggs near sandy river banks. Growing to three metres in length, this species is distinguished by a slender body shape and a narrow snout which is adapted for snapping at more modest prey, including fish, lizards, frogs and smaller birds.

Though there is considerable overlap between freshie and saltie habitat, freshies prefer billabongs and freshwater streams. Their range extends hundreds of kilometres inland along the river system, including those on the plateau where they can be seen basking in waterholes and on the sandy fringes of creeks.

For raw menace few sights compare with being gazed upon by a pair of crocodile eyes breaching the surface of a murky pool. While salties pose a very real threat to anyone foolish enough to stray into their haunts, freshies are, by nature, more reticent and rarely attack people unless cornered or provoked.

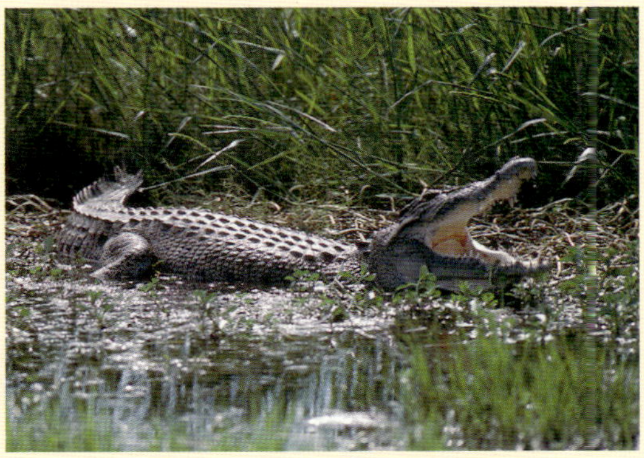

Permanent swamps and billabongs become important habitats for salties as the dry season tightens its grip.

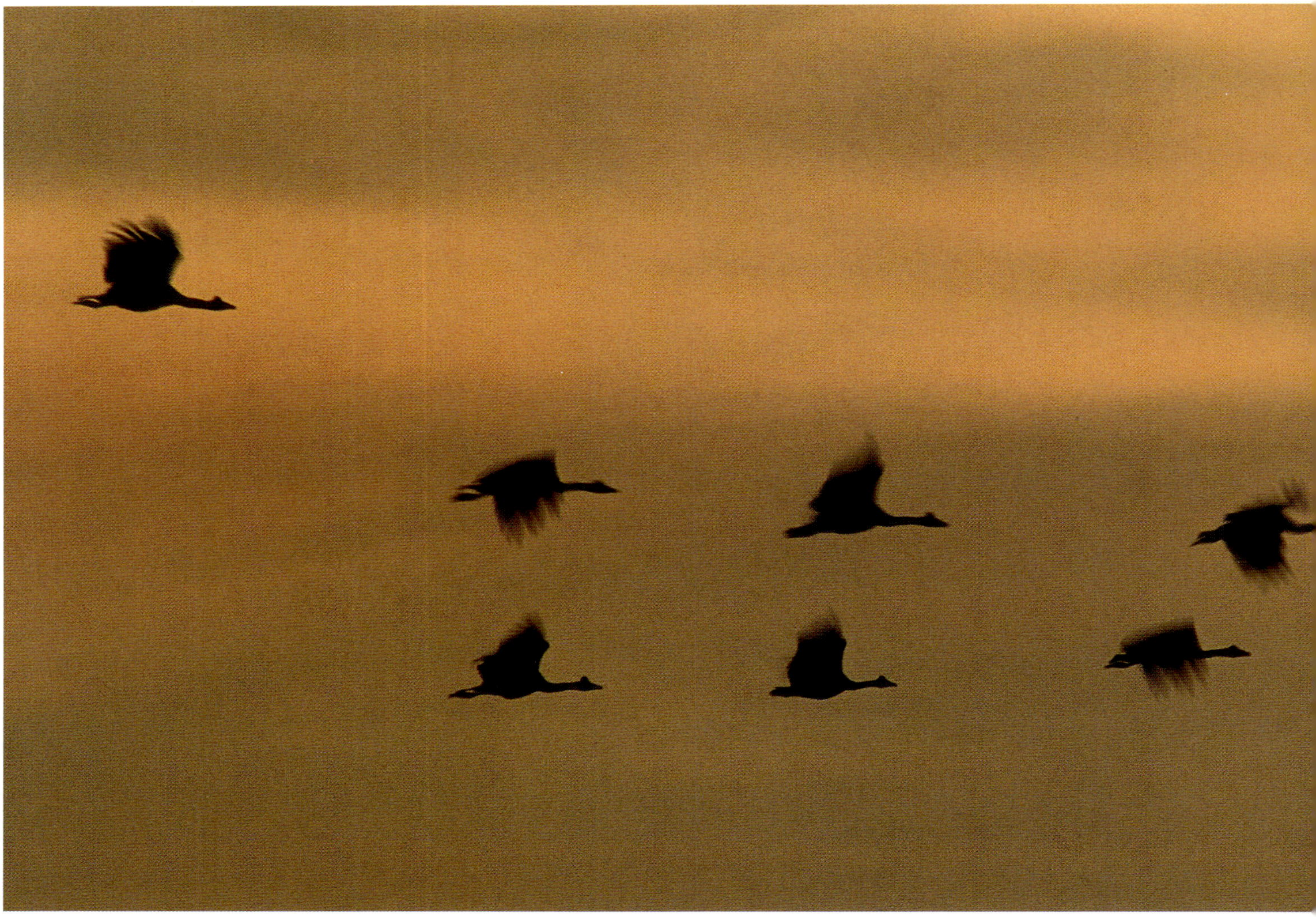

ABOVE Huge flocks of Magpie Geese traverse the floodplains throughout the year.

RIGHT The Darter (Anhinga melanogaster) *is often seen drying its wings while perched on wetland trees.*

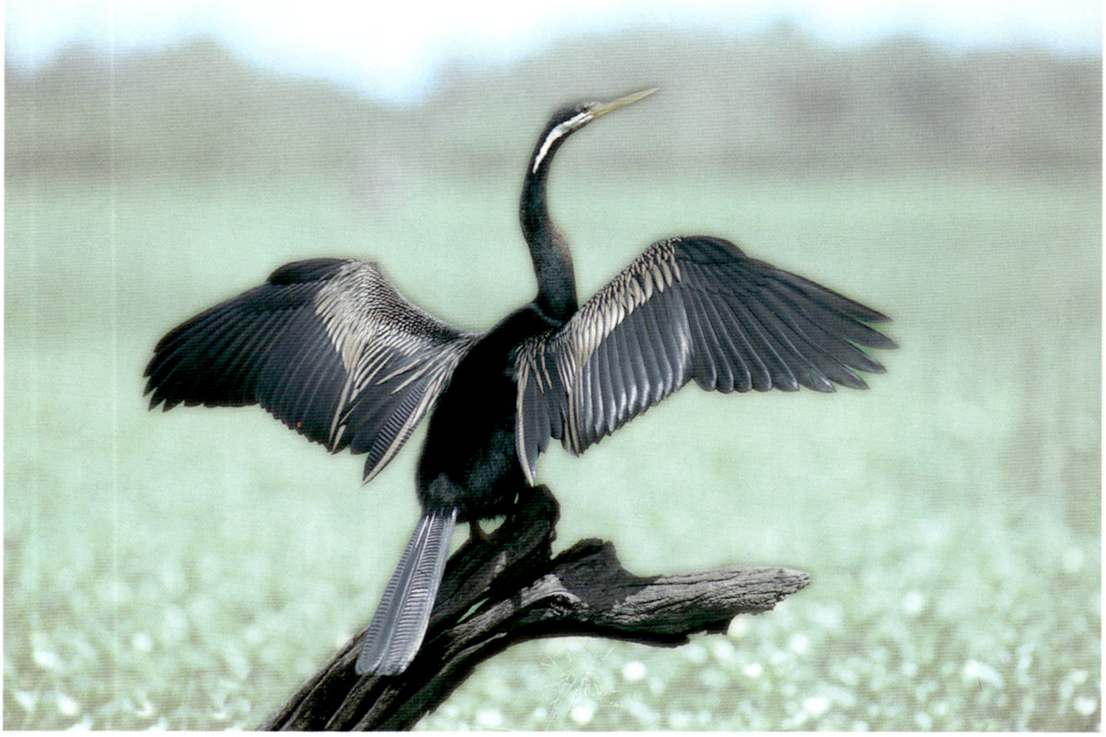

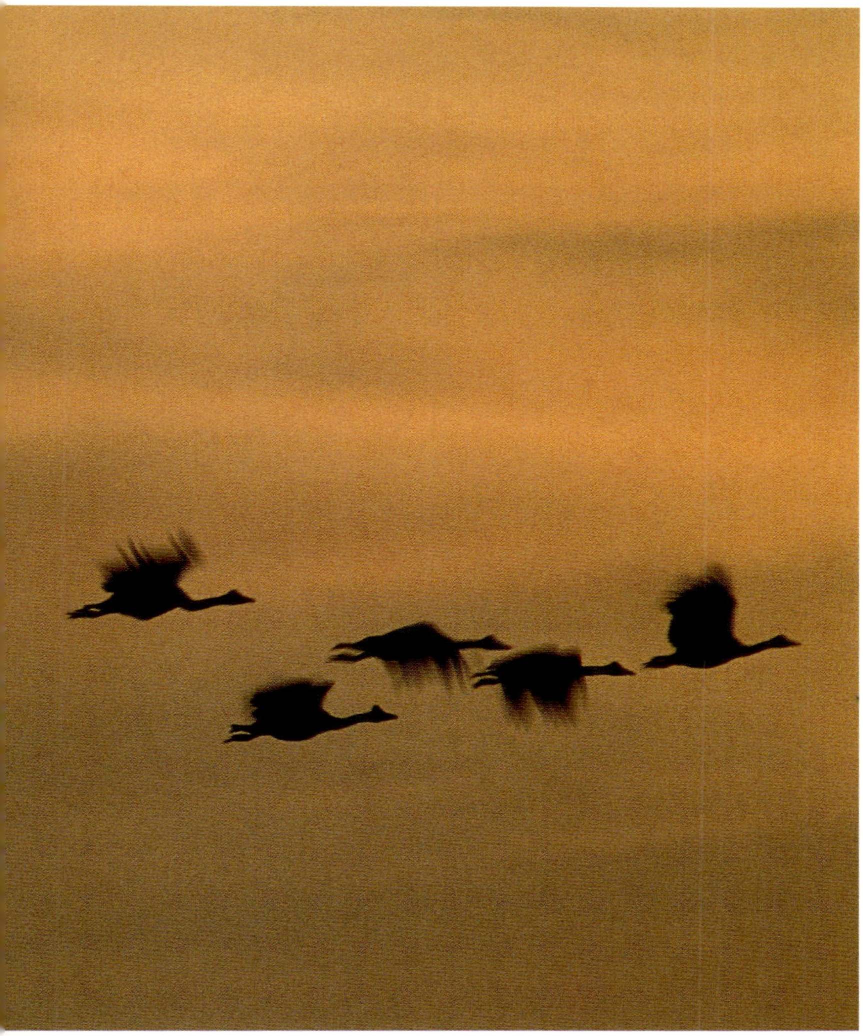

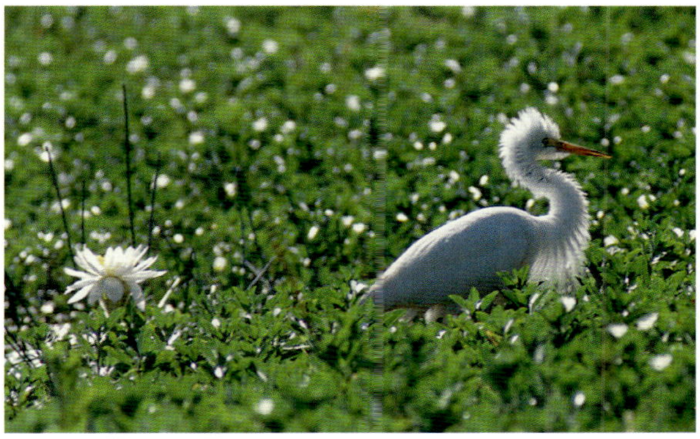

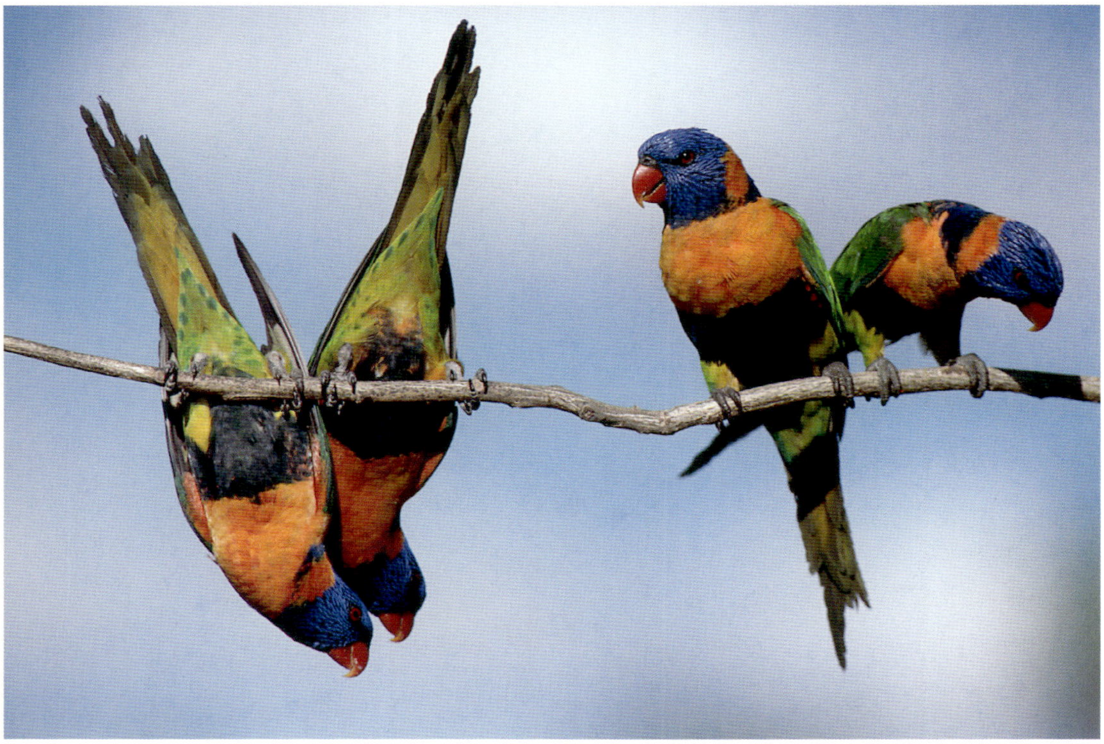

ABOVE *Intermediate Egrets* (Ardea intermedia) *frequent the wetlands.*

LEFT *Red-collared Lorikeets* (Trichoglossus rubritorquis) *are noisy and conspicuous inhabitants of the woodlands.*

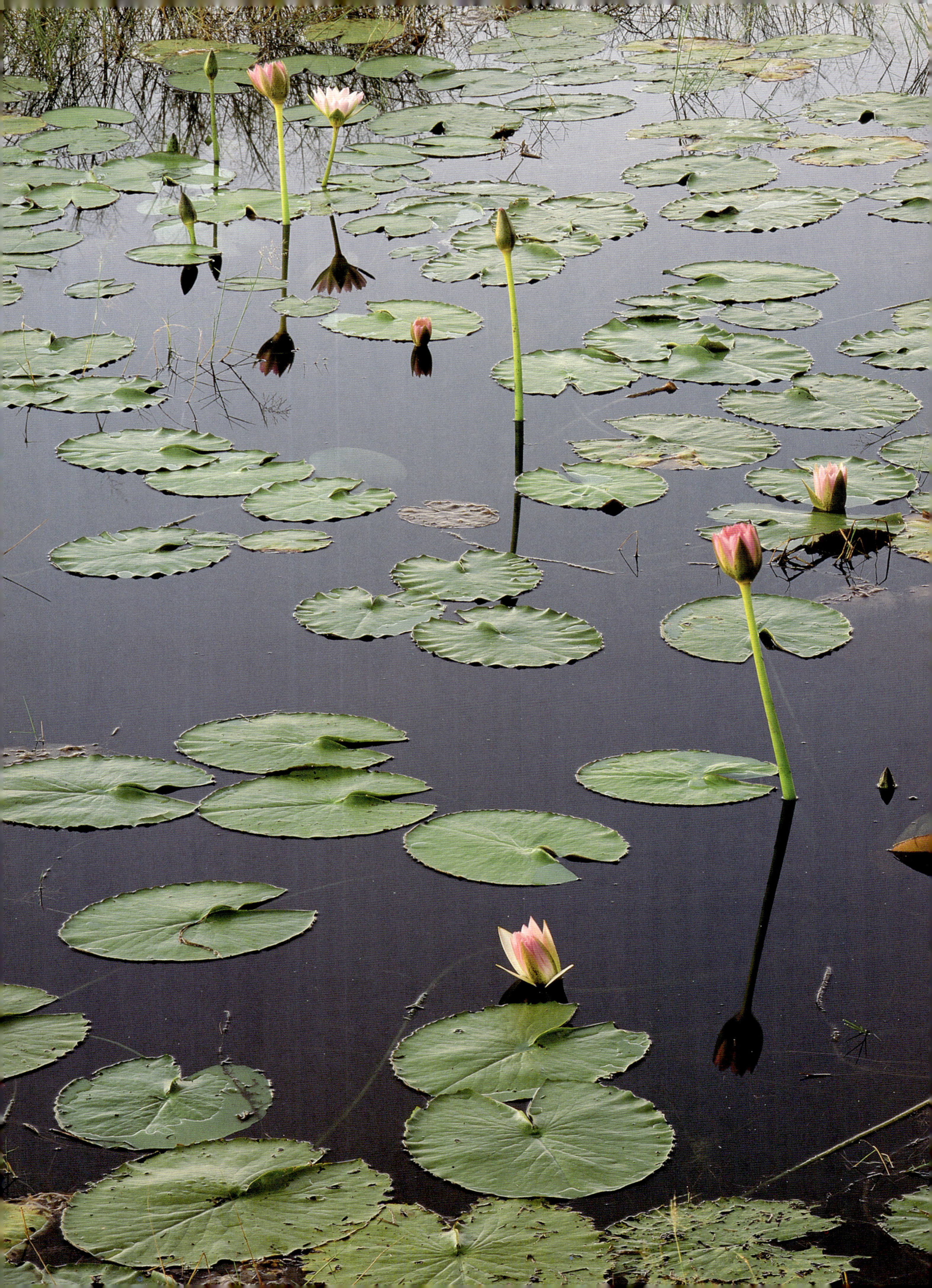

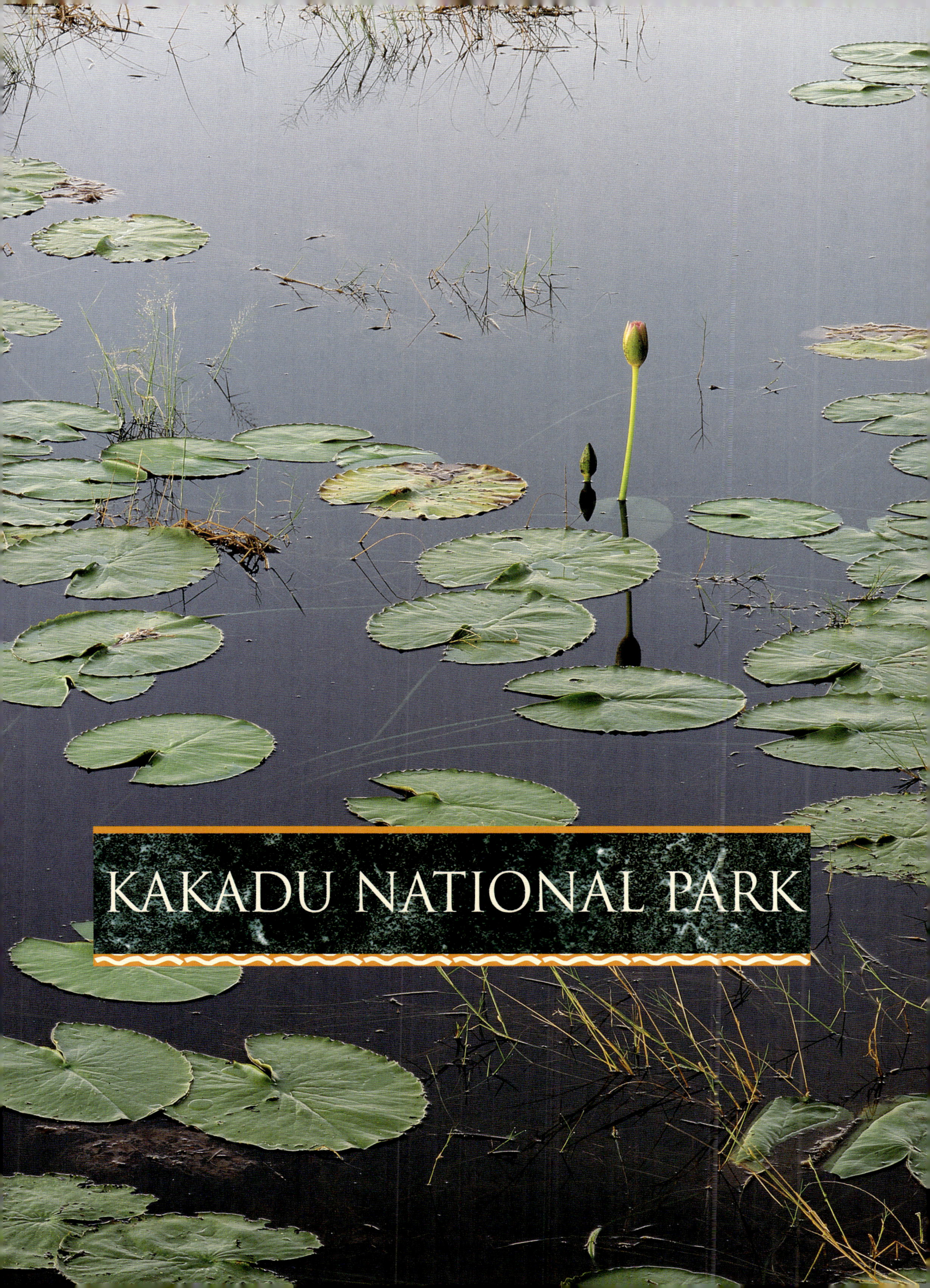
KAKADU NATIONAL PARK

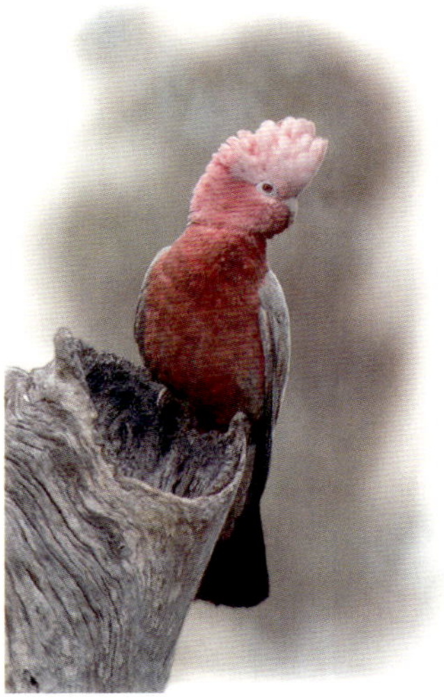

Tree trunks originally hollowed by industrious termites provide nesting sites for a large variety of woodland birds including the Galah (Cacatua roseicapilla).

PREVIOUS PAGE *Morning light over a tranquil Mamukala billabong invites the flowers of the Pink Lotus Lily to greet the day.*

KAKADU NATIONAL PARK

For its traditional owners, Kakadu has always been a place to respect and celebrate. Recognition from the outside world is a much more recent phenomenon.

A national park for the Alligator Rivers region was first mooted in the mid 1960's. Twenty five years later, after innumerable proposals, inquiries and debates, Kakadu National Park finally assumed its current status and proportions. This drawn out process was perhaps understandable, given that plans for a park coincided with the granting of Aboriginal land rights and the discovery of uranium deposits in the region.

Kakadu is Bininj land. Under an agreement signed in 1978 this land was leased back to the then Australian National Parks and Wildlife Service. Stage One of Kakadu National Park was declared in 1979. Further areas were declared during the 1980's. Over this same period Kakadu was also included on the World Heritage List, in recognition of its outstanding natural and cultural significance.

While the original lease has seen many changes, the nub of the agreement remains. This means Kakadu is jointly managed by traditional owners and park staff. This effort is overseen by a board of management with majority Bininj representation. Bininj are also active in the day to day life of the park, both as employees and advisers on a range of issues.

Establishing this co-operative approach has made Kakadu a frontier for redefining what a national park is and how it should work. These definitions have, in turn, been strained to the limit by other less welcome pressures - the most obvious being the anomaly of a major uranium mine lying within the park's boundaries, albeit on a mineral lease.

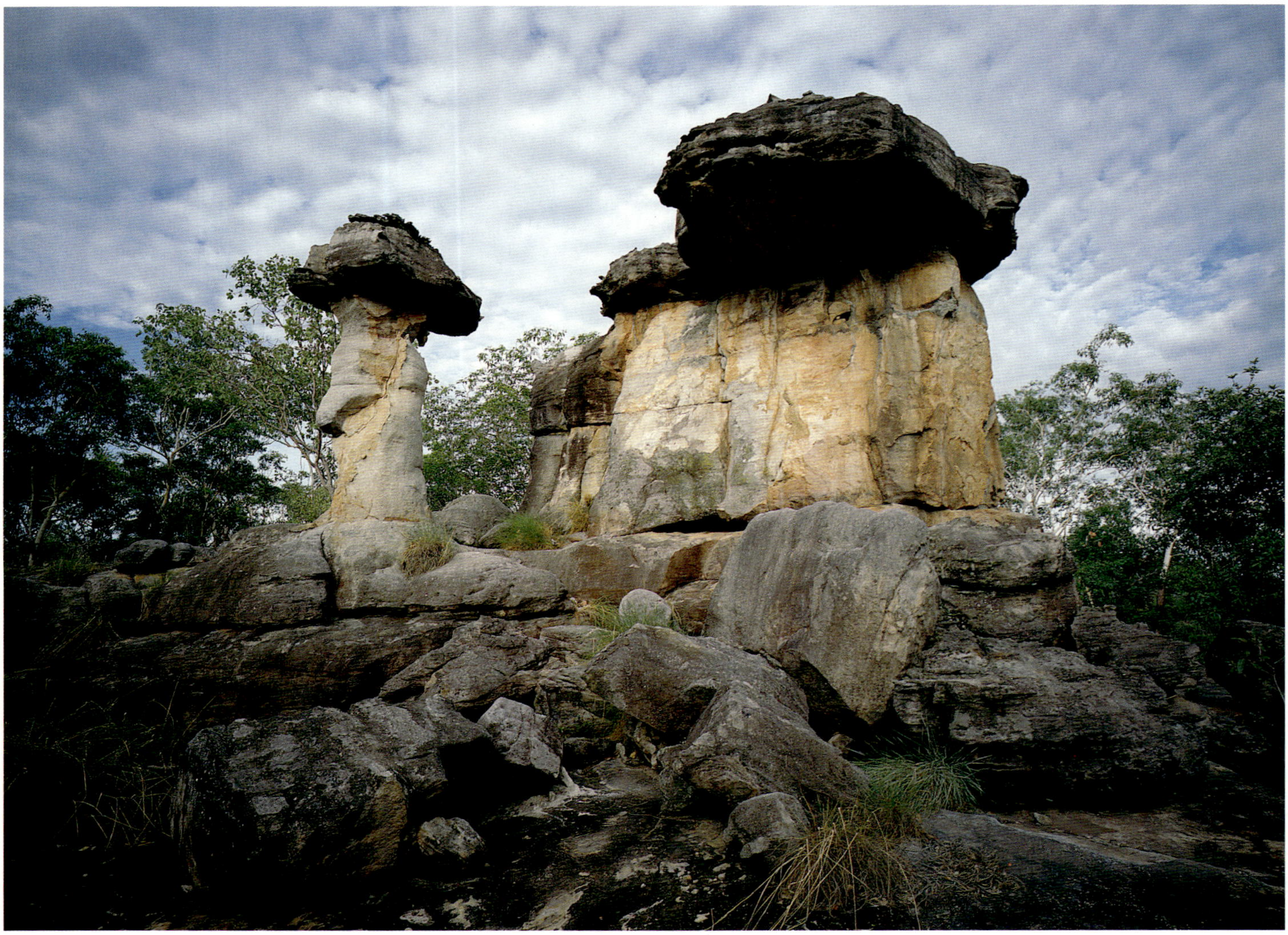

Sentinels in the forest, these pillars are part of the extensive sandstone outcrops flanking the East Alligator River.

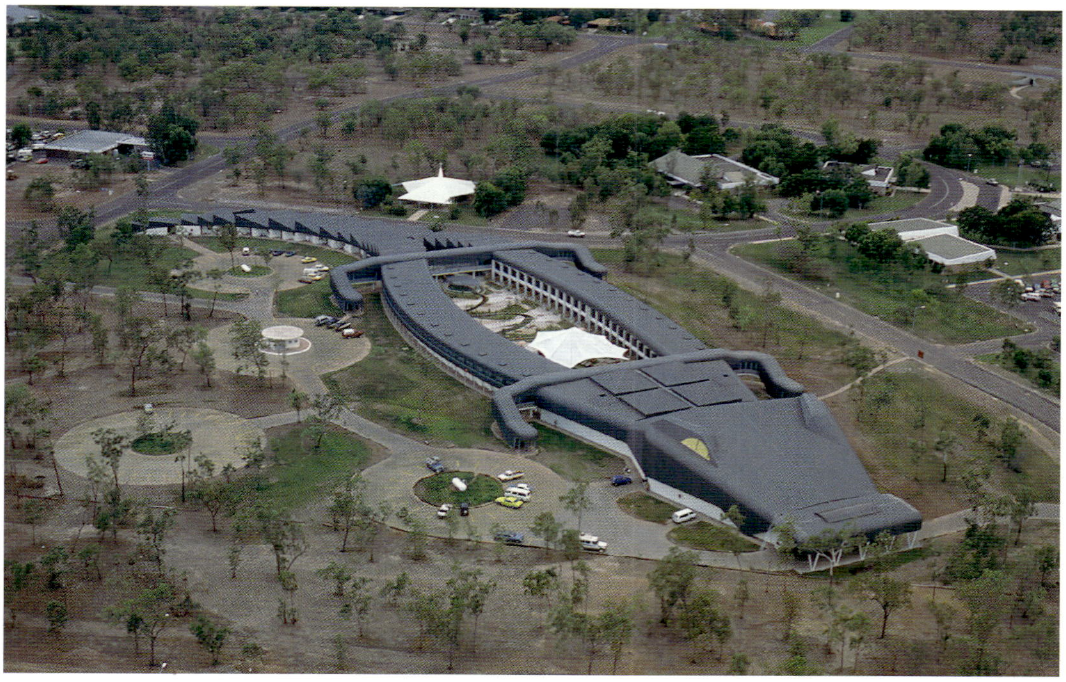

Inspired by Ginga - the saltwater crocodile - this Aboriginal-owned hotel in the township of Jabiru reflects the Bininj ties with the land and its creatures.

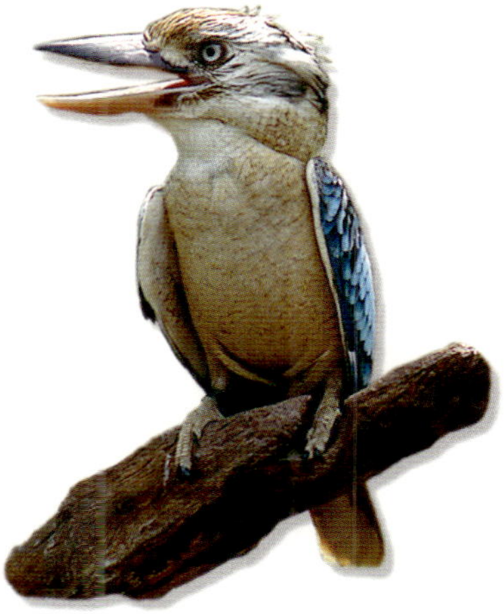

Though not quite as raucous as its southern relatives, the Blue-winged Kookaburra (Dacelo leachii) *is still a keen-eyed woodland hunter.*

In its own way the township of Jabiru is also an incongruous presence in the heart of a World Heritage Area. Established in the early 1980's to accommodate mining workers and their families, it has since become a lively service and tourism centre. Enthusiasm for developing Jabiru into a major commercial town has to be tempered by concerns about how this will affect the park and its wider community.

While the struggles to reconcile the interests of traditional ownership, conservation, mining and tourism remain thorny philosophical questions, they also present daily concerns for those who live and work in the park. For operational purposes Kakadu is divided into five districts - South Alligator, East Alligator, Nourlangie, Jim Jim and Mary River. Providing services and facilities to the seasonal flood of visitors keeps rangers busy in all these districts. Another key aspect of their work is helping to present and protect Kakadu's cultural heritage. As well as liaising with traditional owners, practical tasks include conservation of significant sites, especially exposed rock art sites.

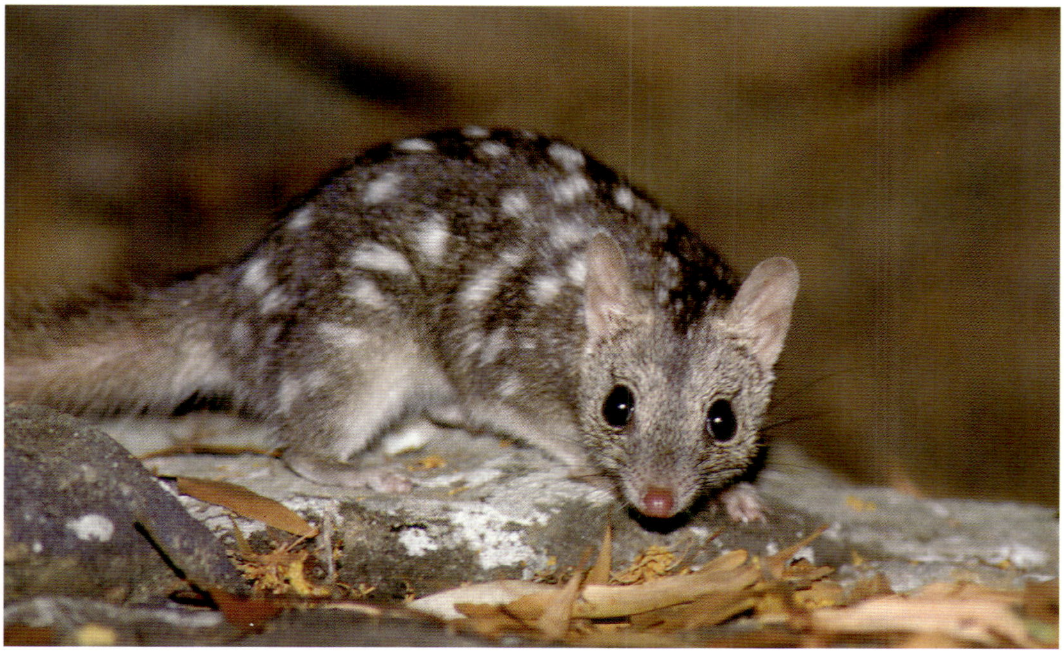

A ferocious insectivore and scavenger, the Northern Quoll (Dasyurus hallucatus) *is a nocturnal feeder, occasionally seen near campgrounds.*

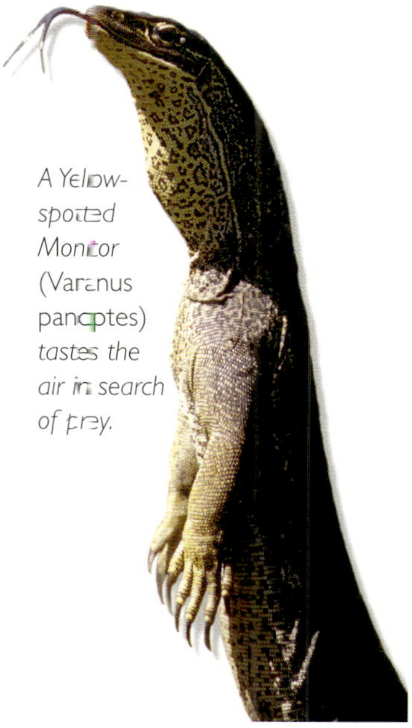

A Yellow-spotted Monitor (Varanus panoptes) *tastes the air in search of prey.*

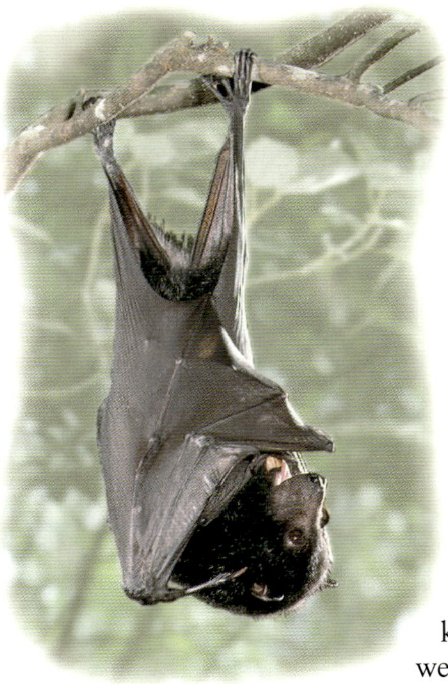

Large populations of the Black Flying-fox (Pteropus alecto) migrate among the forest canopies in search of fruits.

Much of the energy of park staff is directed to the care of Kakadu's natural assets. Fire management has become an essential strategy in restoring the vigour of plant and animal communities. At the same time, native flora and fauna face grave threats from alien species. Eradicating water buffalo was a priority in the park's initial years. An estimated 60,000 in number, these burly intruders caused havoc in wetland areas, disturbing drainage patterns with their wallows and grazing heavily on native vegetation. The buffalo may be all but gone but other ferals such as pigs, cats and domestic dogs are not so easy to remove. Meanwhile the cane toad advances closer to the park's borders each year - a potentially devastating incursion.

The annual flooding of the wetlands also reveals Kakadu's vulnerability to invasion by introduced plants. Some of the most insidious weed species include the spiky shrub mimosa, salvinia - an aquatic fern that forms thick floating mats, and para grass, a floodplain invader.

Much has been learnt about Kakadu's natural order - and its bouts of chaos - over the past two decades. Yet the ecology is still only dimly understood by science. Even attempts to intervene can have unforeseen results. So, for example, removing the water buffalo - a creature who consumes around 40 kilograms of food a day - has allowed the spread of some introduced grasses, as well as causing a build-up of fuel and potential fire risks in floodplain areas.

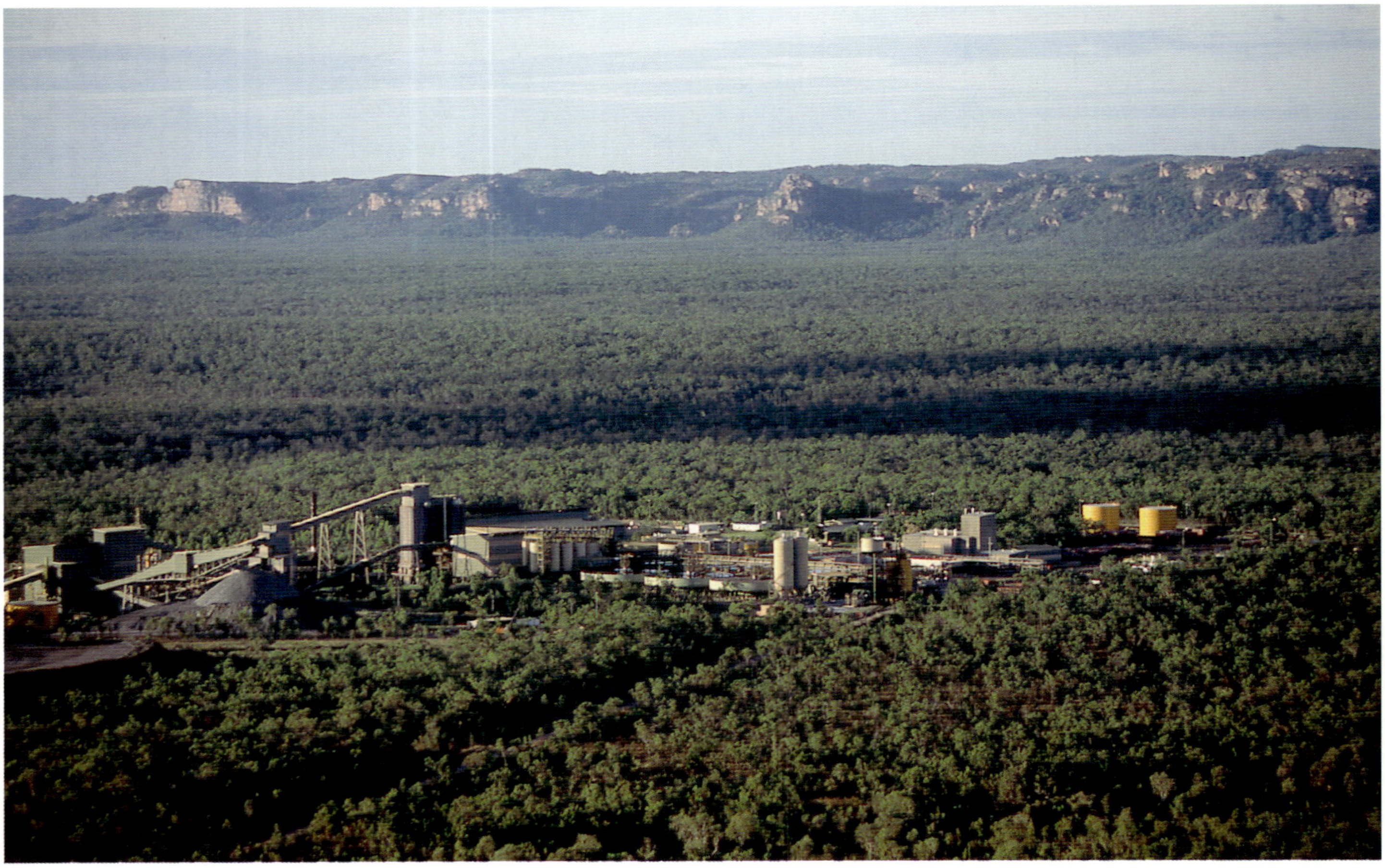

Rising from wooded plains near Magela Creek, the Ranger Uranium mine is an incongruous sight amidst Kakadu's natural splendour.

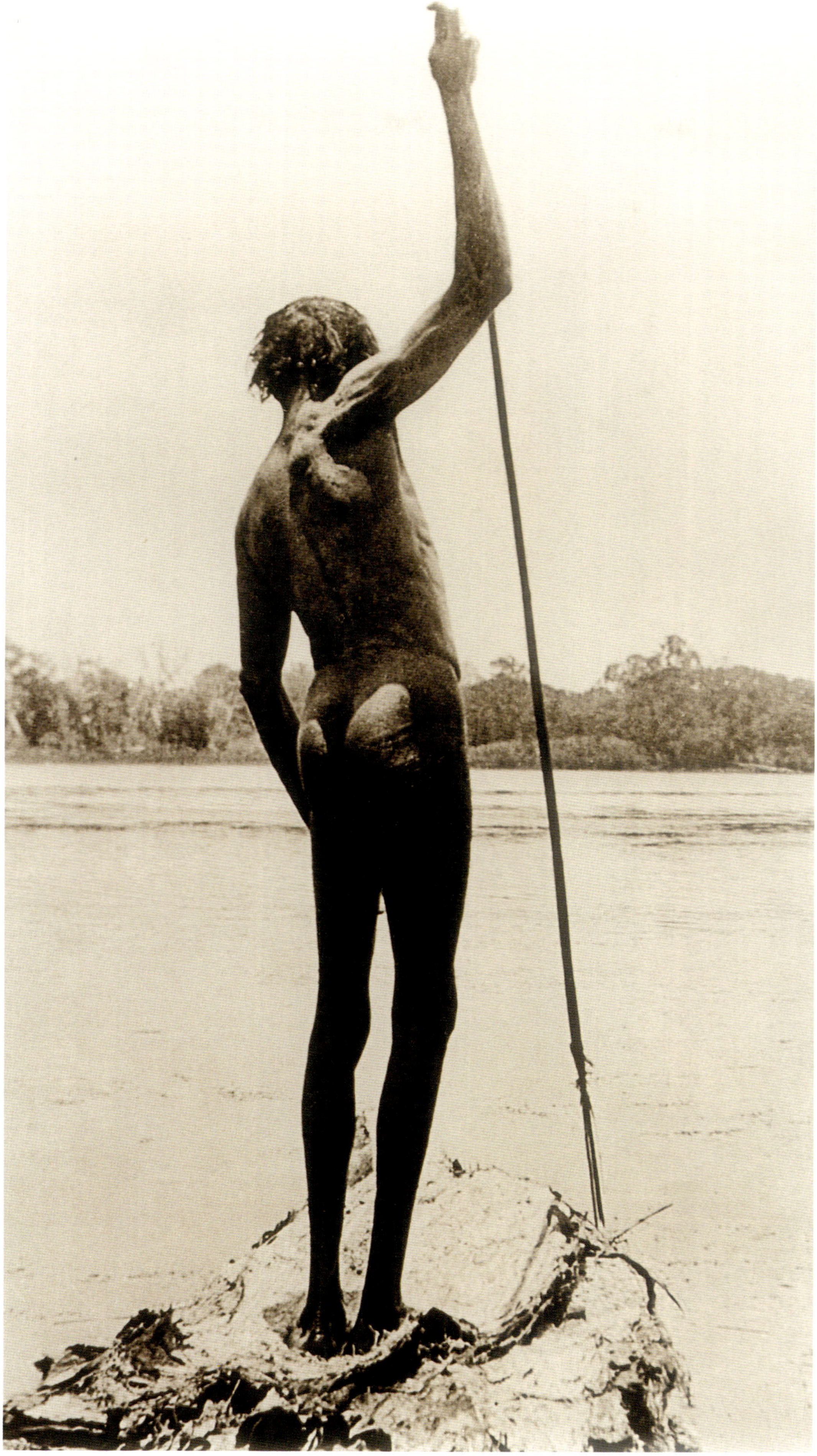

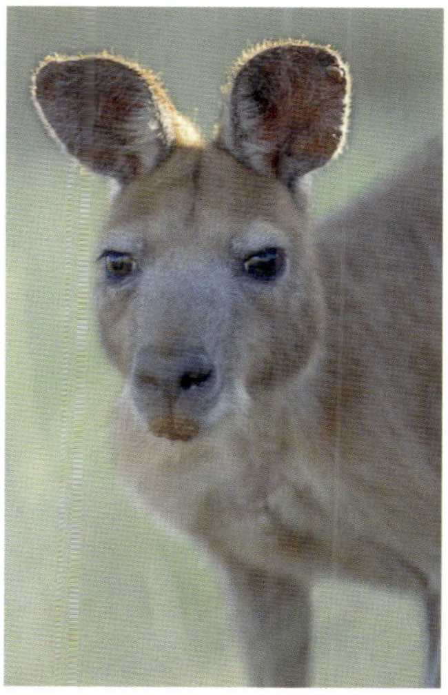

The Common Euro (Macropus robustus).

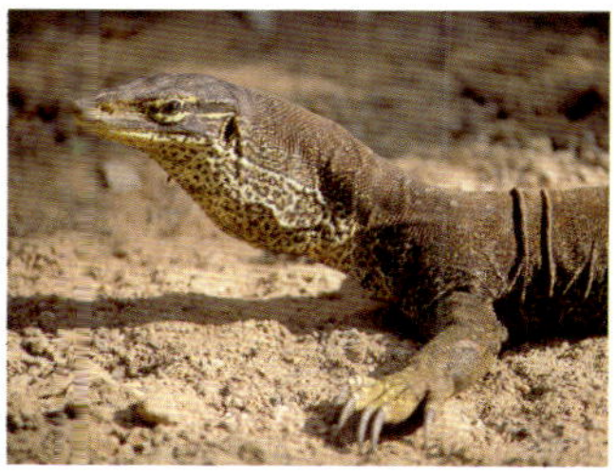

The Yellow-spotted Monitor or Northern Sand-goanna (Varanus panoptes).

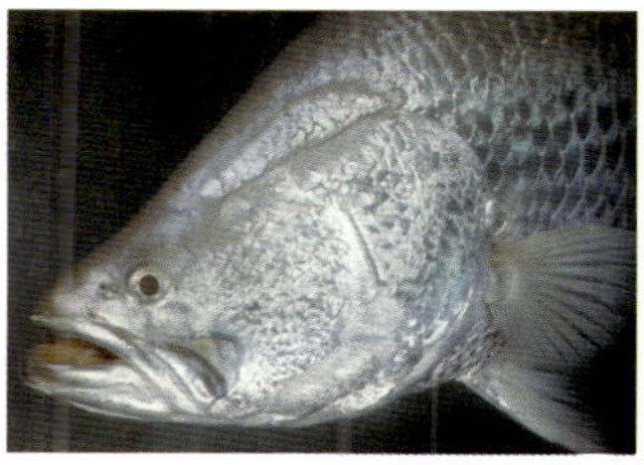

The much-prized fish of northern Australia, the Barramundi (Lates calcarifer).

Traditional Bininj life featured a great many hunting strategies. On the East Alligator River a fisherman poised on a paperbark raft prepares to spear his quarry.

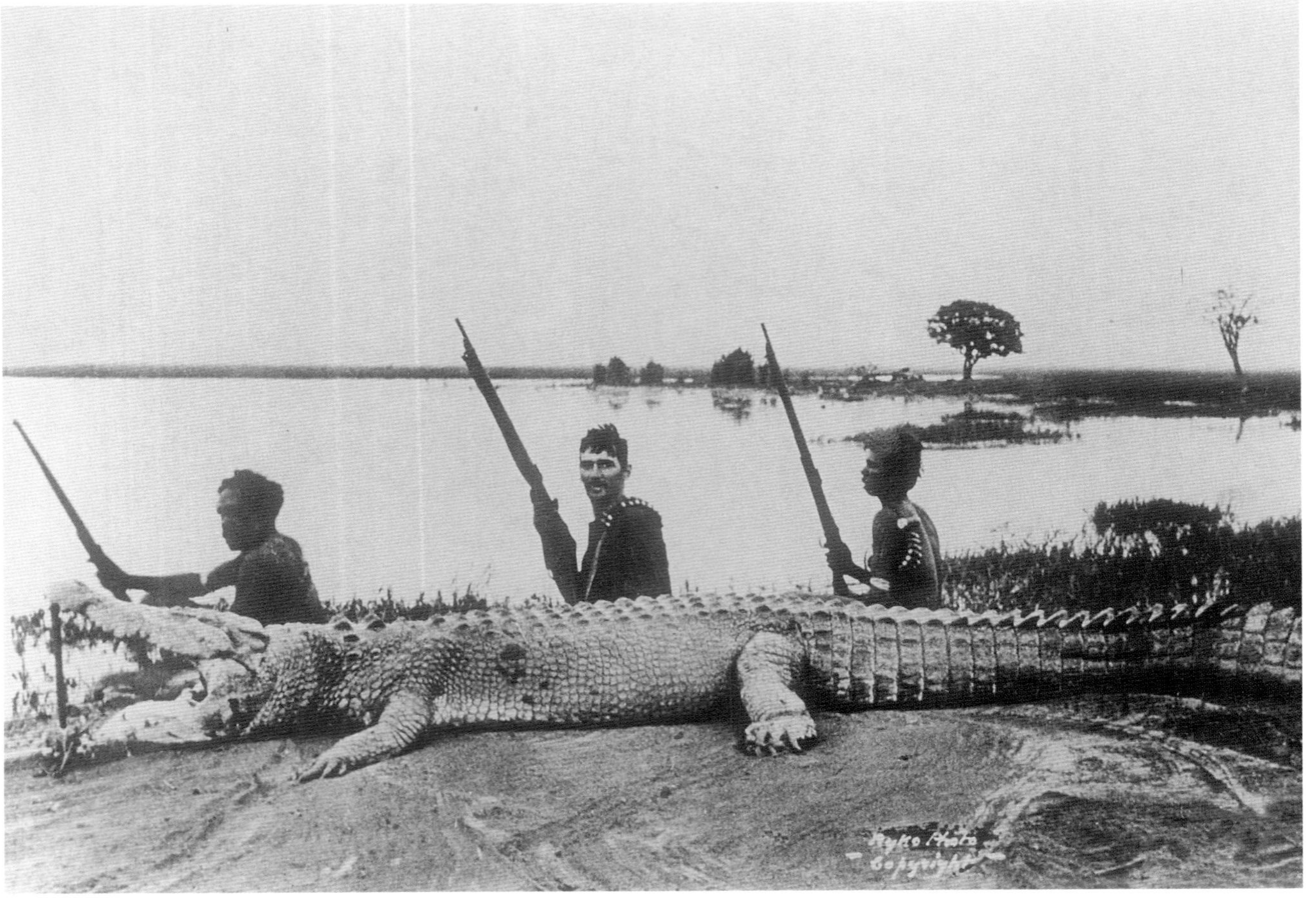

Crocodile hunting became one of many small Balanda industries in the early days of European occupation in the Alligator Rivers region.

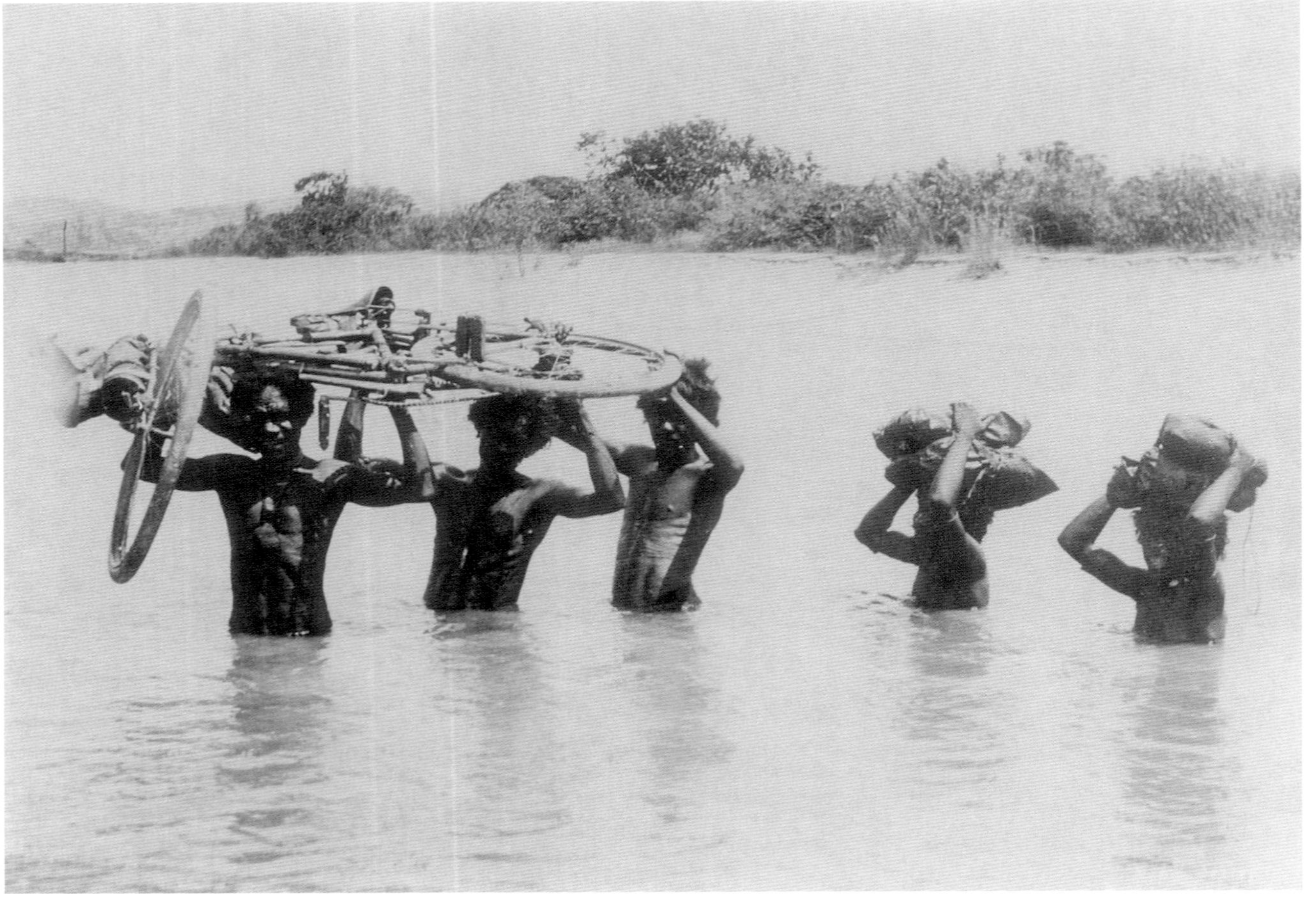

Through the work of Paddy Cahill, the country around the East Alligator River became an important meeting place of Balanda and Bininj life. Here, two-wheeled transport and provisions are ferried across the floodwaters.

THE COMING OF BALANDA

The Kakadu landscape has only been a part of European knowledge for 150 years. Over this time there were several attempts to settle and farm parts of the region, but these were largely frustrated by the rugged terrain and seasonal challenges. Nevertheless, the changes associated with the arrival of Europeans - the Balanda - were profound, even more so than those brought by the Macassan fishermen who, from the early seventeenth century, made voyages to these shores to gather the sea slug trepang.

The party led by Ludwig Leichhardt in 1845 was the first European encounter with the full spectacle of the stone country and the bountiful rivers below. Twenty-seven years earlier the navigator Phillip Parker King had surveyed the coastline and named its three main rivers. But it was the accounts of overland explorers like Leichhardt and later John McDouall Stuart that attracted outside interest in the region.

By the late 1880's the initial enthusiasm had subsided and most Balanda activity in Kakadu was confined to hunting buffalo which had become widespread since being introduced to the Coburg Peninsula in the 1820's. The most famous of these operators was local legend Paddy Cahill, an active trader in buffalo hides who established a small settlement at Oenpelli. This later became a dairy farm and in 1925 was taken over to become a Church of England Mission which carried on its work for 50 years.

Kakadu may not have been subjected to wholesale European colonisation but the seasonal buffalo hunting and a sustained missionary presence, as well as nearby mining and pastoral enterprises, all had a major impact on Aboriginal life. Bininj have a strong association with the cattle and buffalo industries. Many operations relied heavily on their consummate bush skills and local knowledge.

At the same time, social changes and the rapid spread of diseases and introduced drugs, such as tobacco and alcohol, caused severe hardship and dislocation. Around the time of the coming of Balanda the human population of the Alligator Rivers region was around 2000. By the 1970's it is estimated that the number of Aborigines living in the area of the park had dropped to less than 100.

In the face of these disruptions to clan life, Bininj maintained many customary links with country. Despite all the upheavals over the past 150 years, the land and its people have proven to be remarkably resilient.

Kakadu's rock art provides a fascinating record of early contact between Aboriginal culture and the outside world. Here is depicted a prahu, one of several hundred such vessels sailed by Macassan fishermen who arrived each year with the north-west monsoons – a seasonal migration that continued for at least 400 years.

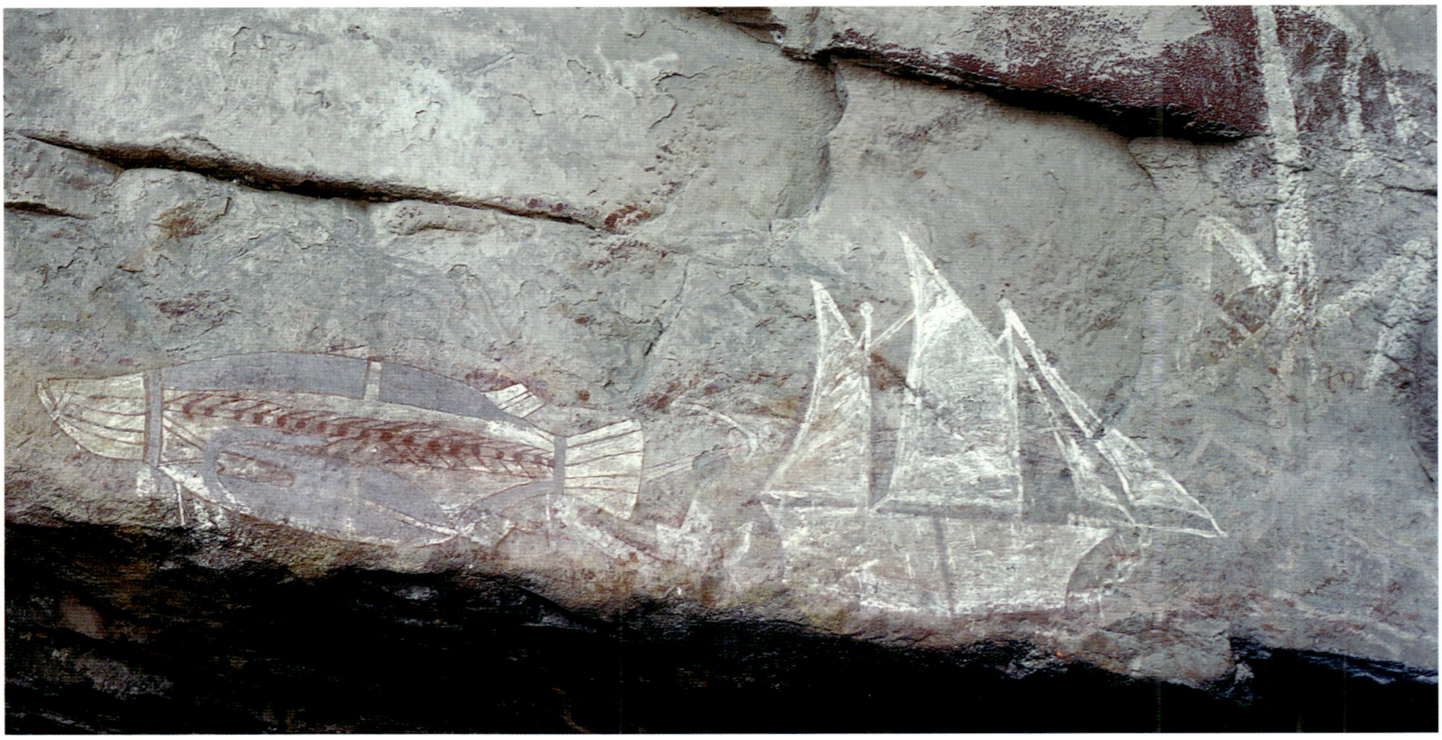

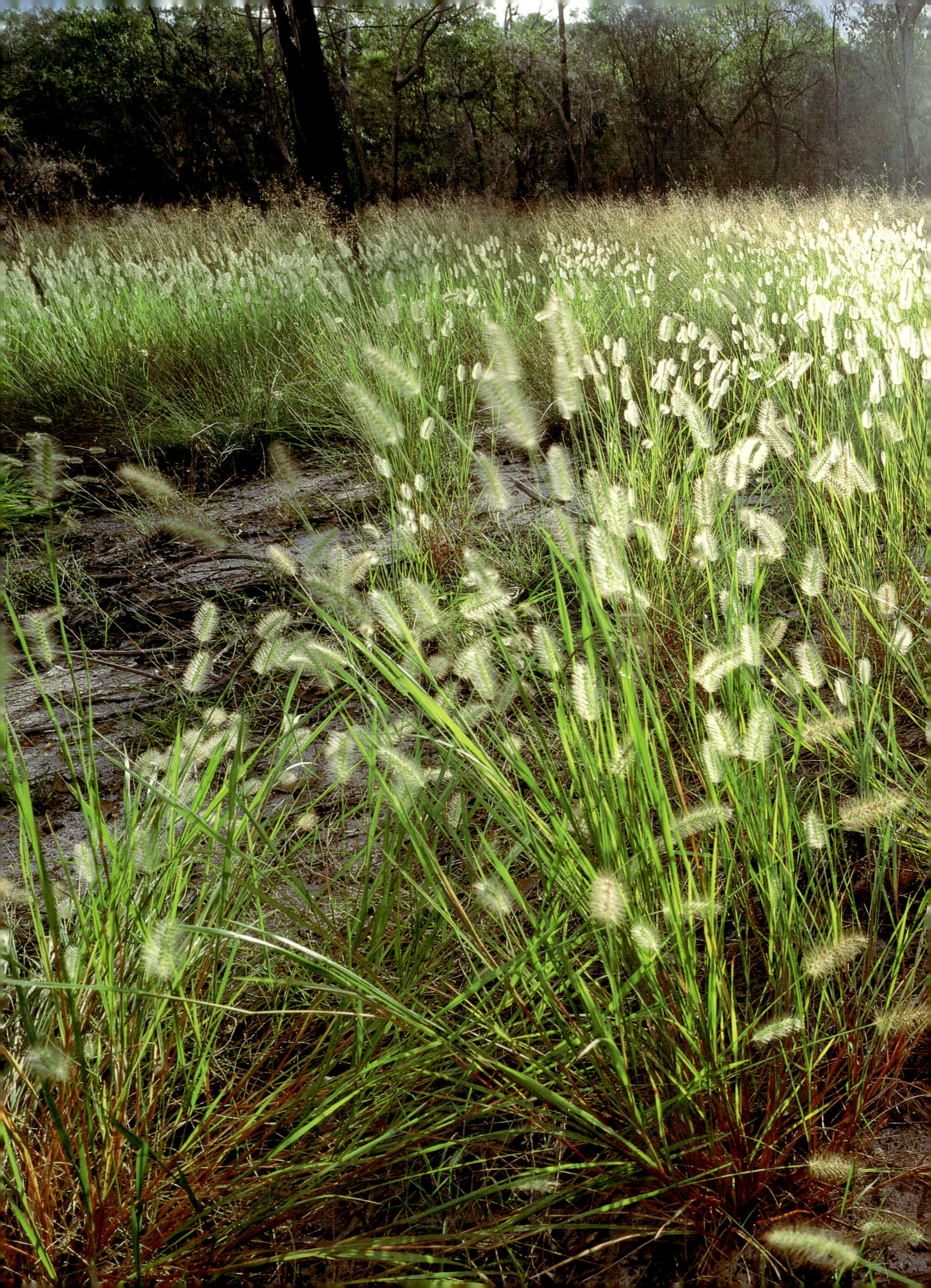

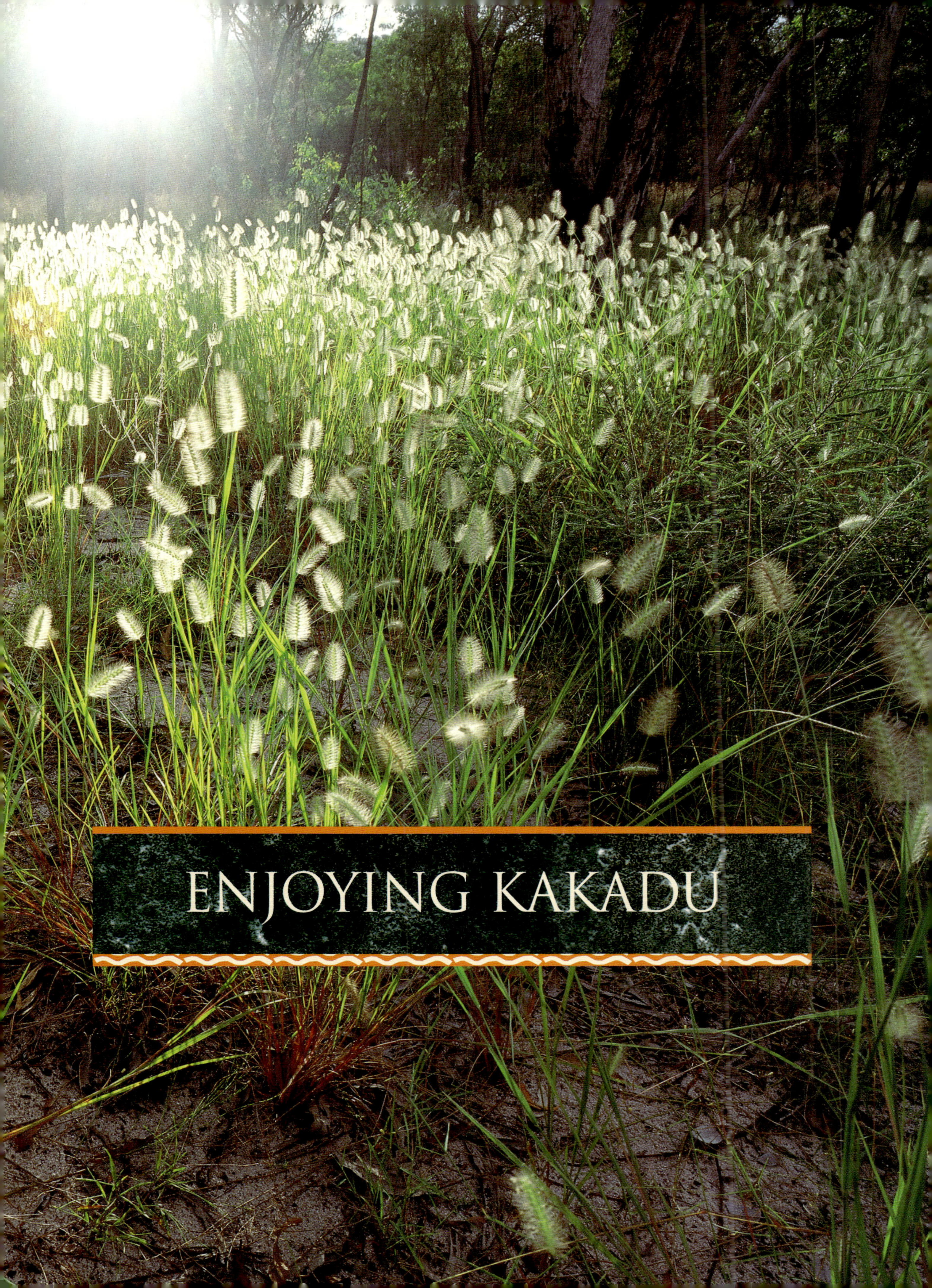

ENJOYING KAKADU

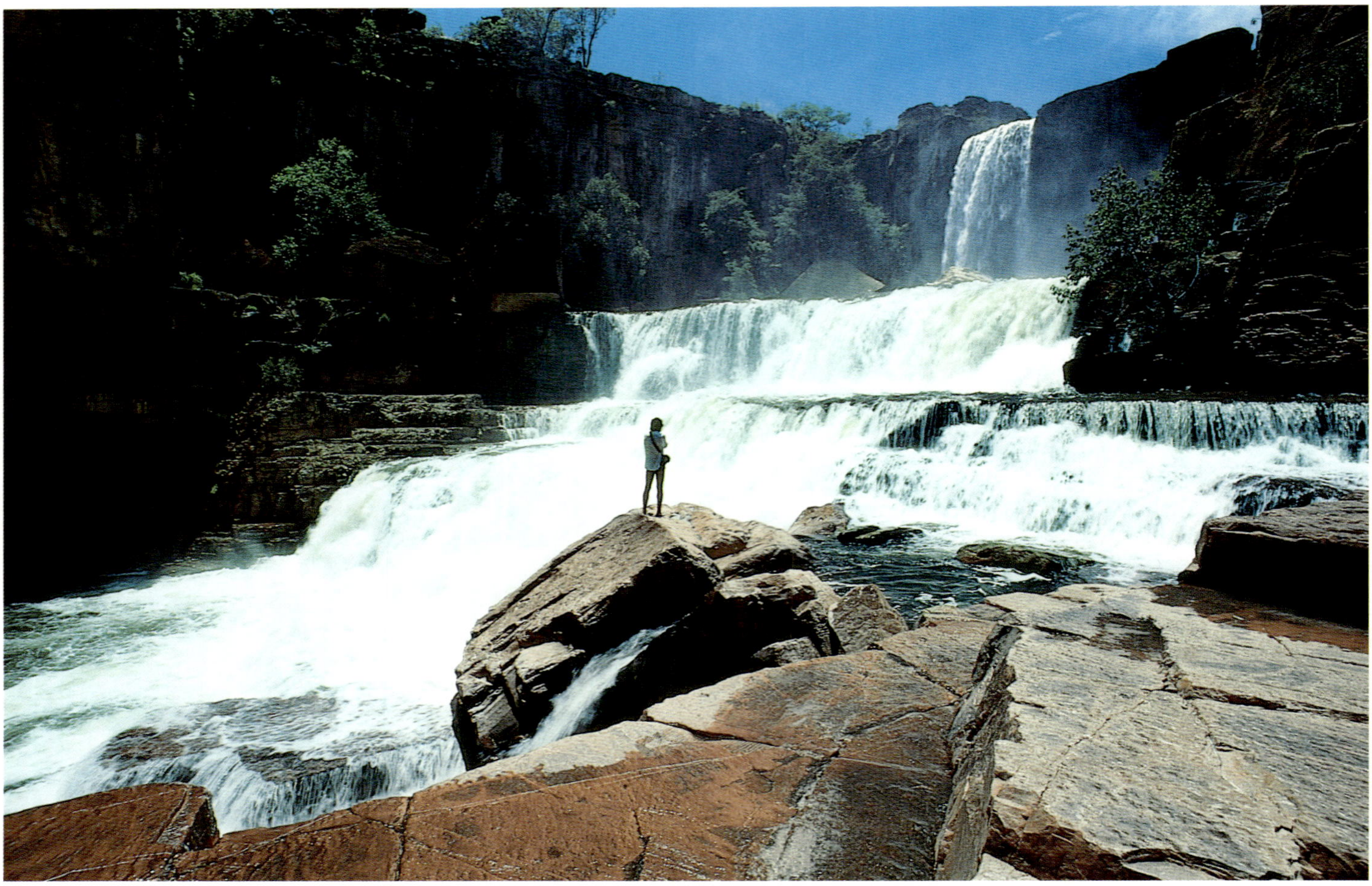

A lone bushwalker is dwarfed by the upper cascades of Twin Falls.

ENJOYING KAKADU

PREVIOUS PAGE Sunlight raking through a woodland clearing catches the feathered tops of late wet season grasses.

Kakadu does not yield its secrets easily. Most travellers to the park will never have encountered a landscape quite like this. The day-time heat and dazzling light, the daunting feeling of space and even the strange sounds and smells of the bush can all be overwhelming. Here the natural wonders are scattered over a vast area and the history of the land and its people challenge the imagination. Yet these elements of confrontation and mystery are all part of the experience.

It is possible to see a lot of the park in a day - but only through the window of a car, bus or plane. To appreciate the true power of an art site or the pulse of life in a monsoon forest takes time. The key to enjoying Kakadu is giving yourself the opportunity to respond to your surroundings. This also means adjusting to conditions on the day and the tempo of the season.

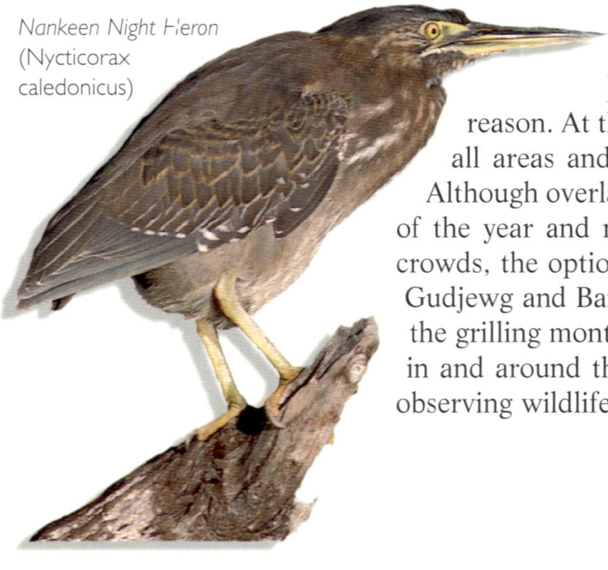

Nankeen Night Heron (Nycticorax caledonicus)

June and July are by far the busiest months in the park, and with good reason. At this time of the year days are milder, it's possible to venture into almost all areas and many plant species still display the benefits of rejuvenating rains. Although overland travel is limited in the wet season, this is perhaps the liveliest time of the year and monsoon cloud brings welcome cover from the beating sun. Fewer crowds, the option of scenic flights and the park's network of all-weather roads make Gudjewg and Banggerreng a worthwhile alternative. Every season has its bonus, even the grilling months of September and October. During this period animals congregate in and around the remaining waterholes, providing many excellent opportunities for observing wildlife.

THE NORTH - RIVERS, FLOODPLAINS & OUTLIERS

As it enters the park the Arnhem Highway traverses a large tract of undulating woodland at the headwaters of the Wildman and West Alligator Rivers. The scene then changes dramatically as you pass through thicker forest to approach the South Alligator River. Here there is the first sight of Kakadu's expansive floodplains.

The upper estuary of the South Alligator is a somewhat stark place, with a narrow strip of trees flanking the silty, churning waters of Kakadu's greatest river. Such vegetated fringes are however a good place to view birdlife, the occasional monitor lizard roaming the grassy banks and possibly even a saltie or two on mud banks exposed at low tide.

Two highlights nearby are the **Gungarre Monsoon Forest Walk**, a gentle 3.6 kilometre loop path through this leafy lowland habitat, and **Mamukala**, where sheltered bird hides provide one of the best vantage points in the park for observing large throngs of waterbirds at close quarters.

Of interest to the more intrepid off-road traveller is the Alligator Billabong Track winding 70 kilometres south from the Arnhem Highway to join the Old Darwin Road, and the 80 kilometre track leading north to remote West Alligator Head, the only overland access to Kakadu's beaches, mangrove communities and coastal forests.

Beyond Mamukala the highway strikes east towards the busiest section of the park where the escarpment meets the East Alligator River and its tributaries. Here outstanding natural features rub shoulders with mining leases, the township of Jabiru and various tourist facilities. The **Bowali Visitor Centre** at the Park Headquarters is a useful place to get your bearings. As well as interpretative displays there is a wealth of information on what Kakadu has to offer.

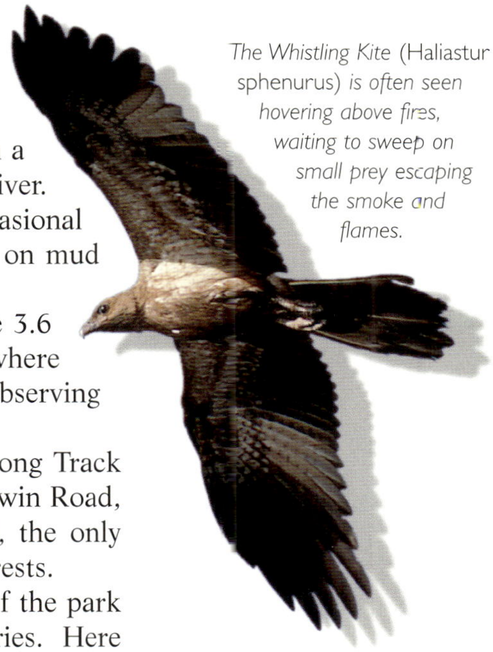

The Whistling Kite (Haliastur sphenurus) is often seen hovering above fires, waiting to sweep on small prey escaping the smoke and flames.

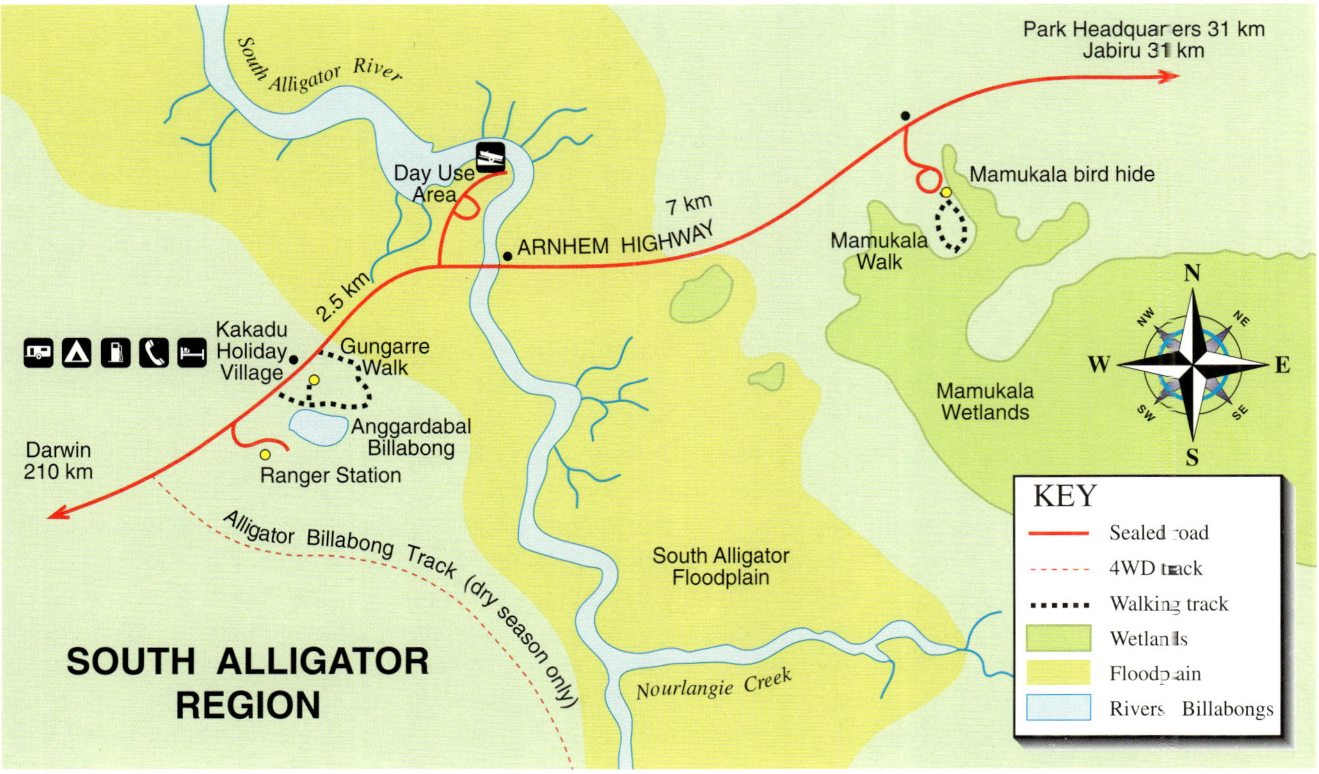

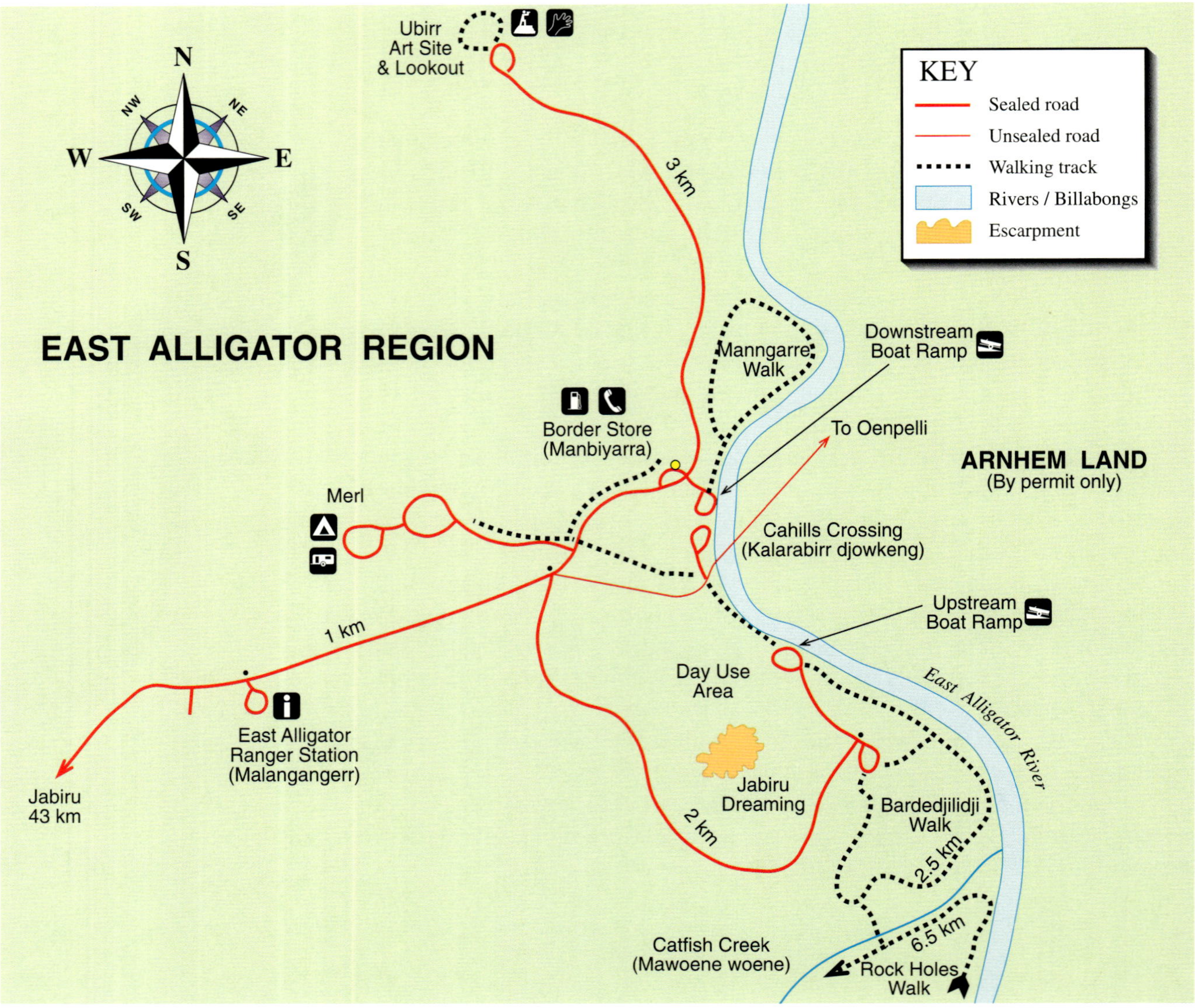

To the north lies Magela Creek, a major branch of the East Alligator River. A sealed road crosses this creek and skirts the Magela floodplain, under the shadow of imposing escarpment outliers - part of the controversial Jabiluka Mineral Lease. A diverse cross-section of habitats is found in the vicinity of the East Alligator. At this point the river forms the boundary of the park and not far from the Merl Campground and Border Store lies Cahill's Crossing, a man-made causeway leading to the Arnhem Land Aboriginal Reserve.

The main drawcard of the area is **Ubirr**, a beautiful cluster of sandstone outcrops housing some of the world's most famous rock art. A short walking circuit links the galleries and includes a climb to a lookout with spectacular views north across the floodplain to the tree-lined East Alligator River. Stretching to the horizon beyond lies yet more floodplain and outliers: a reminder that Kakadu is merely the threshold to a much larger cultural landscape. As captivating as Ubirr's paintings are, this site was also very much a living place where people found shelter, shared food and handed down stories.

Other East Alligator highlights include the **Manngarre Monsoon Forest Walk**, a short trail exploring the cloistered charms of a riverine monsoon forest, where noisy flying-foxes can sometimes be seen roosting in the tree canopy. Further upstream a network of walking trails - among them the **Bardedjilidji Sandstone Walk** - takes you past the river's mighty paperbarks and into the craggy sandstone outcrops nearby. **Guluyambi**, a boat cruise with Aboriginal guides, offers a fascinating look at the East Alligator River environs as well as traditional foods and hunting methods.

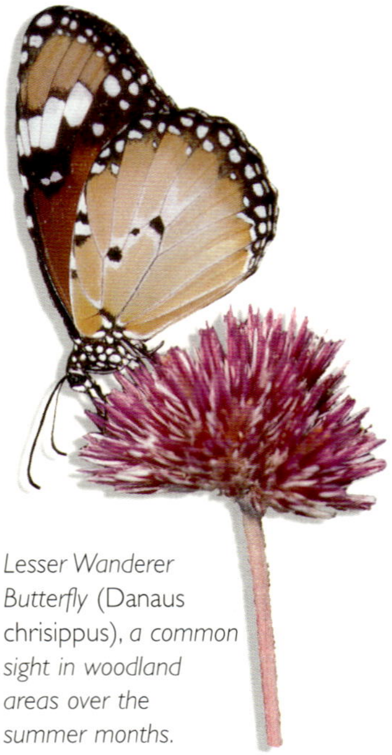

Lesser Wanderer Butterfly (Danaus chrisippus), *a common sight in woodland areas over the summer months.*

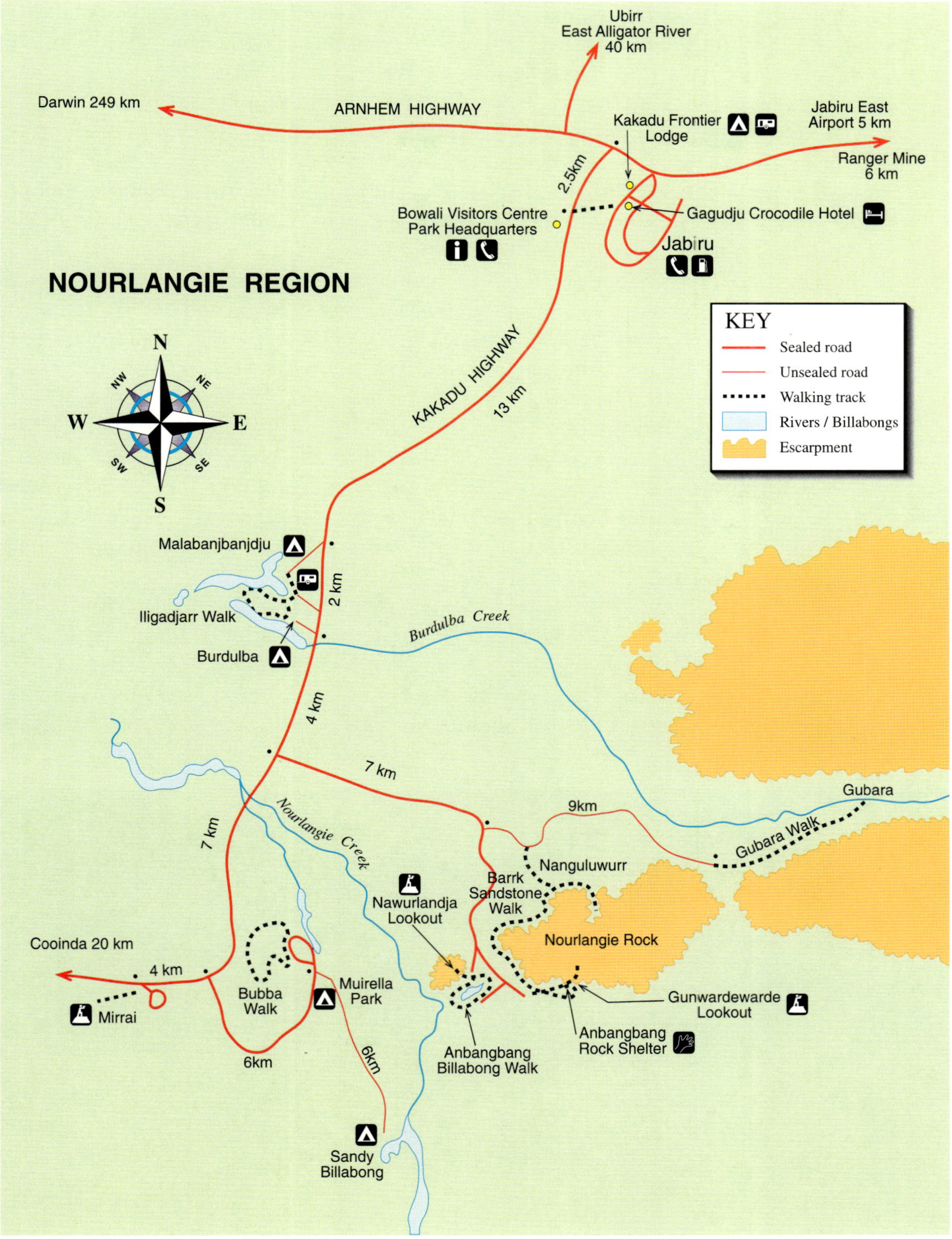

THE CENTRE - WOODLANDS, BILLABONGS & ESCARPMENT

South from the Park Headquarters the Kakadu Highway crosses Burdulba and Nourlangie Creeks, tributaries of the South Alligator River. These creeks are fed by run-off from the escarpment and outliers, the most accessible of which is **Burrunggui (Nourlangie Rock)** - another principal rock art site on display in the park. The highlights of this monumental formation are the Anbangbang Shelter, an important occupation site and the dramatic paintings at nearby Anbangbang Gallery.

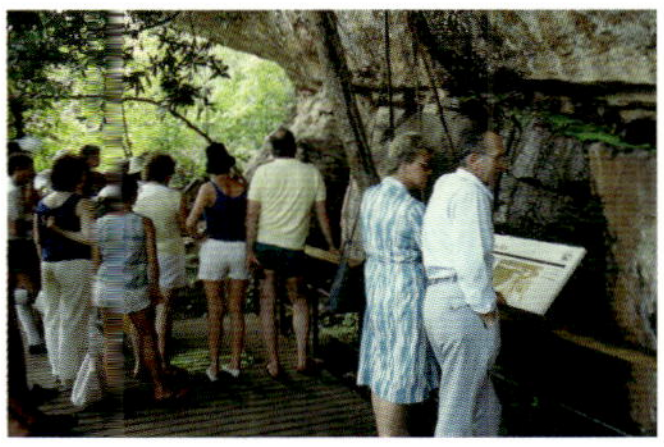

Park visitors viewing the rock art at Anbangbang Gallery.

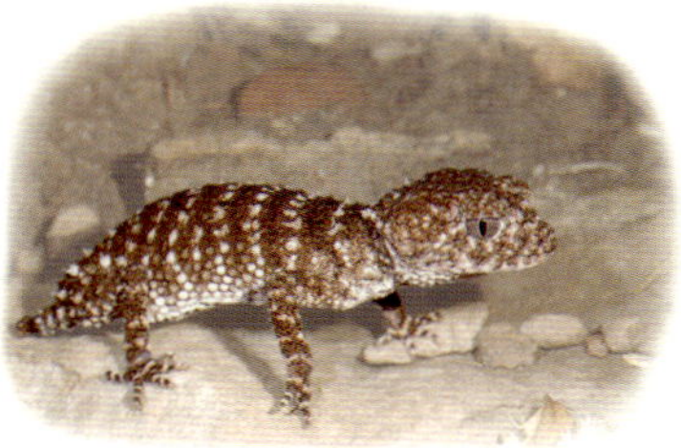

Rough Knob-tail Gecko (Nephrurus asper), *one of 16 geckos found in the park.*

There are several walking trails in the area. The **Nanguluwur Gallery Walk** visits an interesting painting site on the western side of Nourlangie Rock. This gallery can also be reached as part of the **Barrk Sandstone Walk**, a more challenging 12 kilometre circuit taking in the western end of Nourlangie Rock and offering superb vistas of the surrounding country and the escarpment. To the south lies the smaller outlier known as **Nawurlandja** where you can climb for views of Burrunggui or wander around Anbangbang Billabong. Further to the north of Burrunggui the three kilometre **Gubara Pools Walk** explores the beautiful enfolding monsoon forest and permanent waterholes of Burdulba Creek.

Jim Jim Creek to the south is the third main watercourse originating in this stretch of the escarpment. The creek winds through a large area of woodland before joining the South Alligator system at **Yellow Water**. This complex of wetlands and deep river channels is one of Kakadu's outstanding wildlife attractions. Regular boat cruises visit the billabongs which teem with waterbirds and a host of other animal life, notably fish, snakes and saltwater crocodiles.

Warradjan, the Pig-nosed Turtle (Carettochelys insculpta).

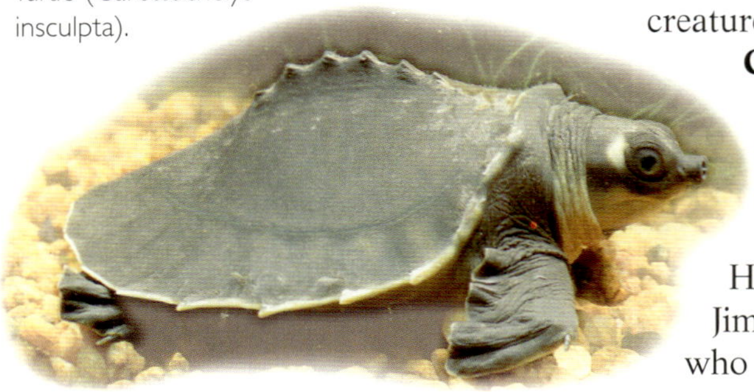

These billabongs are also home to Warradjan the elusive Pig-nosed Turtle, a creature well known to Bininj, and the inspiration for the **Warradjan Cultural Centre** near Yellow Water. Here there are excellent displays explaining creation stories, bush tucker, the clan system, language groups and customs.

Yellow Water is by no means the only wetland feature in this section of the park. There are many turn-offs from the Kakadu Highway giving access to billabongs on Burdulba, Nourlangie and Jim Jim Creeks. These are fine places to witness birdlife and other creatures who frequent the surrounding paperbark forests and eucalypt woodlands.

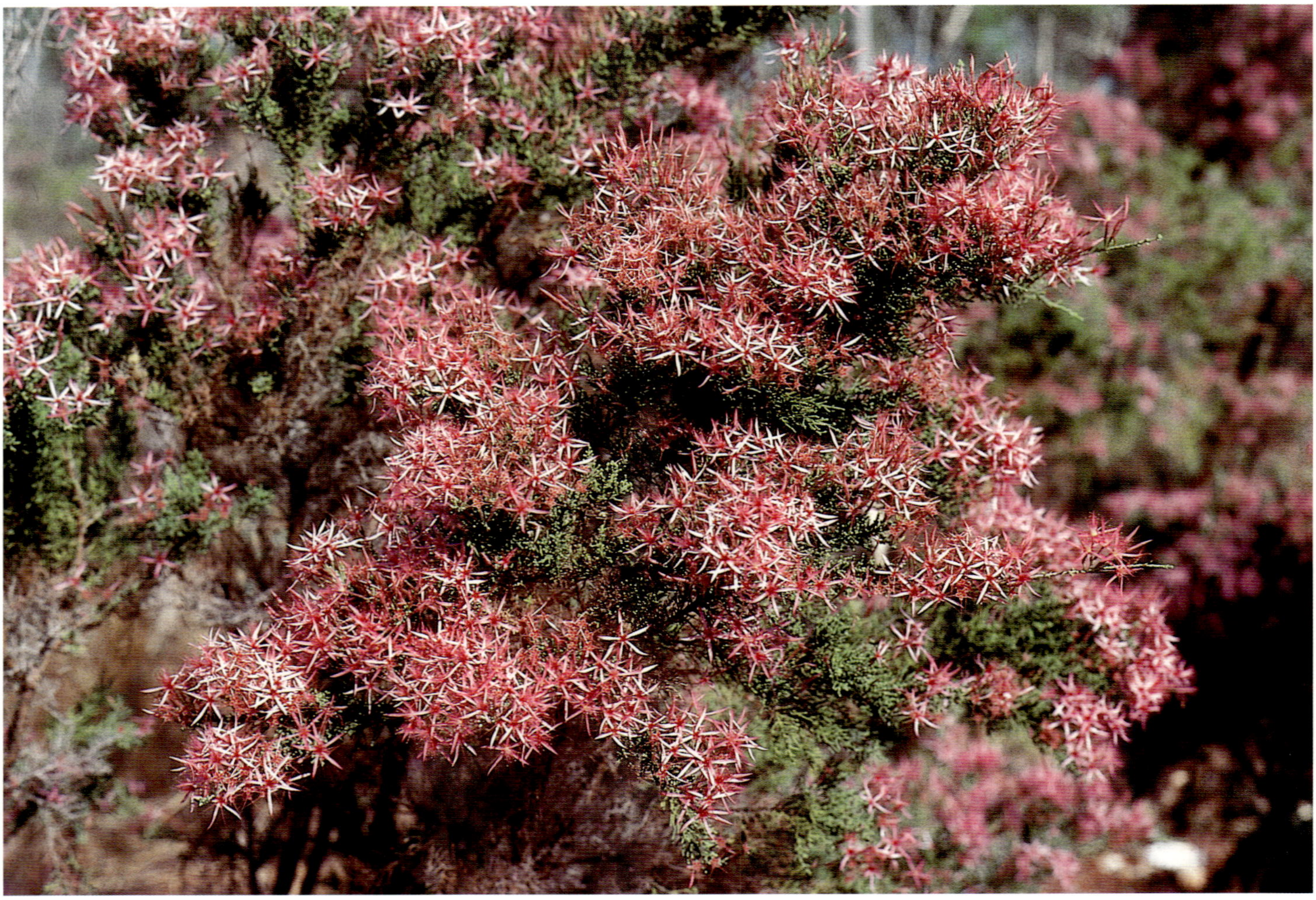

The spectacular Wurrgeng display of delicate flowers belies the hardy nature of the Turkey Bush (Calytrix existipulata).

Gentle walking trails skirt these billabong habitats and many are associated with campgrounds, including those at **Burdulba, Muirella Park, Sandy Billabong** and **Mardugal**.

To witness the escarpment origins of Jim Jim Creek involves an 80 kilometre four-wheel drive journey to the south-east. Even in the dry season **Jim Jim Falls (Barrkmalam)** still makes an arresting sight. The Anbinik forest and deep pools below are full of interest - and often tourists as well. To escape the crowds, keen walkers can tackle the steep marked track winding up a spur to the south to gain the top of the falls. Ten kilometres further south by road stands **Twin Falls (Gungkurdul)**. Access is via a stiff climb to the rim of the escarpment or by navigating three long pools in the magnificent gorge below.

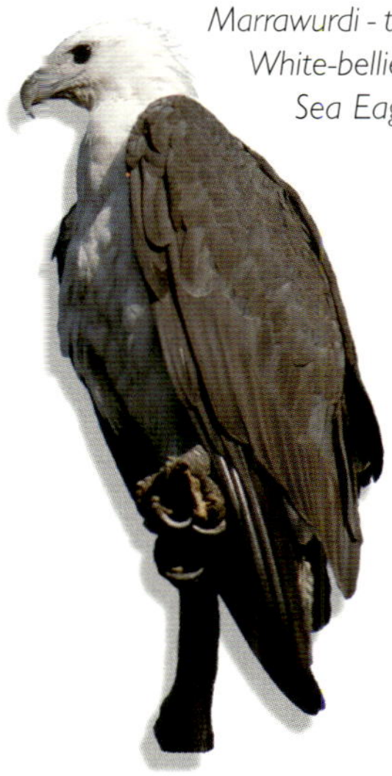

Marrawurdi - the White-bellied Sea Eagle.

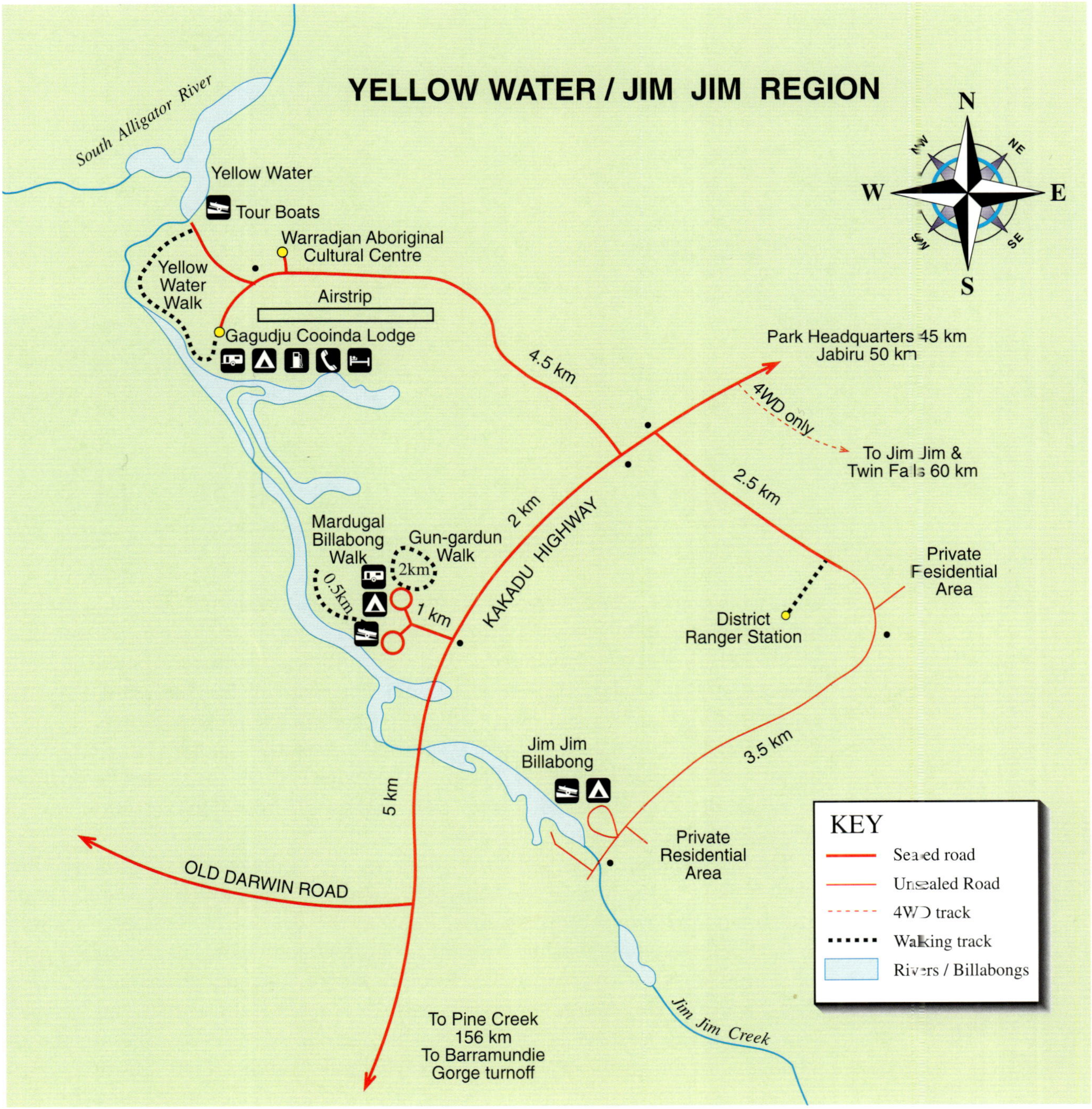

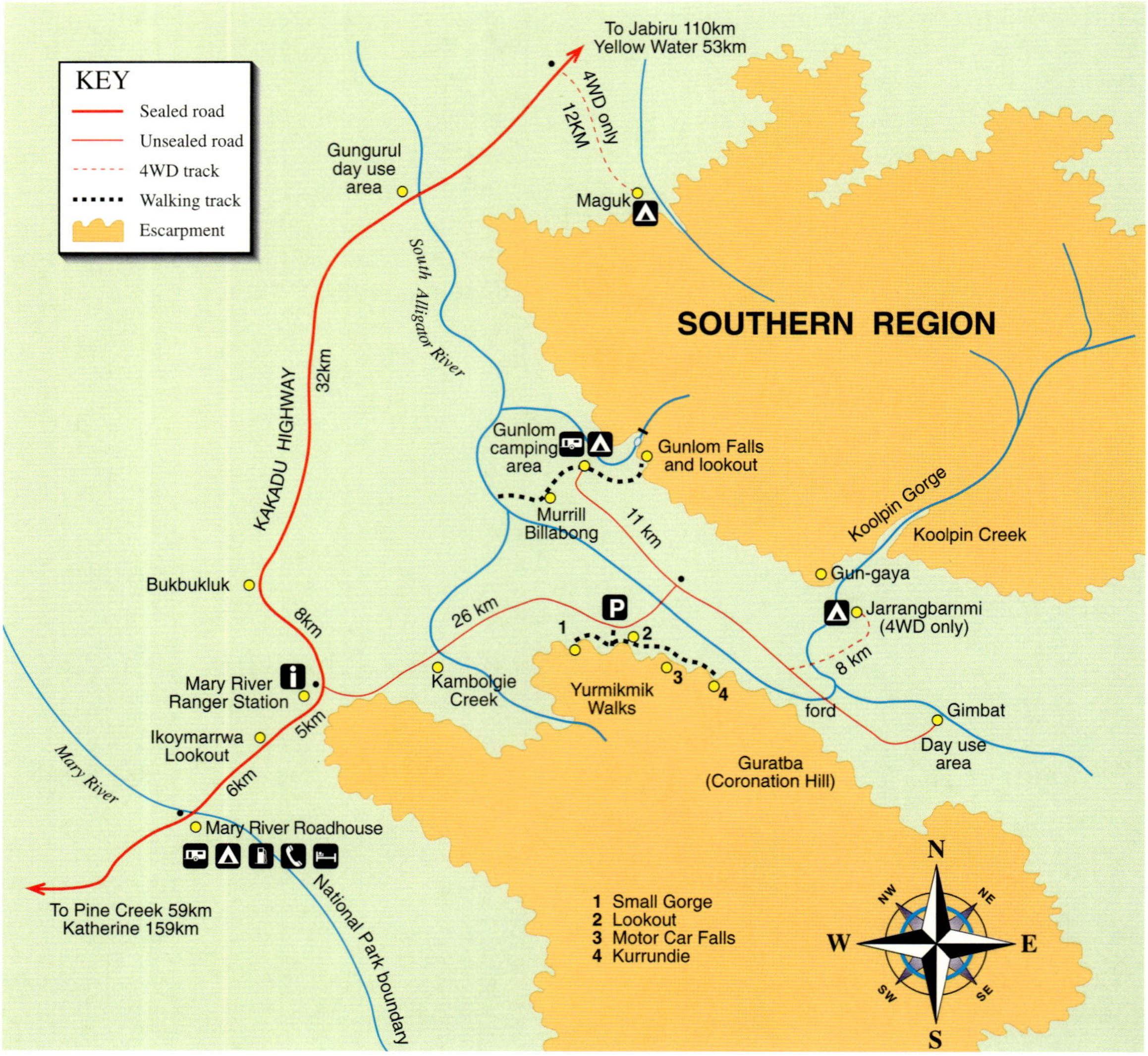

THE SOUTH - RUGGED HILLS, GORGES & WATERFALLS

Twin Falls marks a turning point on the escarpment. From here a major peninsula of the plateau extends westward into the park. This forms the upper catchment of the South Alligator River, a secluded world where the age-worn escarpment is fretted by creeks and slender gorges. Beyond lies the watershed of the Katherine River and an expanse of broken hills and ridges - the heartlands of the Jawoyn people.

As the Kakadu Highway heads south towards this complex region, it crosses Barramundie Creek. A 12 kilometre four-wheel drive track leads upstream to **Barramundie Gorge (Maguk)** with lush monsoon forest flanking the creek and an impressive pool at the top of the gorge.

The prime cluster of gorges in this southern area of the park is reached via a highway turn-off close to the Mary River Ranger Station. **Gunlom Falls** is one of Kakadu's best known landmarks and camping sites. Pools at the base of the falls and upstream are popular for swimming and the lookout trail offers good views of the area. Further up the South Alligator River valley lies **Koolpin Gorge (Jarrangbarnmi)**. This and nearby **Gun-gaya (Freezing Gorge)** are reached via a four-wheel drive track and exploring the gorges involves sections of rugged walking terrain. More accessible are the natural highlights on the various stages of the **Yurmikmik Walking Trail**. Starting just off the entrance road to Gunlom this marked track links a series of interesting diversions to gorges, lookouts and waterfalls.

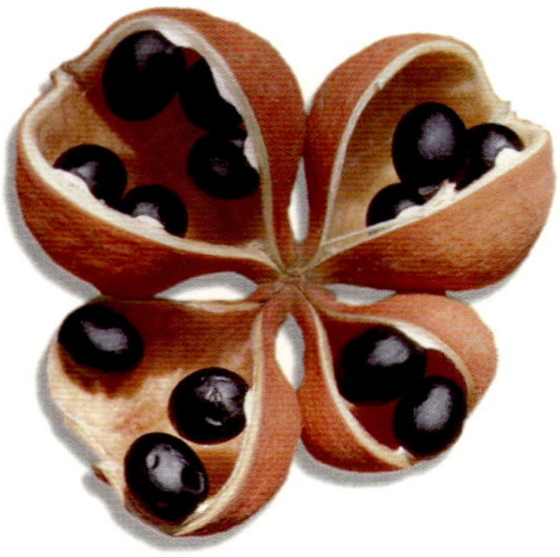

Distinctive seeds of the Peanut Tree (Sterculia quadrifida).

KAKADU BY FOOT & BY BOAT

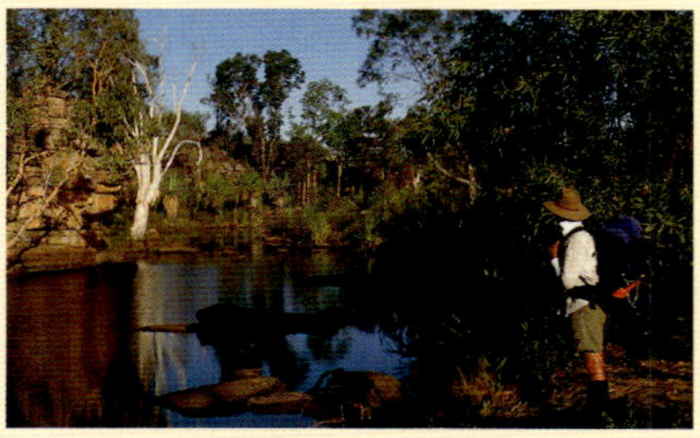

Even late in the dry season there are still welcoming pools in the farther reaches of the plateau such as these high in the Twin Falls creek system.

The best way to experience Kakadu's special sense of place is to travel on foot. Even strolls lasting just an hour or two are worthwhile for capturing moods and aspects often missed in the headlong rush to 'see the sights.' Observing details in the natural world - plants in flower, animal behaviour and weather changes - is also essential to appreciating the traditional Bininj view of the world.

There are more than 20 marked walking tracks in the park. Many are brief excursions to lookouts or through forest, billabong and wetland habitats. Some tracks take you into the heart of traditional art and occupation sites. Others offer a fascinating window on wildlife. The longest outings are all-day affairs rewarding those prepared for rocky scrambles and long climbs.

Even at the 'cool' time of the year temperatures are still warm for walking. For anything more than a brief wander through leafy forest it's best to travel in the cool of the morning or evening. Take precautions against the heat and light by wearing a hat, loose clothing and sunscreen. Above all else carry ample drinking water for the journey.

Indeed, given the climate, water is one of the main attractions for those who enjoy leisurely treks. The gorges and waterfalls in the south of the park are popular for day trips where walking stages are punctuated by cooling rest stops in shady pools. In this section of escarpment hinterland there is virtually unlimited scope for extended bushwalks, however permits are required and it's necessary to apply at least seven days in advance if you want to do a walk involving overnight camping. An alternative is to join one of the commercial bushwalking tours such as those offered by Willis's Walkabouts.

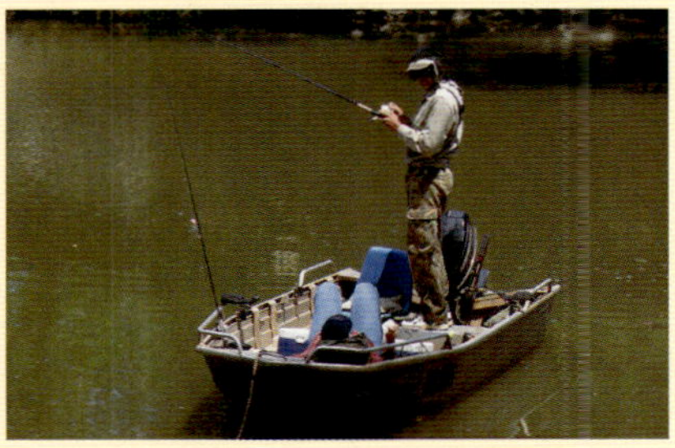

A keen fisherman braving the fierce midday sun warming the soupy waters of the East Alligator River.

Given its impressive rivers and large billabongs it's not surprising that Kakadu is also a popular park for boating. There are boat launching ramps on both the South Alligator and East Alligator Rivers, as well as at Yellow Water, Jim Jim Billabong and Mardugal. While boat travel is an ideal way to experience the river and wetland habitats, strong currents, tides and crocodiles make it potentially hazardous. Fishing is permitted in specified locations. For current restrictions contact the Bowali Visitor Centre or the nearest district ranger station.

KAKADU ROCK ART

For many visitors the most important pathway to appreciating Bininj life and traditions is through encounters with rock art. To linger in a natural stone shelter as the soft evening light plays upon the painted images can be a mesmerising experience. These feelings are all the more potent for the realisation that such sites are more than just galleries: from generation to generation these shelters have regularly served as ancestral family homes, open-air classrooms and natural cathedrals.

The art is scattered all through the stone country. Five thousand painting sites have been recorded in Kakadu - which represents barely half the estimated total. This abundance is testimony to both the prosperity of the land and the extraordinary history of the culture it sustained. The paintings themselves range from haunting images of ancestral figures from the time of creation, to graphic depictions of important birds, fish, reptiles, mammals and insects.

The various artistic styles and subjects form a vivid chronicle of traditional life. In documenting the sites, researchers such as George Chaloupka have pieced together an evolution of painting styles which reflects the profound environmental changes affecting Kakadu over the past 50,000 years.

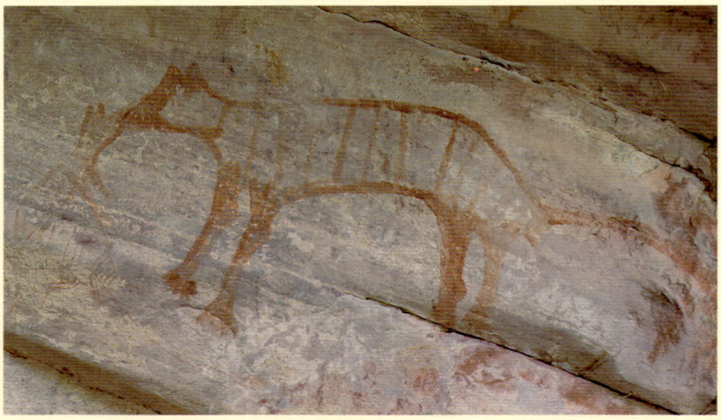

Many paintings provide clues about life in the region during earlier times, including this painting of a Tasmanian Tiger or Thylacine, long-extinct in Kakadu.

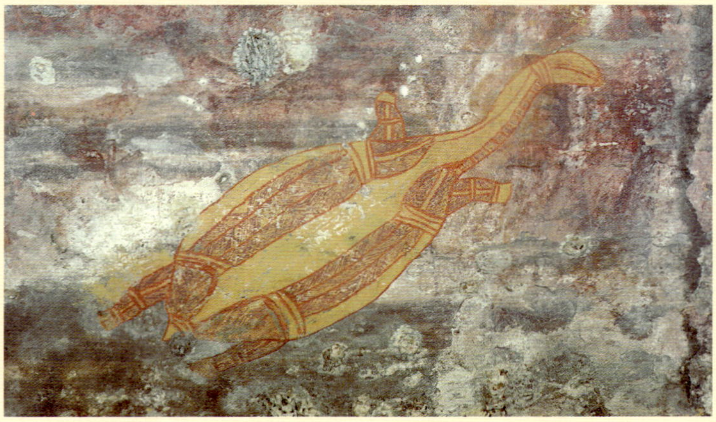

A Long-necked Turtle, an important food source and frequent painting subject.

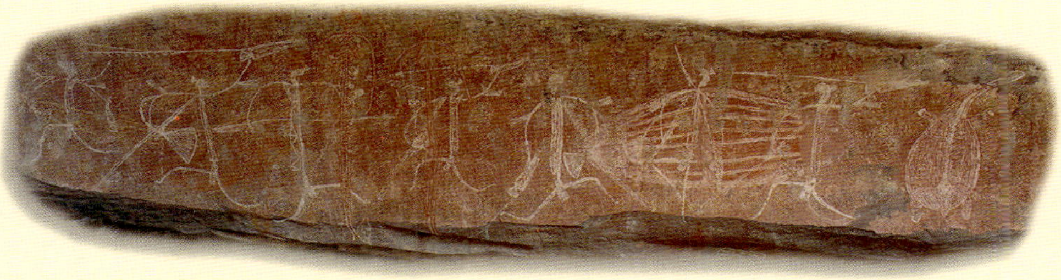

Spectacular hunting scenes such as this frieze are just some of the highlights at Ubirr's rock art galleries.

The art can thus be grouped into four main phases. The Pre-estuarine Period prior to 8000 years ago features early animal paintings, hunting scenes, hand prints and dynamic figures. With the rise in sea level that commenced around 8000 years, new subjects appeared, including yam figures, the Rainbow Snake and an array of fish and other saltwater creatures. This Estuarine Period saw the development of Kakadu's famous X-ray painting style where the animal's internal structures are rendered as part of the image. The subsequent transformation of the floodplains from a marine to freshwater habitat around 1500 years ago ushered in the Freshwater Period, featuring images of freshwater flora and fauna. Art produced in response to Macassan and European influence is grouped as work belonging to the Contact Period.

While many paintings reflect great artistic skill and draughtsmanship, the chief function of the art has less to do with individual expression or decoration than with renewing rituals, knowledge and beliefs. Hence, at many sites, images overlie one another or have been repainted many times. In the case of some ancestral figures, these are thought to be not so much representations as the living embodiments of the beings themselves.

The numinous power of Kakadu's rock art is most accessible in galleries at Ubirr and Burrunggui. Those who are able to spend extended time walking the escarpment stone country cannot help but encounter many more examples of this remarkable legacy.

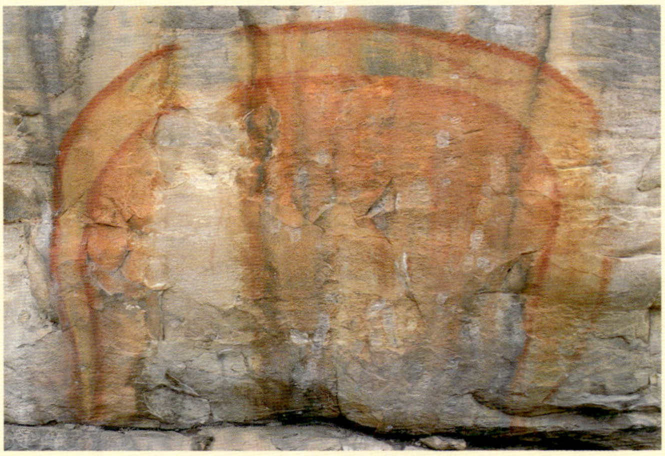

The Rainbow Serpent is one of the most powerful of all creation beings and is widely depicted at art sites throughout the stone country.

PHOTOGRAPHING KAKADU

The key to photography in Kakadu is understanding the light. Conditions vary dramatically according to the time of year. So, for example, the cloudless, dry season days of Wurrgeng offer little respite from the blazing sunlight. By contrast, during the cloudy monsoon months of Gudjewg there are stretches of three or four days in a row when you are lucky to see the sun at all. Seasonal fluctuations such as these provide a range of challenges and opportunities for the visiting photographer.

When taking pictures on all but the most overcast days the first thing to remember is the harshness of the midday sun. Shadows are dark and devoid of much detail, while at the same time highlights may wash out in bright areas. Landscape views photographed with the sun hovering high in the sky will usually appear flat and two dimensional, the light taking on a 'cold' quality which makes prints appear bluish. Special places such as monsoon or paperbark forest need the softer light of a cloudy or overcast sky. If photographing these habitats in the speckled light of a sunny day a disappointing mix of bleached highlights and deep shadows will be the result.

The early and late hours of the day offer better opportunities. With the sun at a more pronounced angle, trees and escarpment views take on a more three dimensional aspect with prints having more 'life' in them. Birds and animals of the billabongs offer great subject matter at all times of the year, although finding wildlife in the monsoon season can be difficult, as animals disperse over a much wider area. Long lenses are definitely an advantage when photographing wildlife, though at places like Yellow Water and Mamukala the birds have developed a tolerance of onlookers.

The golden light of dawn and dusk are special times for photography. As the sun sets the spectacle of the west-facing escarpment glowing with the intensity of a furnace is challenged only by the riot of colour splashed across the clouds of a dramatic wet season sky. Remember too, that the sunset ignites the colours twice. With the last rays of direct sun, tree tops and escarpment take on a glow, but some 10 or 15 minutes later the afterglow from higher up beams down an extraordinary intensity of subtle colouring. During the wet season, it can be a truly remarkable display. Night falls quickly in the tropics, so be prepared for a brisk return, or risk being stranded in the dark.

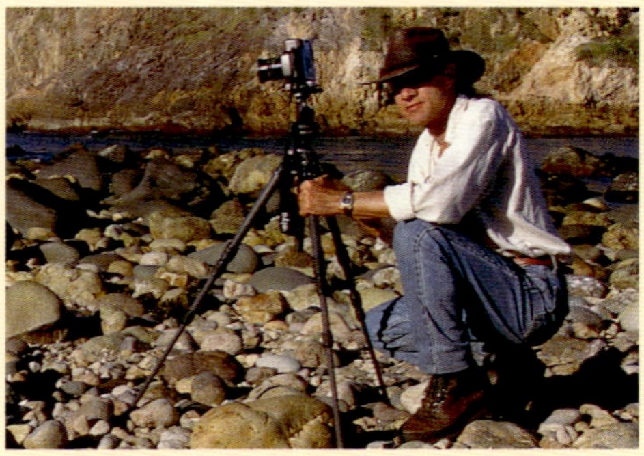

Photography can be a good reason to linger in your favourite environment. As you immerse yourself, listen and feel the spirit of nature. The call of the wild will reward you with memories of a magical moment.

Photographer, Peter Jarver.

INDEX

Entries in **bold** are photographs.

ABOUT PETER JARVER

Peter Jarver has photographed in Kakadu for nearly 20 years. He is a photographer with a long standing commitment to the environment. His large format images have appeared in numerous books including the best selling title *The Top End of Down Under*. The recipient of several major awards, he gained the Master of Photography honour in 1994, a level achieved by only a few Australian photographers.

AUTHOR'S BIOGRAPHY

Quentin Chester is the co-author of *The Outdoor Companion*, *The Kimberley Horizons of Stone* and *Australia's Wild Islands*. He also writes regularly for outdoor magazines and a collection of these stories forms his most recent book, *The Wild Calling*.

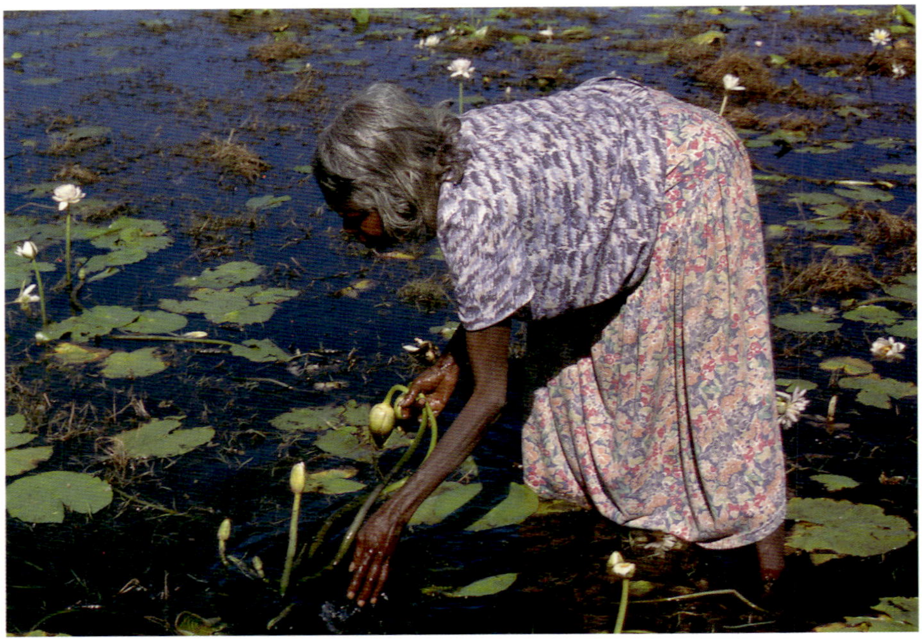

Collecting edible lily bulbs in the traditional manner.

First published by Thunderhead Publishing 1998
PO Box 549 Kuranda Qld 4872 Australia
Telephone (07) 4093 7171 Fax (07) 4093 8897
Email address: jarver@thunder.com.au
Web Page: www.thunder.com.au

Photography by Peter Jarver,
Master of Photography AIPP
Text by Quentin Chester
Additional photography as follows:
Lochman Transparencies:
Jiri Lochman - 12c, 12b, 13b, 19b, 21b, 28t, 39r, 60t, 61b, 63t, 70b, 72c
Raoul Slater - 31t, 31b
Dennis Sarson - 10t, 21t
Wade Hughes - 11b, 63b
Marie Lochman - 17b, 72t
Hans & Judy Beste - 22t, 57b, 62t
Ian Morris - 45b
The Northern Territory Library - 63l, 64t, 64b
John Brock - 5t, 5b, 25r, 38t, 38c, 39l, 74b
Margaret McGregor - 6, 80
Quentin Chester - 75t

Maps drawn by Michael Smith
Maps courtesy Parks Australia North
Design by Liz Seymour
Separations by Graphic Skills
Printed in Hong Kong by South China Printing Co.

Jarver, Peter
Kakadu, A Guide For All Seasons
ISBN 0-958-90678-5

TRAVEL INFORMATION:
Darwin Regional Tourist Association
Ph (08) 8981 4300
Kakadu Visitor Organisation Ph (08) 8979 2548
Katherine Regional Tourist Association
Ph (08) 8972 2650
Willis's Walkabouts Ph (08) 8985 2134

FOR FURTHER INFORMATION ABOUT KAKADU CONTACT:
Kakadu National Park Ph (08) 8938 1100 or write to the Park Manager Kakadu National Park, PO Box 71 Jabiru NT 0886.
Northern Territory Tourism Commission, Darwin Ph (08) 8999 3900